LEGENDARY LOCALS

OF

THE NORTHERN OUTER BANKS

NORTH CAROLINA

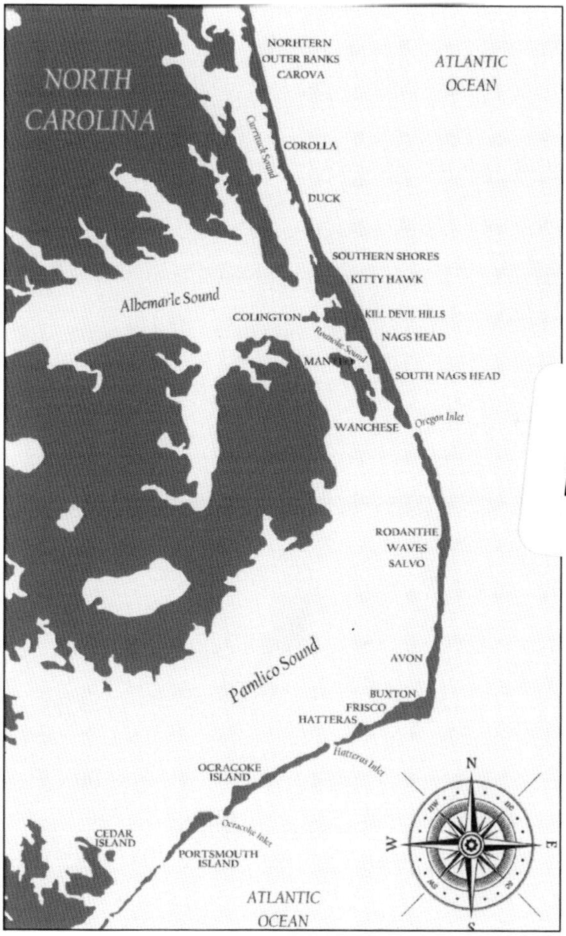

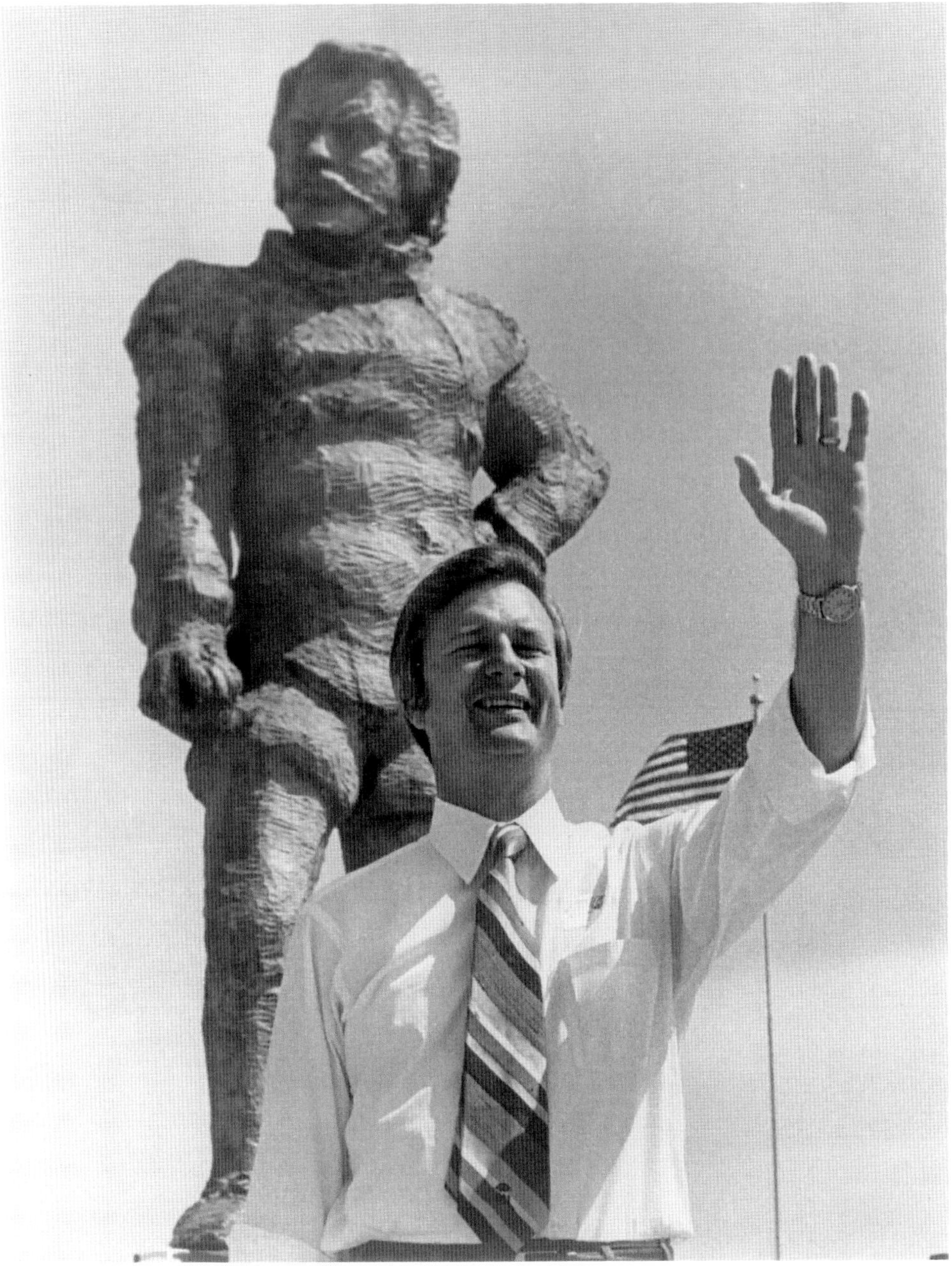

Two Prominent Men
Jim Hunt, former governor of North Carolina, waves at the crowd. The gigantic wooden statue of Sir Walter Raleigh stands proudly in the background. (Courtesy of Manteo Centennial Exhibit Collection.)

Page 1: Map of the Northern Outer Banks
The villages from Corolla to Nags Head, North Carolina, make up the northern Outer Banks, which includes parts of Currituck County and Dare County. (Courtesy of Coastal Impressions.)

LEGENDARY LOCALS

OF

THE NORTHERN OUTER BANKS

NORTH CAROLINA

R. WAYNE GRAY AND NANCY BEACH GRAY

LEGENDARY LOCALS

ISBN 978-1-4671-0185-1

Legendary Locals is an imprint of Arcadia Publishing
Charleston, South Carolina

Printed in the United States of America

Library of Congress Control Number: 2014943480

For all general information, please contact Arcadia Publishing:
Telephone 843-853-2070
Fax 843-853-0044
E-mail sales@arcadiapublishing.com
For customer service and orders:
Toll-Free 1-888-313-2665

Visit us on the Internet at www.arcadiapublishing.com

Dedication
To the spirited and independent people of the Outer Banks

On the Front Cover: Clockwise from top left:
Andy Griffith, stage, screen, and television star (Courtesy of Aycock Brown Collection, OBHC; see page 94), Meagan Agreste, helped form a charter school (Courtesy of Meagan Agreste; see page 91), Jethro Midgett Sr., and helpers, crusade against beach buildup (Courtesy of Aycock Brown Collection, OBHC; see page 121), Paul Green, playwright who wrote *The Lost Colony* (Courtesy of OBHC; see page 72), Georgie Daniels, Crab Slough oysterman (Courtesy of Georgie Daniels; see page 48), Dottie Fry, child participant in World War II effort (Courtesy of D'Amours Collection, OBHC; see page 17), Ladd Bayliss, coastal advocate (Courtesy of Ray Matthews; see page 90), Tshombe Selby, training with famous opera tenor (Courtesy of Melody Leckie; see page 95), Mabel Evans Jones, first superintendent of Dare County Schools (Courtesy of Edna Evans Jones Collection, OBHC; see page 71).

On the Back Cover: From left to right:
David Wayne Light, teenage junior dragster champion (Courtesy of David Light; see page 110), Ken Mann, radio and television personality turned minister (Courtesy of Drew Wilson Collection, OBHC; see page 87).

CONTENTS

ACKNOWLEDGMENTS

For their generous support in the writing of this book, we are indebted to Erin Vosgien and Arcadia Publishing.

This book would not have been possible without the kindness and efforts of many friends, both old and new. We thank all of the people who took time from their busy schedules to give interviews, share histories, and provide valuable photographs, many of which have never before been published.

The staff of the Outer Banks History Center—KaLei Schurr, Sarah Downing, Tama Creef, and Stuart Parks—graciously rendered their time and expertise in searching for information and photographs, which were crucial for our project. They provide a vital service for anyone doing serious research on the Outer Banks, and they offer it cheerfully.

Jill Landon, curator of the marvelous Whalehead Club, opened her archives to us. Jamie Lanier, National Park Service curator, provided important information and photographs, as did Lebame Houston, Roanoke Island Historical Association archivist. Thanks are due to Wanda Lassiter, Museum of the Albemarle curator, who provided us with valuable photographs.

Individuals who provided documents, historical information, and family photographs are represented in credits given in these pages. We apologize to anyone who was inadvertently omitted.

Choosing approximately 140 people to represent the Outer Banks was daunting. During the course of our research, we realized that we could realistically write about a thousand legendary figures to represent our area. So, we also apologize to the hundreds of people who could have easily become a part of our book.

OBHC is used throughout the book under photograph credits as an abbreviation for the Outer Banks History Center.

INTRODUCTION

The Outer Banks of North Carolina is made up of a string of barrier islands extending from the Virginia border to just south of Cape Lookout, North Carolina. These fragile, constantly shifting islands are little more than built-up sandbars that act as protective beaches for inset areas like Colington and Roanoke Island, North Carolina, which would otherwise be exposed to the harsh nor'easters and hurricanes.

The region has always been blessed with abundant natural resources, yet it is cursed by isolation. Its geographical location as the easternmost point of land on the East Coast, bordered on all sides by water, and buffeted by severe weather patterns, contributed to its lack of development for many years. Before the advent of tourism, the area was dependent on subsistence fishing, farming, hunting, wrecking (claiming goods that washed ashore from wrecked vessels), and progging (foraging for any way to make a living).

From the beginning, living on the Outer Banks for the early settlers was a struggle. Their livelihood depended on living off the land and the sea in a harsh environment. It was a hard life, but a rewarding one. Their isolation made for a fierce circular family and community, which exist today.

In addition to its wonderful natural resources and isolation, the Outer Banks is truly a land of beginnings. It has celebrated many firsts, such as being the first nonpermanent English colony in the new world, the birth of Virginia Dare, the first American child of English descent, Fessenden's wireless radio broadcasting experiments, the all-black-member lifesaving station, the Wright brothers, and many more. It is a land rich in mystery, adventure, and history. With the building of roads and bridges connecting Outer Bankers to the outside world, the tourist industry began and changed the atmosphere and culture of the still untouched beauty of the place.

This book addresses the northern Outer Banks, which is the designated area from Carova to Nags Head, North Carolina. This area was a beautiful wilderness first inhabited by the Algonquians, natives who hunted, fished, and grew crops for their survival. They lived in temporary places on the Outer Banks and had a complex social structure. They had their own customs and religious beliefs. When the colonists arrived, the natives did all they could to make them welcome. However, in the end, the negative actions and threats of the colonists eventually ousted them.

Some 75 years later, the early settlers began moving into the area and making it their home. The first land grant by the Lords Proprietors of North Carolina was the beginning of the first permanent settlement.

About the time the Civil War ended, a boon to the local people came through the building of many hunt clubs scattered along the northern Outer Banks, which is rich in the history of waterfowl. The clubs, many of them built by wealthy northern industrialists, were an added boost to the economy. The owners employed locals as builders, guides, cooks, and caretakers. Scores of these clubs were built and maintained for many years, from the last half of the 1800s to the early part of the 20th century. Many famous people came here to hunt and stay at the clubs. The Whalehead Club in Corolla, North Carolina, was the most glamorous and luxurious of all the clubs, with its Tiffany lamps and personal airstrip.

During the apex of the hunt club years, two brothers came to the Outer Banks looking for special weather conditions conducive to their experiments. A few years after their decision to stay, on December 17, 1903, in Kitty Hawk, North Carolina, Wilbur and Orville Wright accomplished what they set out to do—successfully fly an engine-powered heavier-than-air machine. Their lifetime dream came true in accomplishing what men had been attempting to do for centuries. In one of the most isolated spots in the country, they figured out the secret of controlled flight.

At almost the same time, a few miles away, William Fessenden was conducting his experiments. A few years later, Mabel Evans, superintendent of schools for Dare County, was uniting a group to begin celebrating the birth of Virginia Dare. Also, planning began for the 3,000-seat amphitheater for Paul Green's play about Raleigh's colonists who disappeared, *The Lost Colony.*

After World War II, many changes occurred as highways and bridges connected the Outer Bankers to the outside world. The tourist industry began in earnest and changed the atmosphere and culture of the still untouched beauty of the place.

Men like Aycock Brown, Ben Dixon MacNeill, and David and Frank Stick, to name a few, were responsible for positive changes on the Outer Banks. These men and other individuals mentioned in this book altered the course of Outer Banks history.

Today, Jan DeBlieu and Ladd Bayliss are two of many environmentalists who understand the coastal dynamics and the problems facing the Outer Banks in the future. They know we have to protect our coast from overdevelopment and adapt a different way of thinking about development if we are to preserve the still pristine Outer Banks.

* The quoted subtitles in the chapter titles are from the comical and philosophical character Old Tom, from Paul Green's drama *The Lost Colony.*

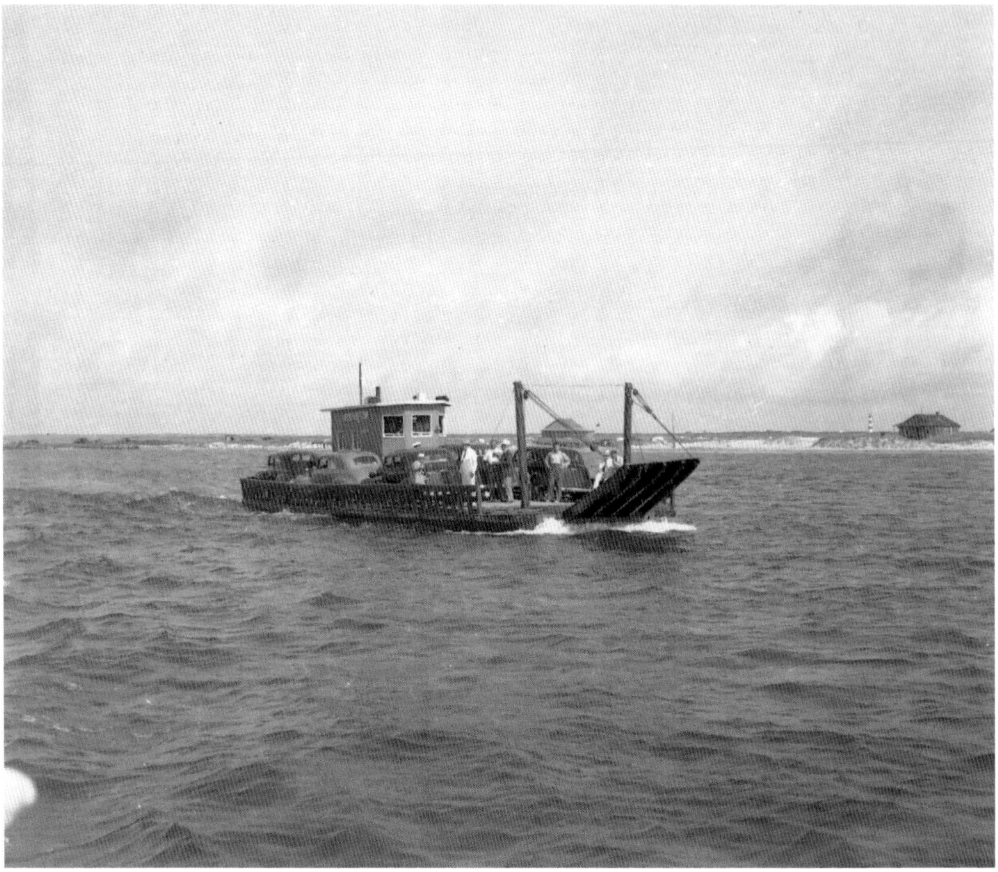

Ferry Crossing
In 1941, Toby Tillett's ferry *Barcelona* crosses Oregon Inlet. (Courtesy of Aycock Brown Collection; Margaret Tillett Daniels.)

CHAPTER ONE

Early Settlement

"Verily, this is a new land of opportunity."

The first inhabitants of the Outer Banks were the Algonquians, who had made it their seasonal home since 500 CE. After the arrival of Raleigh's colonists, these nonpermanent settlers soon disappeared, and the Outer Banks reverted back to the Native Americans until the 1660s, when a few pioneers began arriving. Little is recorded of this period. Families scratched out a subsistence living by fishing, farming, progging, and raising domestic animals. They were isolated and life was hard; the Outer Banks was far from an ideal place to make a living.

More than two centuries later, people like Marshall Collins and Ernie Bowden, living over 30 miles from each other on opposite ends of the northern Outer Banks, were still subsistence fishing, farming, and raising cattle to support their families. A few local businessmen like Richard Gray had mercantile stores that were focal points for their communities. Edward and Marie Knight, like a number of millionaires who came and built elaborate hunt clubs, helped the economy immensely by employing a large number of people in construction and domestic service.

About this time, lifesaving stations began dotting the Outer Banks. Wherever they appeared, entire communities were often built up around them; post offices, schools, and churches became a part of these small villages. The lifesaving service also employed numerous locals such as John T. Daniels and Richard Etheridge, offering them good, secure jobs.

African Americans like Marshall Collins, Richard Etheridge, and the Bias and Hargraves families were sprinkled over the Outer Banks and integrated the villages. These men and families were highly respected and acted as role models for everyone many years before integration was ever established.

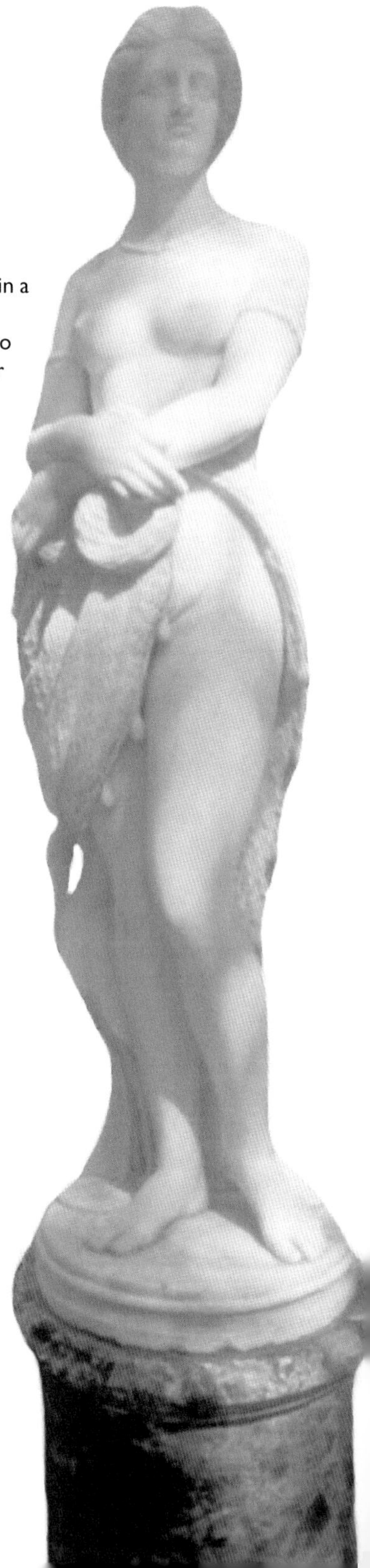

Lady Dare
Sculpted out of white Carrara Italian marble, this statue, clad only in a fish net, graces Roanoke Island's Elizabethan Gardens.

Virginia Dare was the first English child born in America, to parents who came to the New World as a part of Sir Walter Raleigh's experimental colony. Her 18 year-old-mother, Eleanor, and her bricklayer father, Ananias, had her baptized on the day of her birth, August 20, 1587. Virginia Dare's grandfather John White left for England soon after she was born to get more supplies for the colonists. The struggling settlement would go down in history as "the Lost Colony," when the inhabitants were unable to be found upon White's return. It is not known if Virginia made it into adulthood, but this image expresses the hope that she did. (Photograph by Ray Matthews; courtesy of Elizabethan Gardens.)

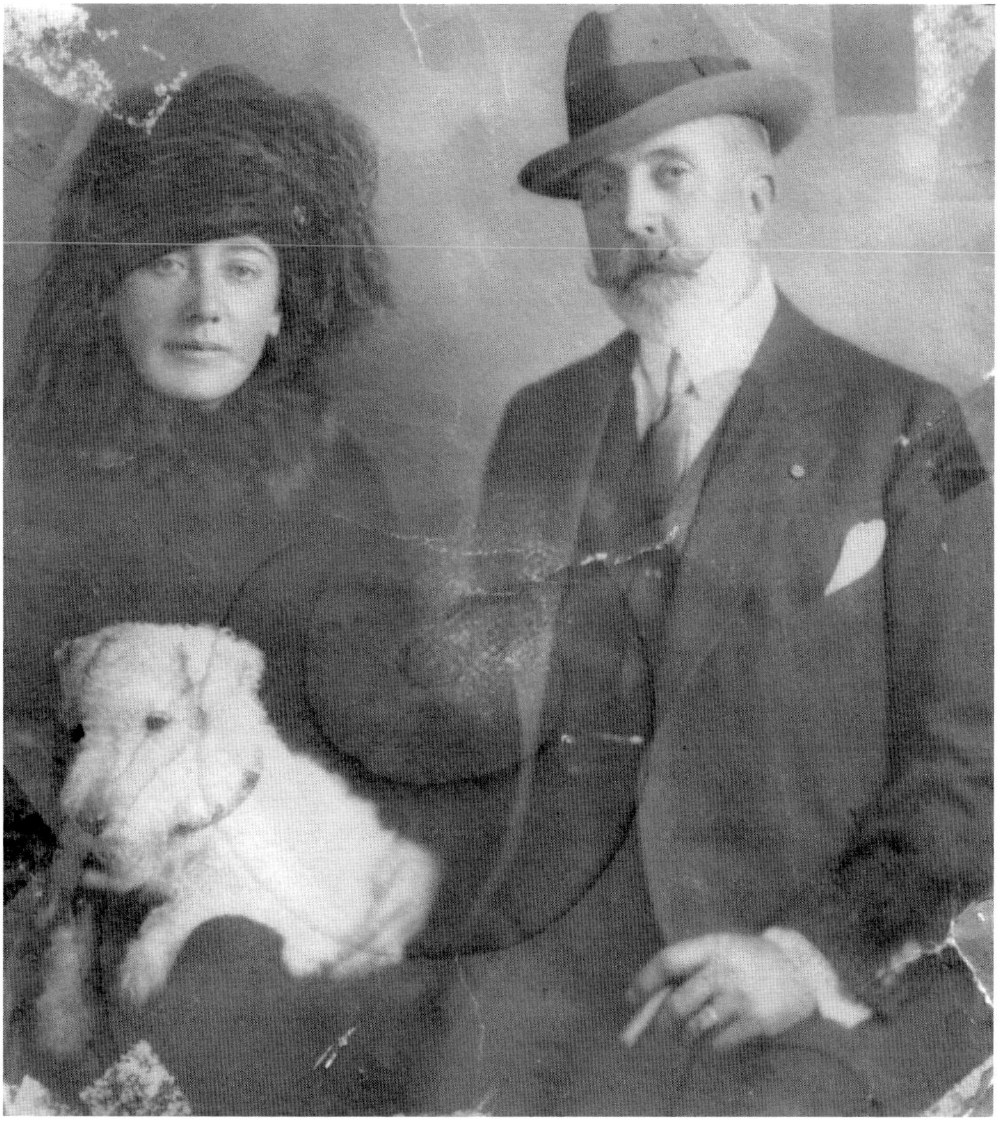

Creating Their Own Paradise

Edward Knight, a railroad magnate from Philadelphia, Pennsylvania, fell in love with the Currituck Banks after a hunting trip. He brought his second wife to Corolla, North Carolina, for their honeymoon and stayed in the Lighthouse Club. However, his wife was denied shooting privileges in the men-only membership lodge.

In 1922, the couple began to build their dream residence, now known as the Whalehead Club, where Marie Louise could hunt. Taking three years to construct at a cost of $383,000, the mansion had unprecedented design and craftsmanship with amenities such as Tiffany lighting fixtures and cork flooring.

The Whalehead Club changed hands many times over. Finally, in 1992, Currituck County bought the iconic building for $2.5 million. Extensively renovated, it reopened in 2002 as part of Currituck Heritage Park. (Courtesy of Whalehead Preservation Trust.)

First Flight Cameraman

When John T. Daniels and the other surfmen at the Kitty Hawk Lifesaving Station first encountered the Wright brothers, they "laughed at them as just a pair of poor nuts. They would sit on the beach for hours, just watching the gulls." However, a friendship formed between the men of the lifesaving service and the Wrights, and the local men were a great help to the brothers who would nail a red blanket on the side of their building when they needed help from the men.

Daniels received instructions from Orville on how to take a photograph of the glider as it ascended and trip the shutter. When the first flight occurred on December 17, 1903, not only was John a witness and a photographer of the event, but it was also the only photograph he ever took with the only camera he had ever seen. A man with a quick wit, he also claimed to be the first person ever to be an airplane casualty. On about the fifth flight that day, a great gust of wind lifted the craft that he was holding (he was known to be an extremely strong man). He got tangled in the wires as the plane crashed and tumbled end over end. The flyer was destroyed, and John had minor injuries.

John was never a publicity hound concerning his association with this famous event, but he was honored with invitations to a number of presentations about the Wrights. In this 1935 photograph, other first flight witnesses, Adam Etheridge (left) and W.J. Tate (right), join John (center) on a flight to a celebration at Greenfield Village, Michigan. Henry Ford had purchased the Wright family home and cycle shop and moved them from Dayton, Ohio, to Dearborn, Michigan, where they were put on display at his museum. (Courtesy of National Park Service.)

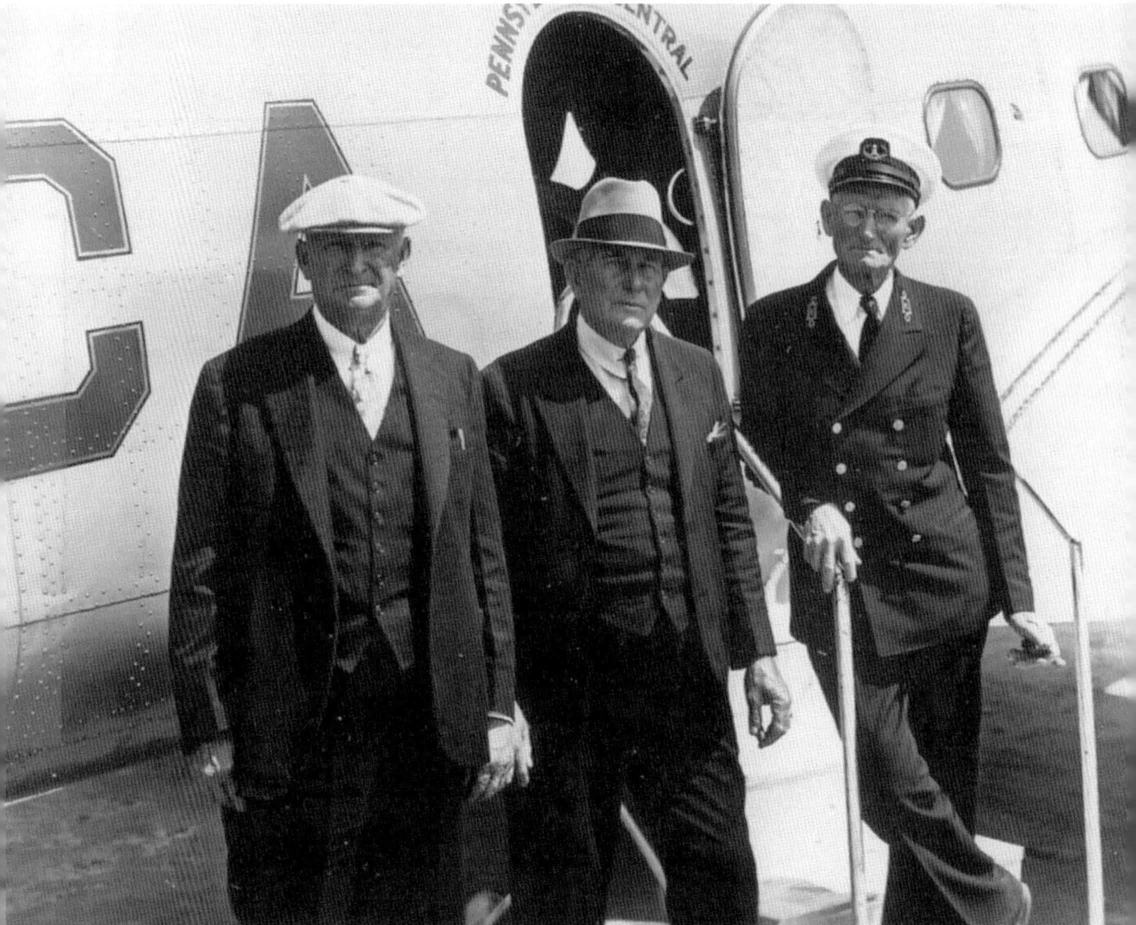

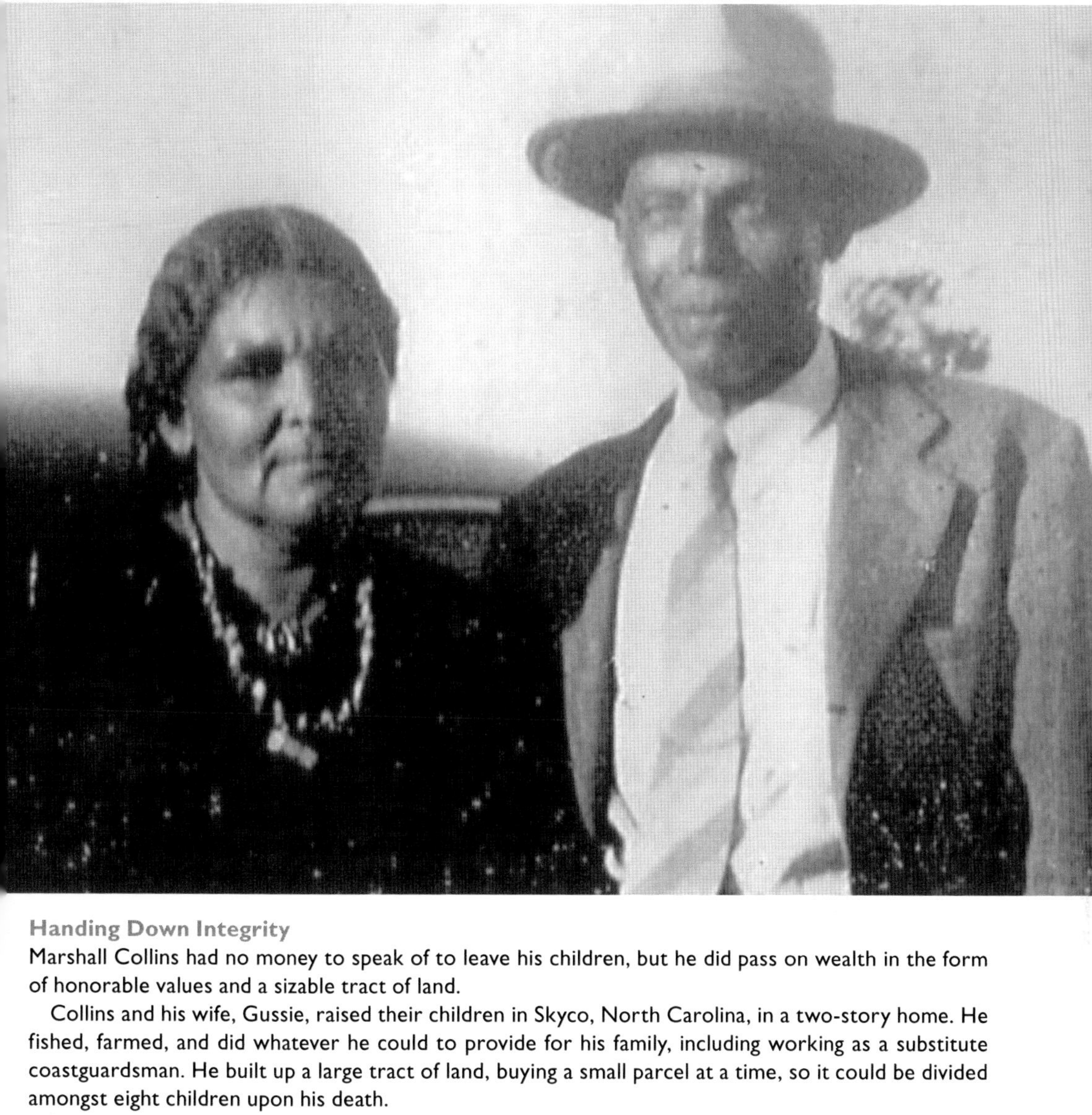

Handing Down Integrity
Marshall Collins had no money to speak of to leave his children, but he did pass on wealth in the form of honorable values and a sizable tract of land.

Collins and his wife, Gussie, raised their children in Skyco, North Carolina, in a two-story home. He fished, farmed, and did whatever he could to provide for his family, including working as a substitute coastguardsman. He built up a large tract of land, buying a small parcel at a time, so it could be divided amongst eight children upon his death.

Decades later, the land was undervalued for a government project. The heirs wisely united and went to court. After a just payment, the family gifted a portion of the land to Dare County for a visitor center and administrative buildings. (Courtesy of Frank Hester.)

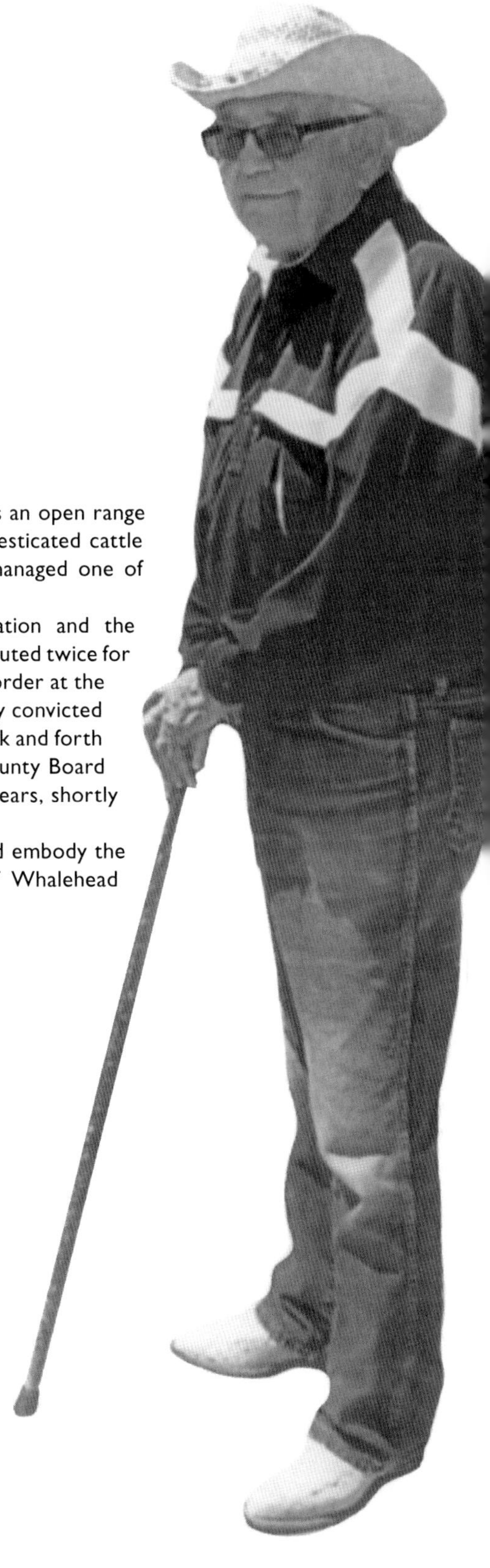

Last of the Beach Cowboys

Before Corolla was a vacation destination, there was an open range between Corolla and Carova. Wild horses and domesticated cattle shared the northern beaches, and Ernie Bowden managed one of the herds.

He became somewhat of a rebel when civilization and the government started pressing in on him. He was prosecuted twice for refusing to pay a fee for a permit to cross a fenced border at the state line through Back Bay Refuge. He was eventually convicted of failing to obey federal laws concerning traveling back and forth to his home. Ernie was elected to the Currituck County Board of Commissioners, a position he would hold for 24 years, shortly before he began his two-month prison sentence.

His independence and refusal to be pushed around embody the spirit of a true American cattleman. (Courtesy of Whalehead Preservation Trust.)

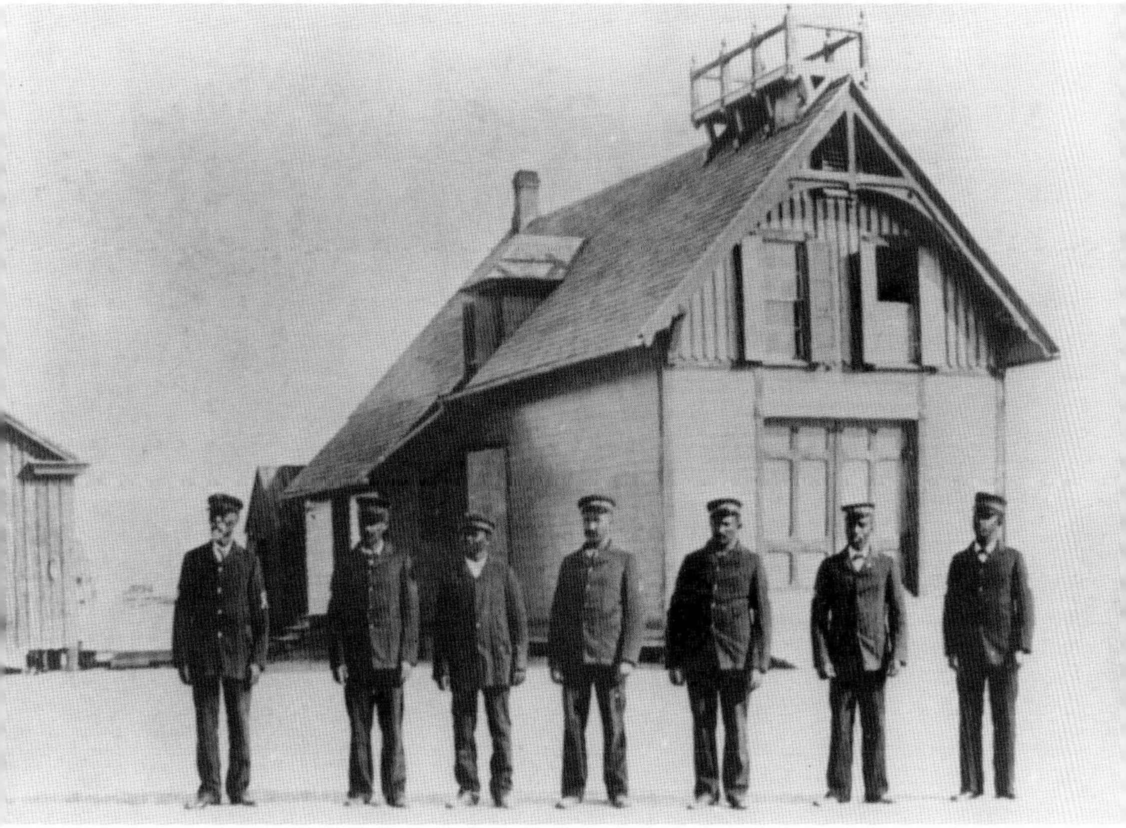

From Slave to Honored Keeper

Good character is forged in the fire of adversity, and Richard Etheridge had enough hardships in his young life to bring about the strong temperament that was needed to meet the challenges of his later years.

Born in 1842 as a slave in Manteo, North Carolina, he was raised as a member of John B. Etheridge's family, taking a place at the table and learning to read and write. As a young man, he worked at farming and fishing, giving him a deep understanding of the weather and the water. He fought in the Union Colored Troops during the Civil War. His bravery and his common sense made more than one officer take notice of this natural leader. He learned during war that he was accountable for his men, so he made them accountable to him.

Many factors converged to cause assistant inspector of the lifesaving service, Frank Newcomb, to choose Richard (left) to be keeper of an all-black Pea Island Lifesaving Station south of Oregon Inlet. Richard had excelled as the number six surfman at Bodie Island station. He could read and write well enough to keep the station's daily journal. Most importantly, he was known as being "a man among men."

Being the first "colored man" to hold this position, he knew his station would be scrutinized for its efficiency and performance. He and his crew became role models as they performed valorously in many rescues, showing heroism in raging seas and storms.

He was keeper for 20 years and died on the job. The station was decommissioned in 1947. The Coast Guard christened one of their cutters *Pea Island* in 1992. In 1996, Richard Etheridge's crew posthumously received the Gold Life-Saving Medal for Heroism in the rescue of the *Newman.* (Courtesy of the National Park Service; OBHC.)

Enticed the Wright Brothers

Perhaps because Bill Tate was postmaster and probably the most educated person in Kitty Hawk at the time, J.J. Dosher of the US Weather Bureau asked him to answer a letter from Wilbur Wright inquiring if the Outer Banks would be a suitable spot for the brothers' flying experiments. Bill replied favorably by describing the area and reporting that there were daily mail and telegram services. Due to the friendly and encouraging response they received, the Wrights decided to come and scout out North Carolina as soon as they read his letter.

Tate and the Wrights were friends for over 40 years. Tate and his wife, Addie, were photographed with her sewing machine that Wilbur used to make alterations in the cloth covering of their 1900 glider. Addie commented that Wilbur's sewing was excellent. (Courtesy of OBHC.)

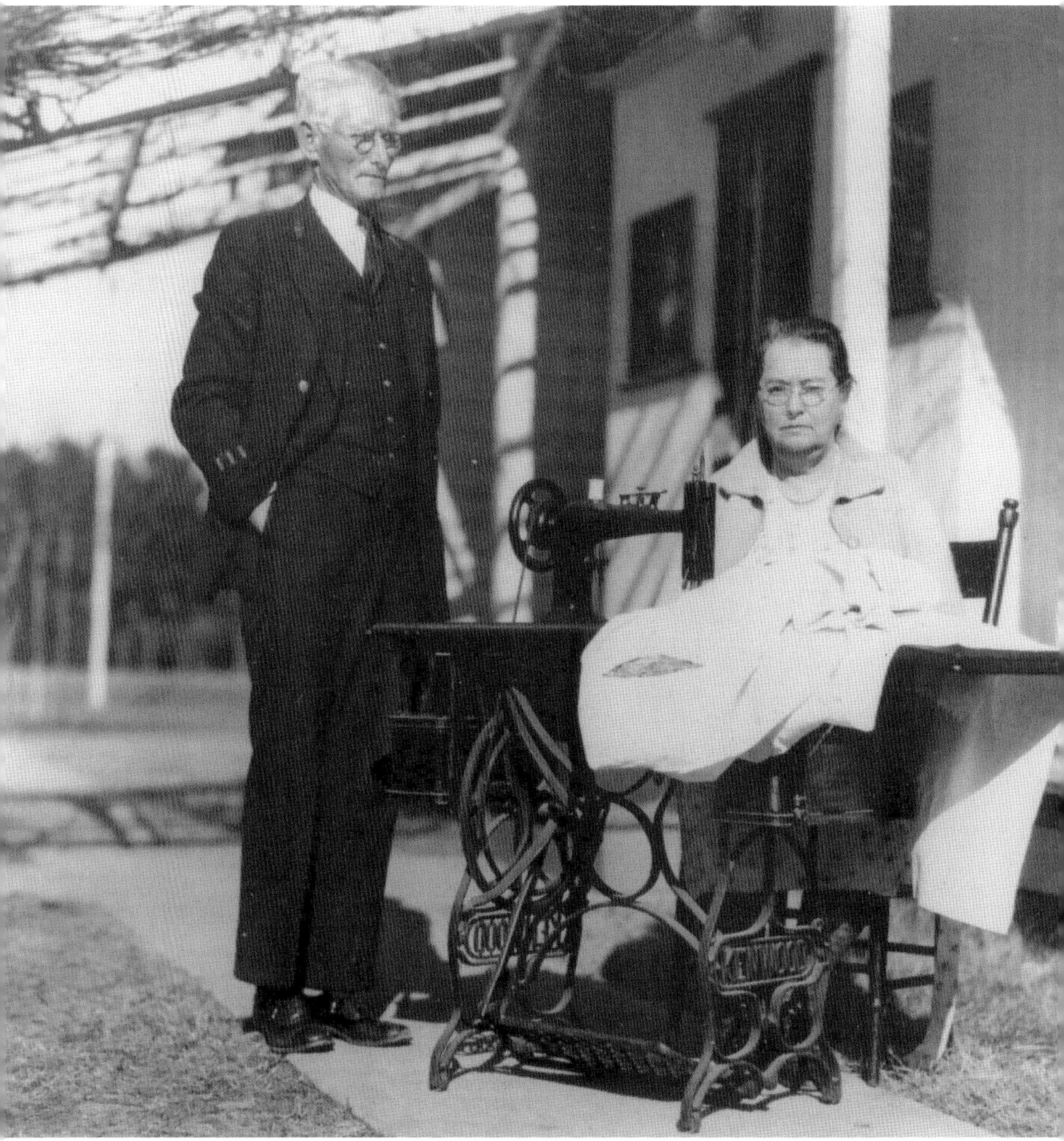

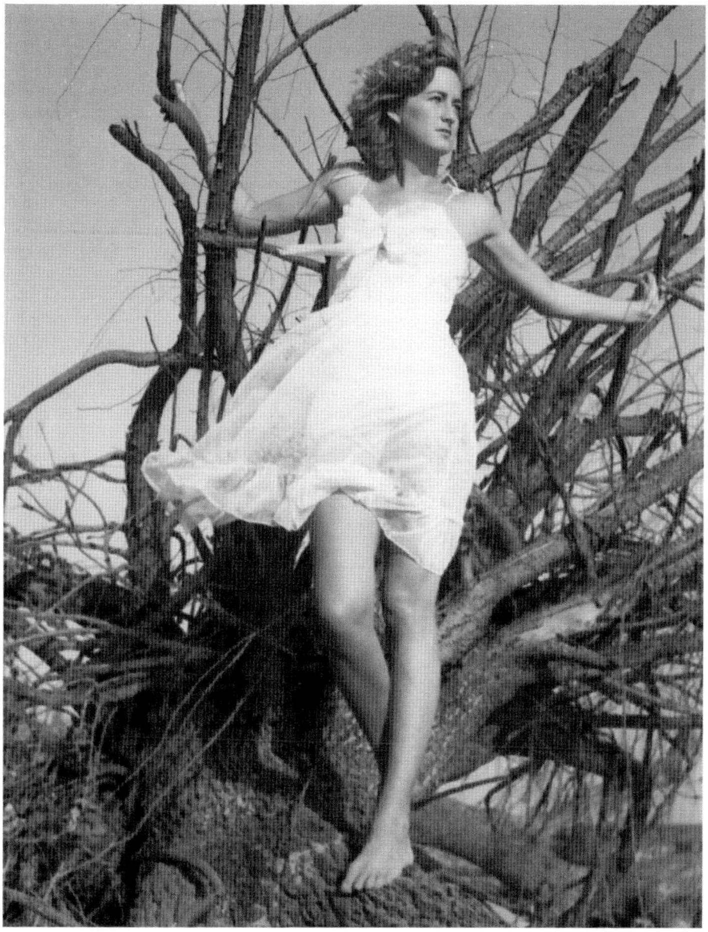

Growing up in Manteo

When Dottie Fry grew up in Manteo, it was a town where no one locked their doors, the roads were unpaved, and almost everyone was related.

The previously isolated community was forced onto center stage during World War II when German U-boats prowled offshore. Dottie told Ekaterina Etheridge, a college writer, that as a youth she had a job that was the envy of her twin sisters. A high watchtower was built in the middle of town that Dottie and other specially trained children would climb to lookout for German planes. They identified different types of planes as they flew overhead and reported questionable ones to the US Army in Norfolk, Virginia. The position was not a paying one, but she felt privileged to wear a military armband.

During the war, Dottie and her sisters met a young couple that drove a nice car and spoke perfect English. They often went to the beach together. The man, always carrying a suitcase with him, would disappear for long spells. One day, Dottie's sister excused herself on the pretext of visiting the pier house bathroom. She followed the man and watched him using a tripod and telescope. They later found out that he was a German spy gathering information about ships passing along the coast. They saw a photograph of their friend in leading newspapers when he was captured and arrested after leaving the Outer Banks.

Dottie played in *The Lost Colony* with other family members for years. Her fun-loving personality made her a favorite model for Aycock Brown's promotional photographs, meant to lure tourists to Dare County. She had many jobs during her lifetime, but, perhaps, none so exciting as her unpaid wartime occupation. (Courtesy of D'Amours Collection; OBHC.)

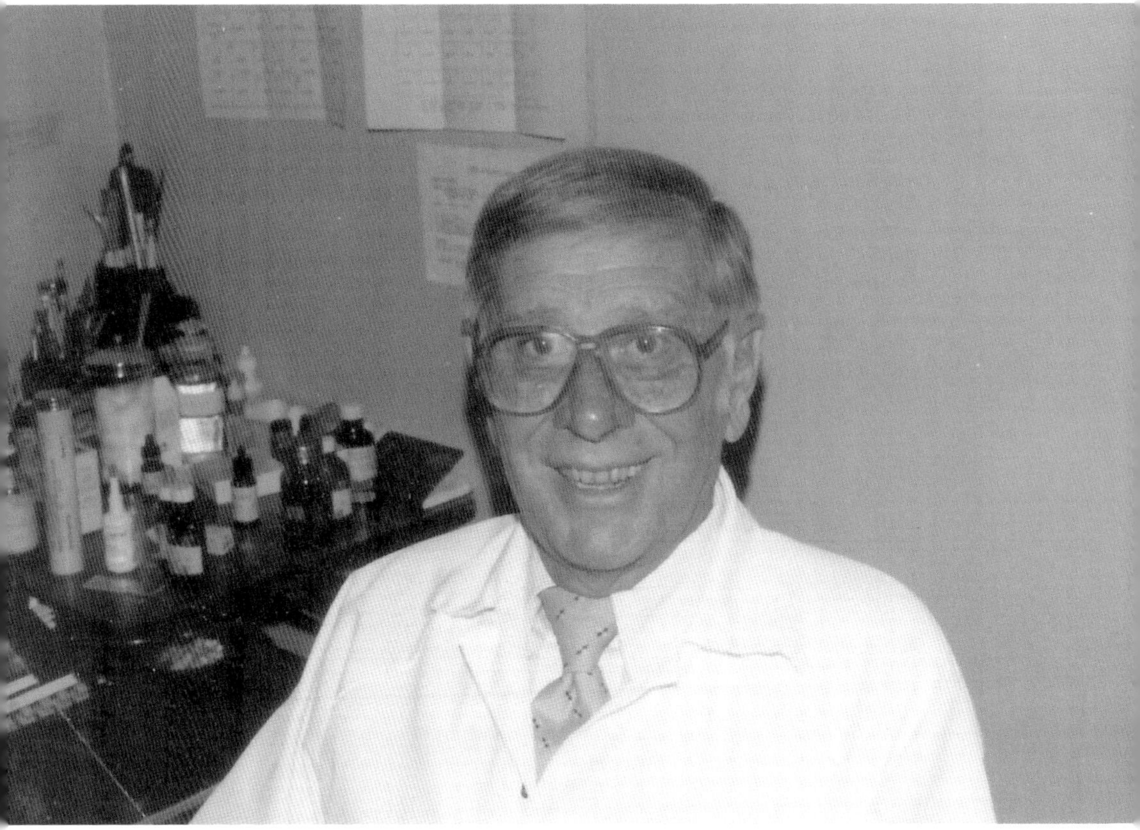

One Thousand Babies

Dr. Charles Wright impacted the Outer Banks during his 43 years of practice like few doctors have before or since. A devoted family practitioner, he believed a shot of penicillin in the rear "would do you right" in most cases.

Aleca Miller once wrote that Dr. Wright had a great sense of humor and would greet many patients with a cheery, "Well, what the hell's wrong with you?" He was known to send a constipated patient to the hospital miles away with an order reading, "F.O.S.!" He dispensed his own drugs, set broken bones, and administered to other ailments for patients as far away as Ocracoke, North Carolina.

His rough humor and chain smoking did not detract from the confidence of the more than 1,000 mothers whose babies he delivered. It is a part of his legacy that Dr. James Owens, who practices across the street from the original Wright Clinic, was delivered by his mentor, Dr. Wright. (Courtesy of Paula Lipman.)

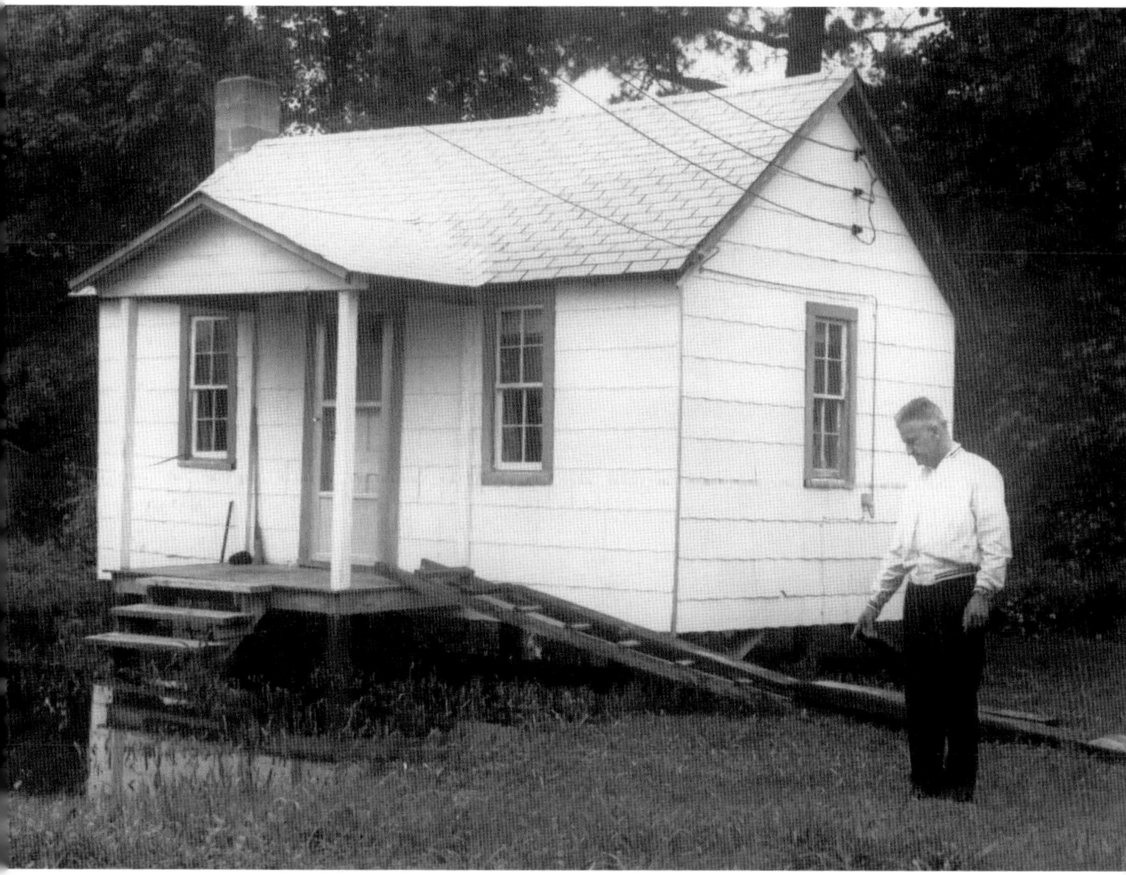

A Gentleman Keeping the Peace

Dare County sheriff Frank Cahoon was a popular and respected public servant. In his 36-year career, only two political opponents dared to run against him. A very quiet man, he never carried a gun or wore a uniform. He was known to simply telephone a man with a warrant against him and convince him to come to Manteo and turn himself in.

With no prior law enforcement experience, Sheriff Cahoon developed his own style of executing his duties. In those days (1946–1982), the sheriff had the responsibility of collecting county taxes. He would travel to the different villages, set up an office in the general store, and meet with all of his constituents as they came in to pay their taxes. In that way he got to know everyone, and every citizen got a chance to ask for things they needed.

His son Jack recalled one night when he and several other high school boys decided to play a prank. They took a 16-foot juniper boat from the waterfront, walked it up the courthouse staircase, and laid it across the pews in the courtroom. As they were making their escape, they came face to face with a patrolman, who called their fathers. Sheriff Cahoon said that Jack was to be kept overnight. The next day, Jack's father said, "I'm your attorney, judge, and jury, and you've been found guilty." Jack was sentenced to split wood for the courthouse for one week, just like the other convicts.

The sheriff would never talk about the details of an investigation, not even with his wife. He was a man who said what he meant, and meant what he said. In this photograph, he is investigating the murder of Shotgun Boogie at the victim's house. (Courtesy of OBHC.)

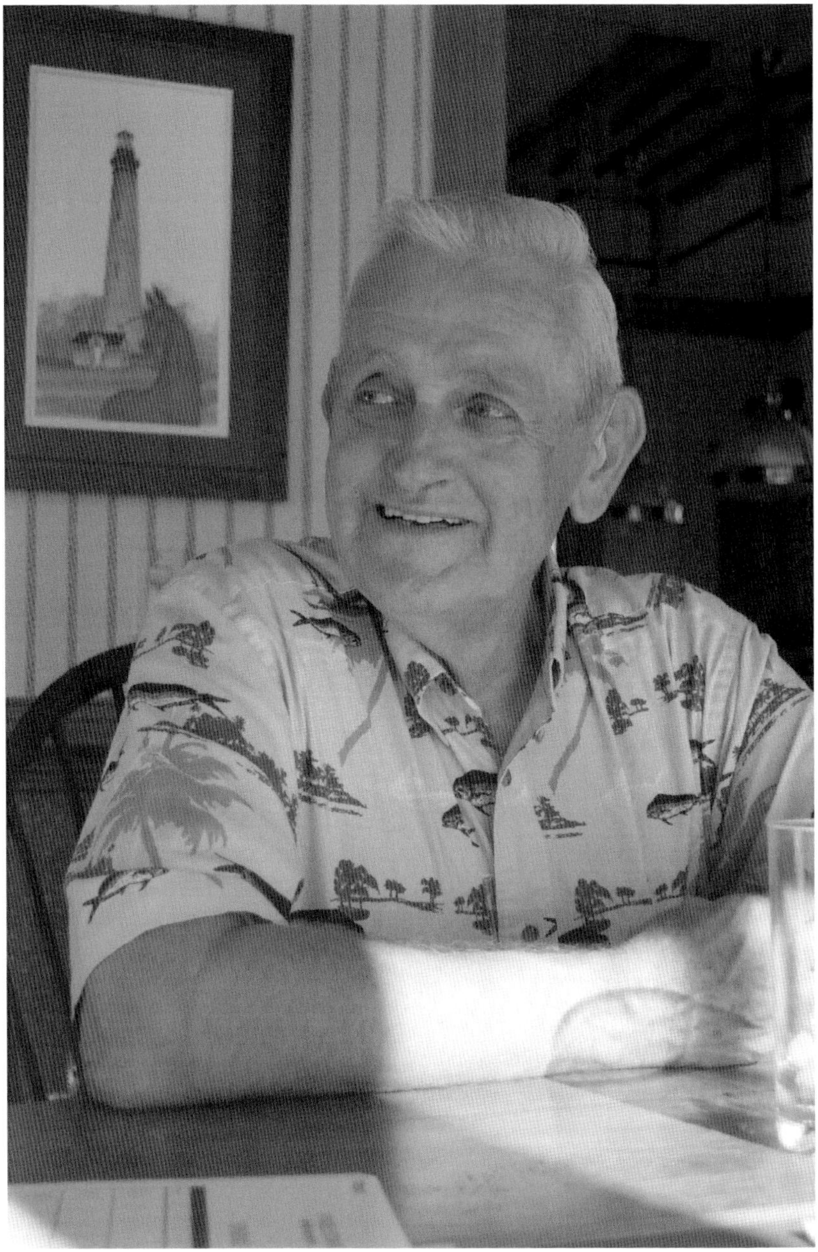

Corolla's Only Living Native

Being postmaster of Corolla must be a good job, because there have only been seven postmasters since the post office began in 1895. Norris Austin's father was one of them until 1959, when Norris took over his father's position. Norris had never wanted to be anything but a postmaster since he was a child. He served in that position for 33 years.

In 1970, the population of Corolla had dwindled to about six families and 25 people because many residents moved away to find work. Norris was zeroed in on the future. He wanted to see a paved road in the village, a school for the children, and the locals profiting from development. In his wildest dreams, he never envisioned the popular, upscale vacationland of today. (Courtesy of Yulia Vozzhaeva.)

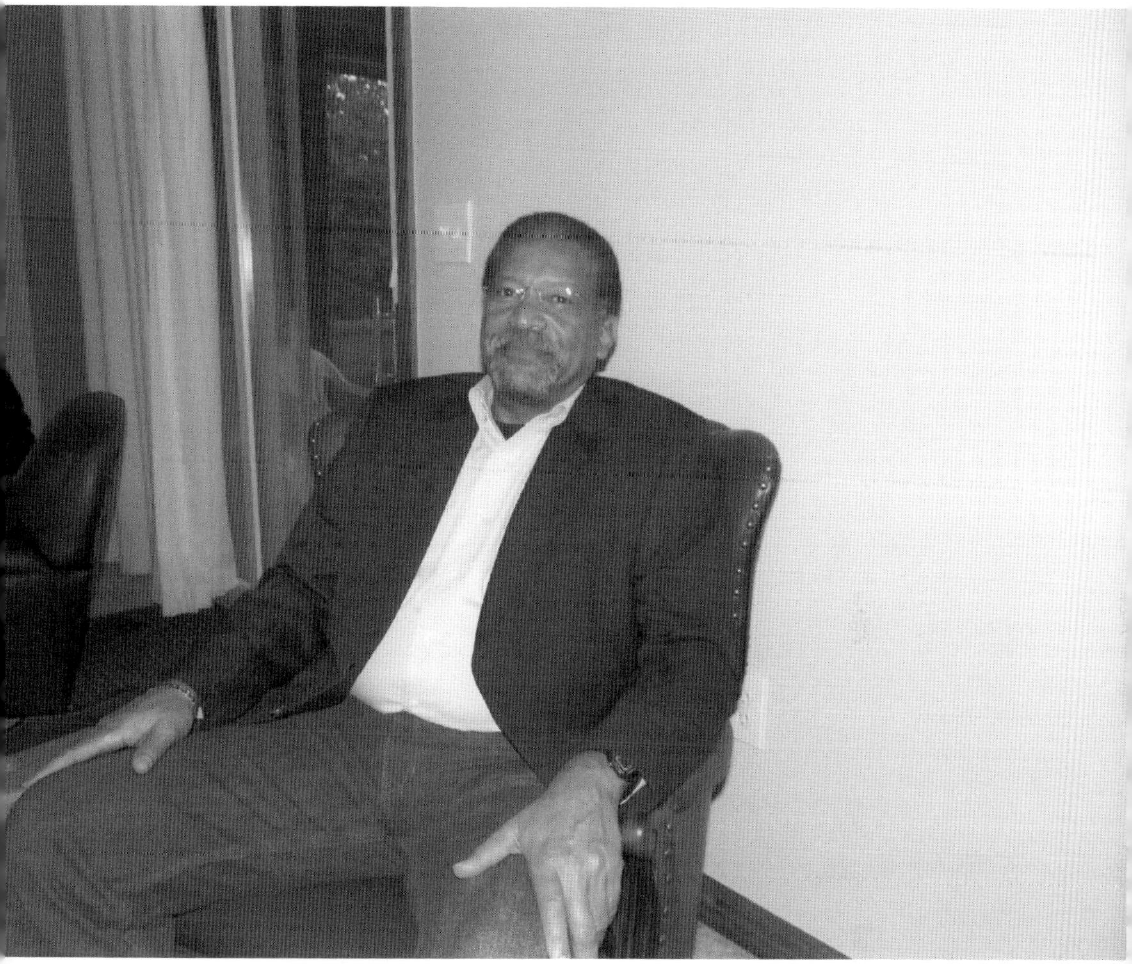

Integrating the Beach

In 1929, Dr. John H. Bias and two friends, Charles Jenkins and Henry Hargraves, purchased 84 acres of property from ocean to sound south of Duck, North Carolina. They paid $2,100 for the land and divided the property into three parcels.

According to research by Shoshannah Roy, Henry Hargraves built a nightclub on the sound side of his property in 1950. It was a place where African Americans who worked as domestics and in hotels and restaurants went to relax, drink, and dance after hours. Henry's land became an area known as Hargraves Beach.

John Bias's children developed his parcel into Bias Shores, a small, affluent neighborhood. The Bias family is a family of educators, many of whom have taught at Elizabeth City State University, where several buildings have the Bias name. In a small way, the northern beach became racially integrated before other areas.

Pictured here, a grandson of Dr. John Bias, James Cofield, is at home in Bias Shores. (Courtesy of Shoshannah Roy.)

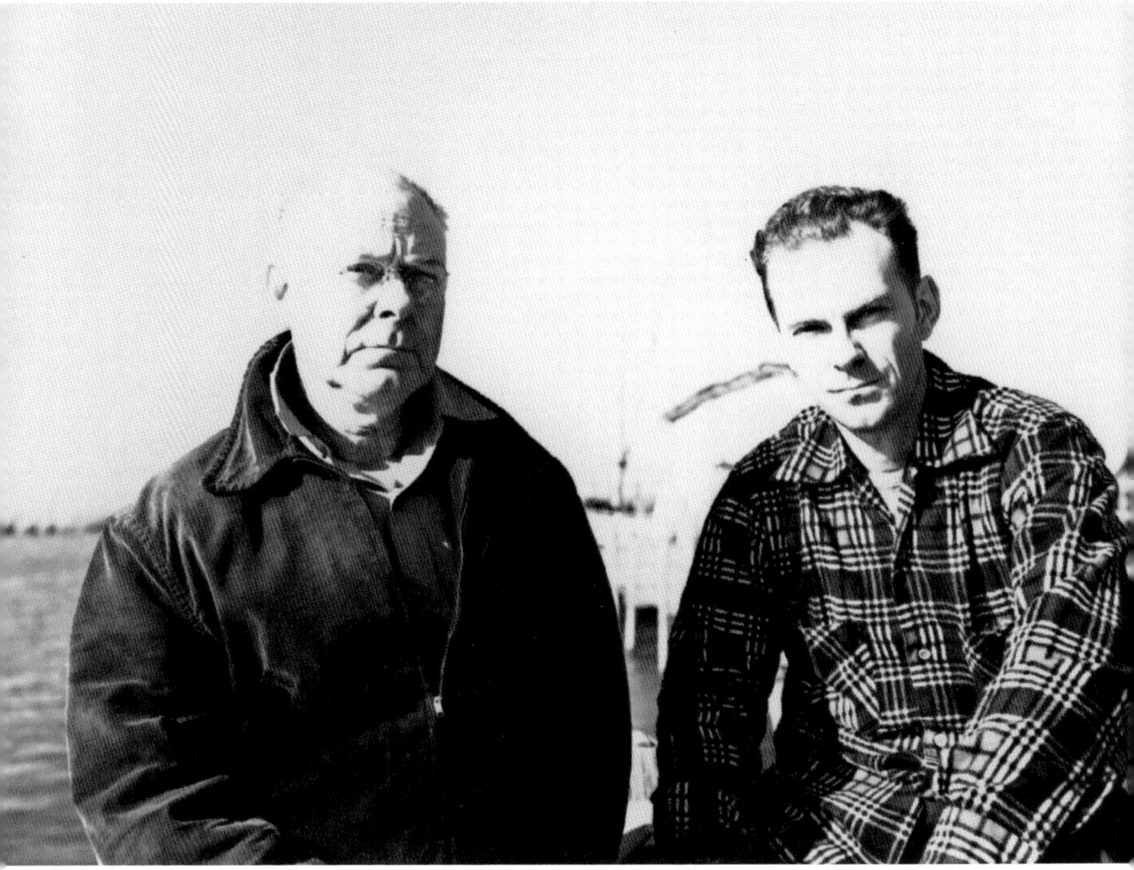

Accepting the Job for Life

When the owners of the Globe Fish Company put the word out that they were looking for a hardworking young man of integrity and honesty to operate the main wharf complex in Wanchese, North Carolina, Richard Gray, a young man from Buxton, North Carolina, was suggested. Only 17 at the time, he accepted the job and moved from Hatteras Island to Roanoke Island.

In 1911, Wanchese Wharf consisted of a series of docks, tram tracks, a large freight house, and a hotel. The owner of Globe Fish Company, E.R. Daniels, made this wharf the main depot on his Wanchese Line.

Gray married E.R. Daniels's niece Daisy, who grew up down the road from the wharf. Pictured here with his son Don, "Mr. Richard" worked as stationmaster for over 65 years, rarely missing a day. Under his diligent direction, Wanchese Wharf was a hub of activity when commercial fishing was the primary occupation of Outer Bankers. (Courtesy of Jane Gray.)

CHAPTER TWO

The Changing Face of Communities

"I will be remembered."

In the villages along the Outer Banks, changes came about rapidly as roads and bridges were built to connect the villages with the mainland and the villages to each other. Also, as a result of this infrastructure, tourism began to take a foothold. Manteo became the county seat of Dare, and communities began to incorporate. Locals such as R. Bruce Etheridge, Victor Meekins, W.O. Saunders, John Wilson, and Billy Parker helped the communities move forward with their politics, news reporting, preservation, and conservation. People were now able to pull together and make a living without depending on small-scale farming and fishing.

Many communities were becoming beach resorts, and a new way of life had begun. Settlements that had sprung up around lifesaving stations disappeared when the stations were decommissioned. Other villages on the extreme northern Outer Banks were discovered, seemingly overnight. Duck and Corolla are now major tourist attractions with only a few native residents left. These two summer boomtowns become almost ghost towns in the winter. Tourists and developers from northern states bought entire villages in a matter of years. Carova, the northernmost hamlet, is situated on the North Carolina/Virginia line. It is accessible only by boat or four-wheel-drive vehicle. There is no paved road for the approximately 12-mile stretch of beach leading there, yet real estate prices are already sky high.

However one views the Outer Banks—for better or for worse—change, in the name of progress, marches steadily forward.

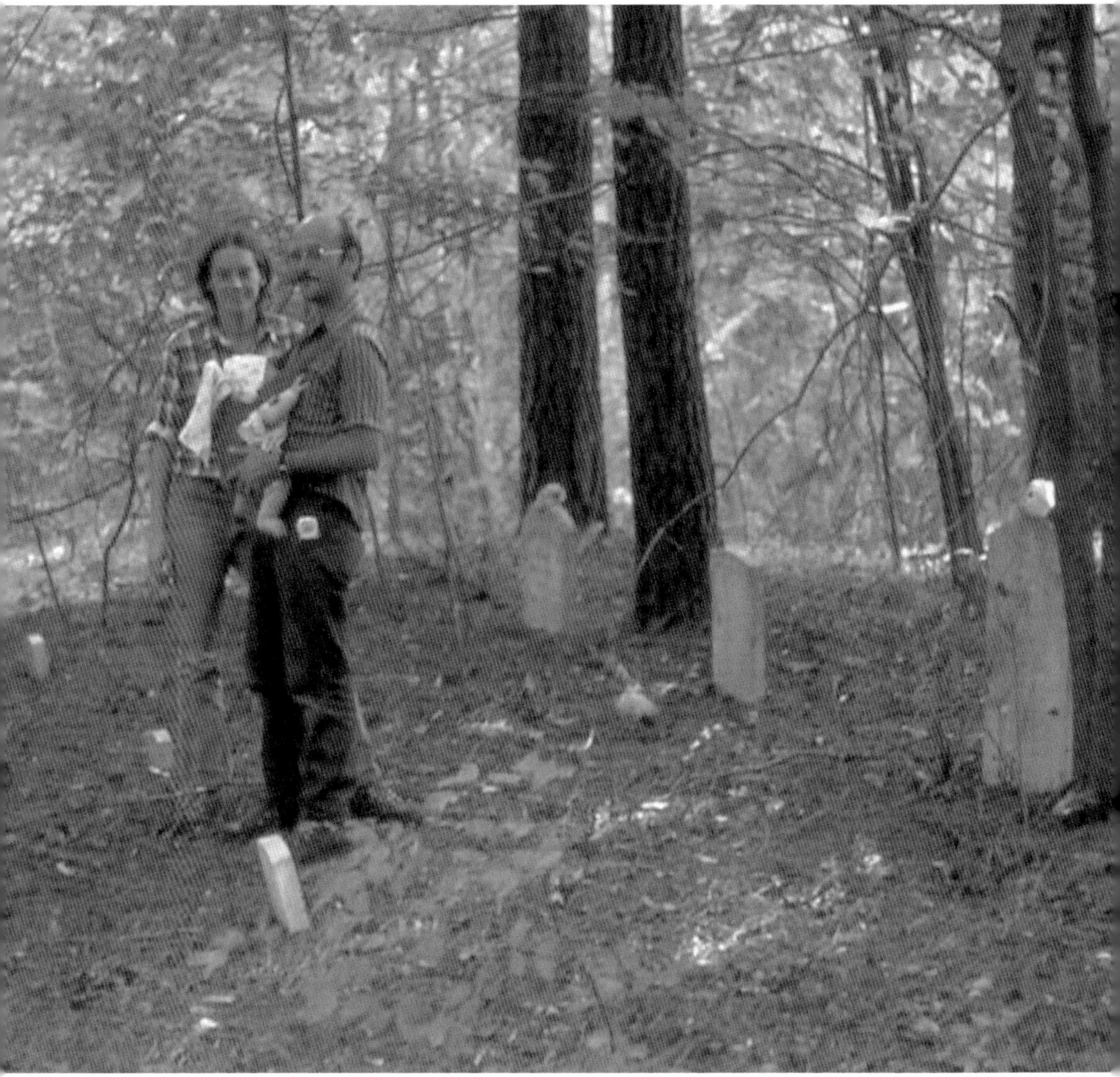

Maritime Forest Preservationists

It was Henrietta List's mother who first introduced her to the unique environment of Nags Head Woods, a maritime forest with hardwoods and vegetation not usually found growing on a tiny, ocean-exposed sand strip.

A movement began when a garden club member asked Henrietta if she knew of an area that could be a conservation project for them. In 1978, a combination of Henrietta's persistence and the input of many key players resulted in the North Carolina Nature Conservancy hiring Jim and Henrietta List as director and steward to implement a protection plan for the woods and keep it in an undisturbed state.

With their two young sons in tow, they expanded trails, built boardwalks, and helped construct a visitors' center and managers' residence. They left their magical paradise in 1988, but still feel the call of the mysterious woods. (Courtesy of Henrietta List.)

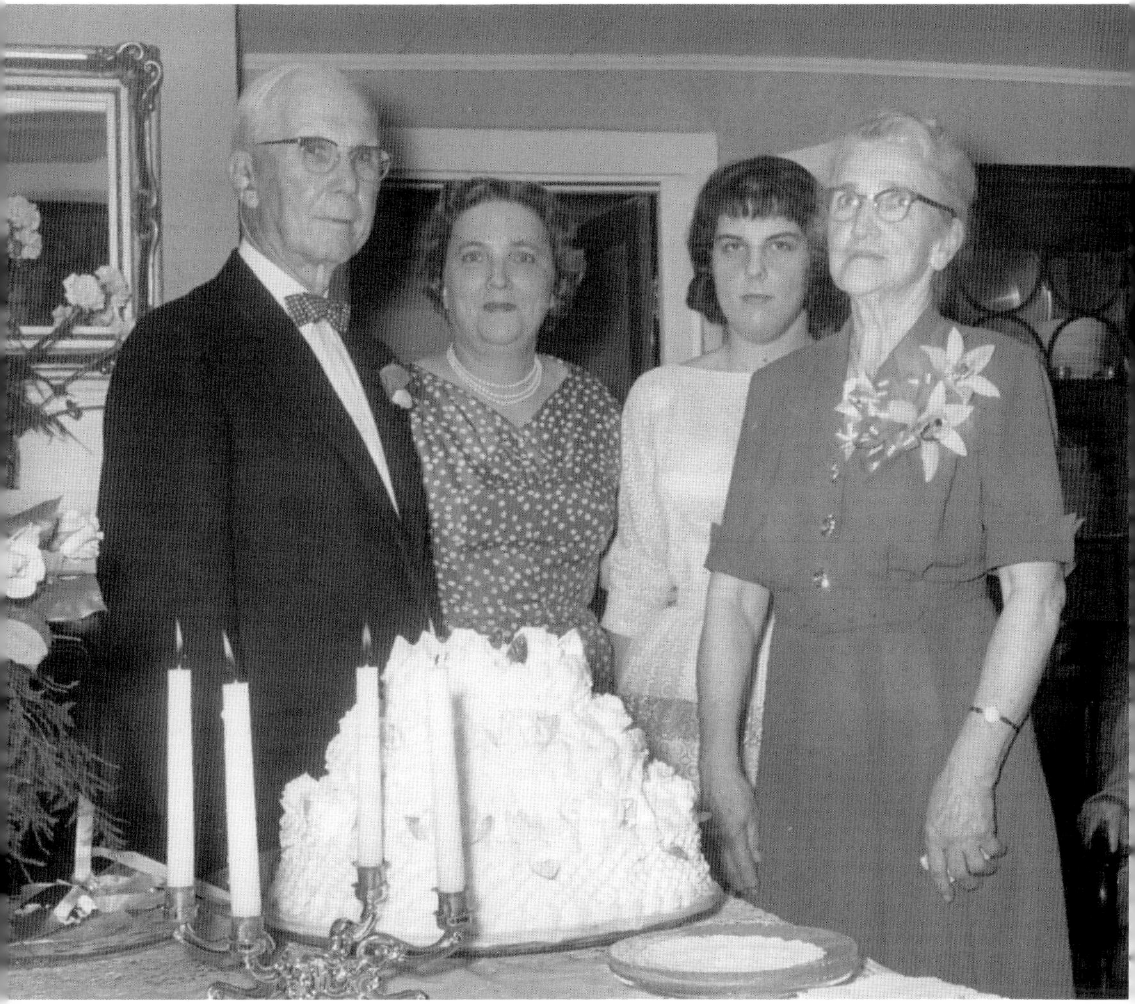

Duke of Dare

His stately demeanor and life spent advocating for Dare County caused home folks to call R. Bruce Etheridge "Uncle Bruce." Fellow legislators in the North Carolina General Assembly called him the "Duke of Dare."

North Carolina historian William Powell aptly described R. Bruce Etheridge as "never content to be involved in a single occupation." He worked as superintendent of schools, clerk of superior court, Manteo postmaster, president of the Bank of Manteo, and as a partner in an insurance and realty venture all while serving a half century in the North Carolina General Assembly, primarily in the House of Representatives. As one of the founders of the Roanoke Island Historical Association, he commemorated the Roanoke Voyages and continuously promoted *The Lost Colony* drama. He used his 13-year position as director of the Department of Conservation and Development to help advertise North Carolina as a tourist destination.

For promoting his community so well, a North Carolina ferry was christened *R. Bruce Etheridge*. His family christened two of his granddaughters with the middle name Bruce. (Courtesy of Betty Bruce Stratton.)

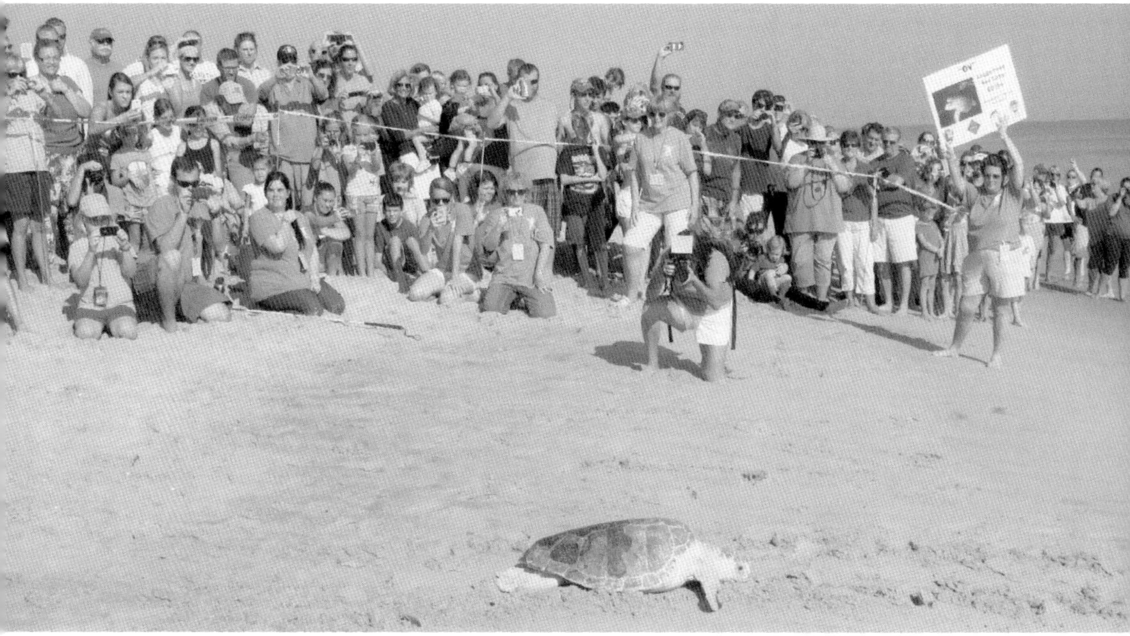

Returning Turtles to the Water

The Network for Endangered Sea Turtles (NEST) began when a small group of citizens became concerned about an injured loggerhead. Their volunteers devote themselves to monitoring nesting season on the Outer Banks by conducting daily morning patrols along 53 miles of oceanside coastline.

NEST partnered with the North Carolina Aquarium on Roanoke Island, and after receiving a grant from the Outer Banks Community Foundation, they built a small rehabilitation center on the grounds of the aquarium. Marine patients suffering from sickness, injuries, or cold-stun are cared for until being released back into the wild.

To the delight of the gathered crowd, a loggerhead turtle is set free. (Courtesy of the North Carolina Aquarium on Roanoke Island.)

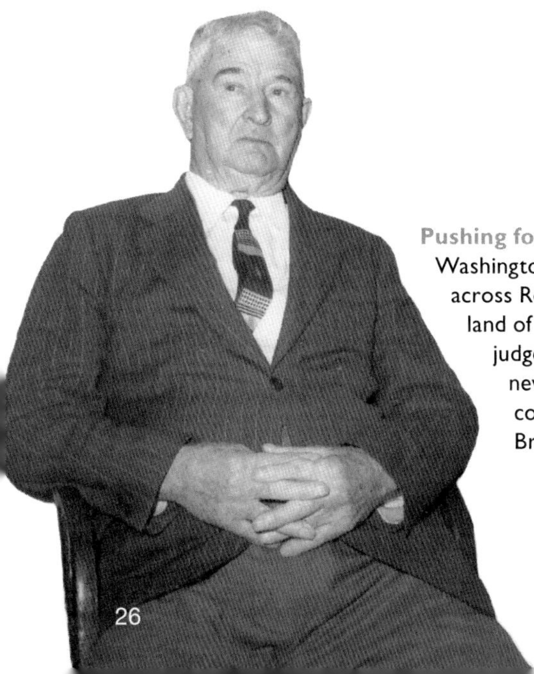

Pushing for Progress

Washington Baum led a drive to see the first toll bridge constructed across Roanoke Sound. His plan was to make Dare County a new land of opportunity. He held the position of recorder's court judge from 1928 until 1962. The year he stepped down, a new concrete bridge to replace the old wooden span was completed and named in his honor. (Courtesy of Aycock Brown Collection; OBHC.)

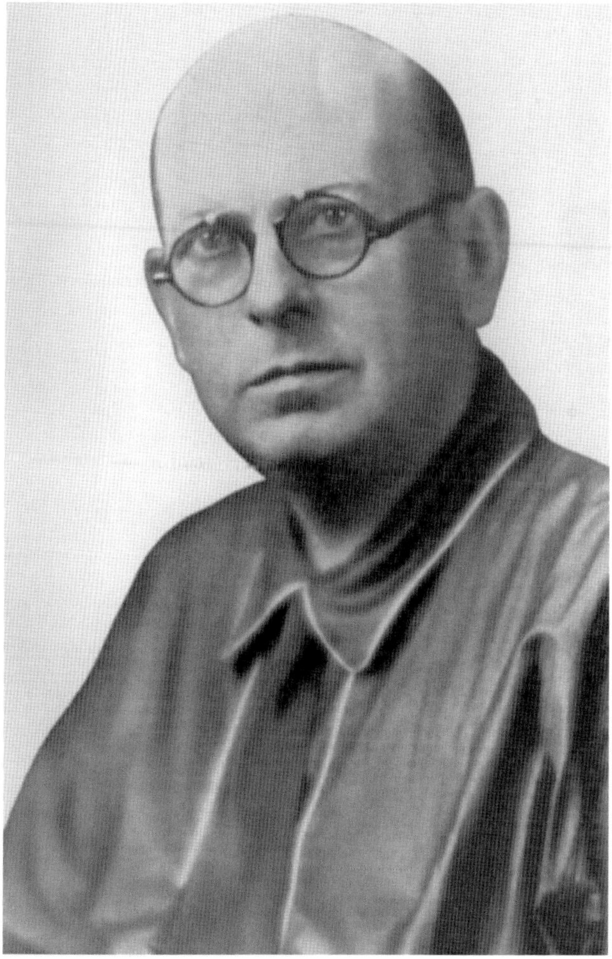

The Independent Man

The great American critic H.L. Mencken once wrote, "If the South had forty editors like W.O. Saunders . . . its problems would disappear within five years." He was referring to the editor of the weekly *Independent* newspaper in Elizabeth City, North Carolina.

W.O. Saunders was a hard, outspoken editor who deliberately offended many people he wrote about if he felt they were corrupt businessmen, politicians, or religious fakes. He championed the rights of African Americans, women, and the downtrodden. He was shot at twice and beaten up several times as a result of his caustic editorials.

He began a campaign to build a monument to the Wright brothers in 1927. Congressman Lindsay Warren had a funding bill passed, a group of people from New Jersey donated land, and work was begun on the monument by 1931. He was also an advocate for bridges to be built in an effort to encourage tourism on the Outer Banks.

One of the incorporators of the Roanoke Island Historical Association, in an editorial entitled "A Real Idea," Saunders promoted the creation of a drama, not just a pageant, to tell the story of the lost colony. He suggested they hire a professional playwright and have some kind of park where the settlement could be replicated. In 1937, the symphonic drama *The Lost Colony* opened, commemorating the 350th anniversary of Virginia Dare's birth, with seating for 3,000 at the site of the original Fort Raleigh. America's longest running outdoor drama owes a debt of gratitude to one of its greatest promoters. (Courtesy of the Museum of the Albemarle.)

Bought Ink by the Barrel

As editor of his own paper, the *Dare County Times,* Victor Meekins used his money, time, and editorials to advocate change for the betterment of his community. As a former sheriff and as a member of many groups, he lobbied for better roads and building the Manteo Airport. In this August 1941 photograph, Meekins (left) is talking with Gov. J. Melville Broughton aboard Toby Tillett's ferry that plied the waters of Oregon Inlet.

Six years earlier, Victor and Catherine Meekins borrowed $75 to buy used printing equipment to go into business as the area's first newspaper. Now known as the *Coastland Times,* it is operated today by granddaughter Susan Simpson. (Courtesy of OBHC.)

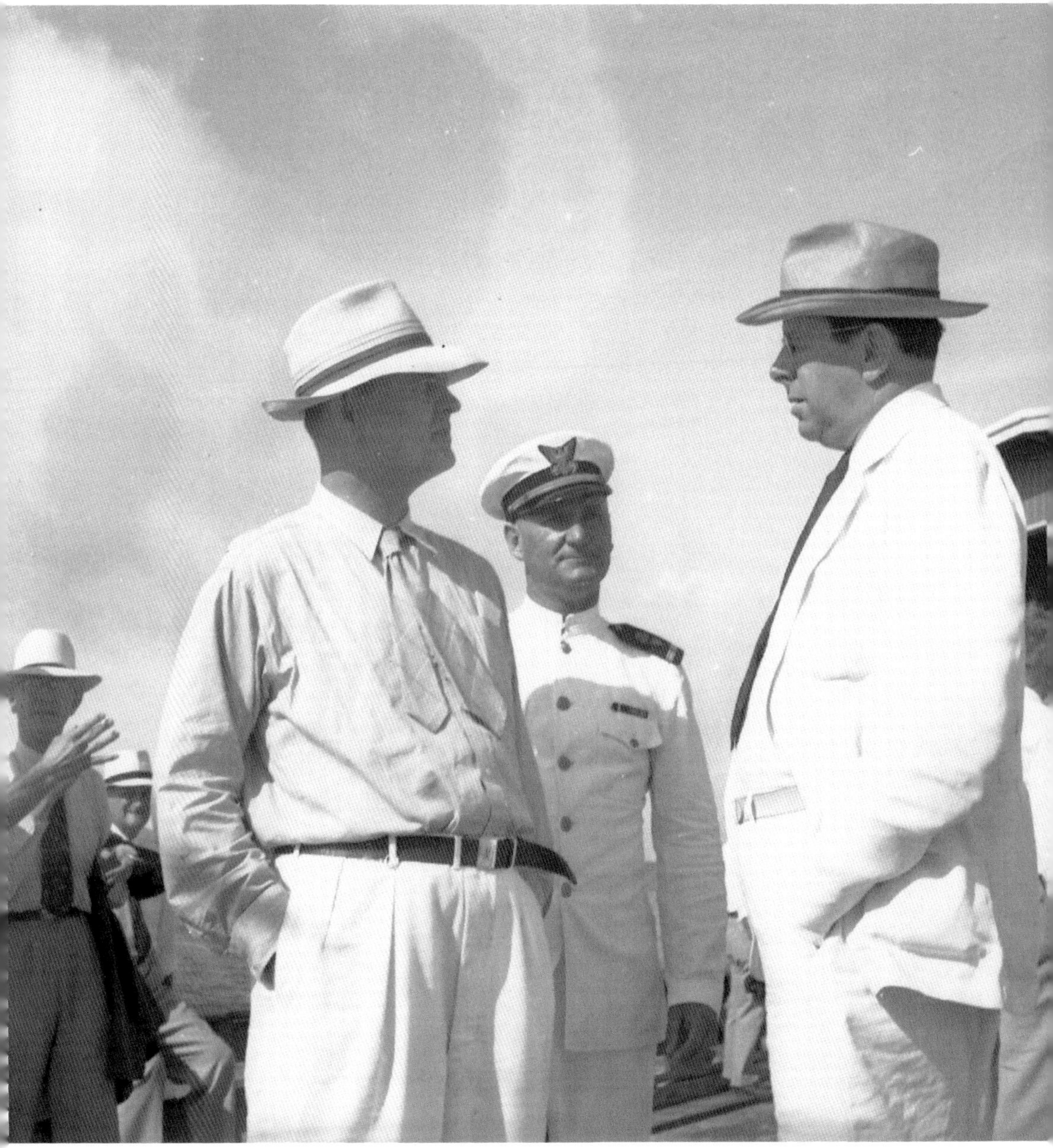

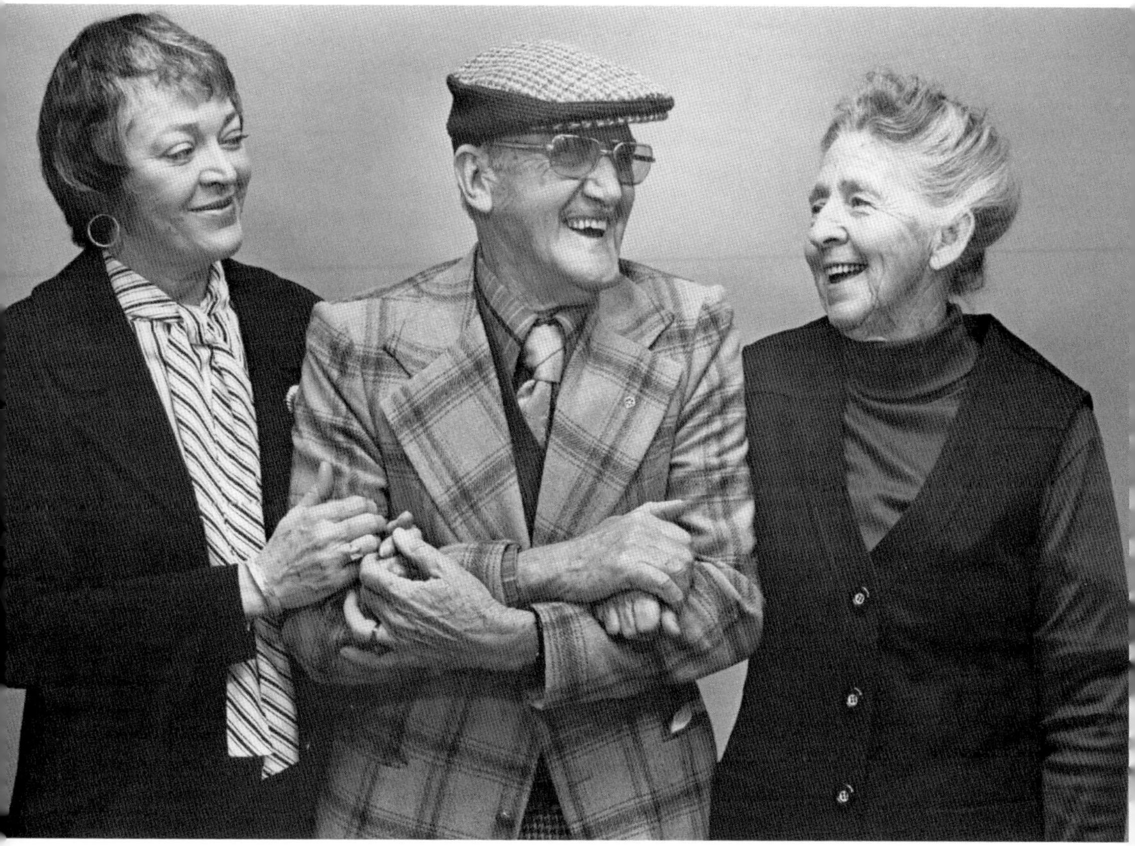

Pretty Girls and Dead Fish

Slight and spry with a straw hat, trademark moustache, and numerous cameras around his neck, Aycock Brown was an Outer Banks fixture. He was seen everywhere taking photographs of everything. Largely as a result of his efforts, the mid-20th century history of the Outer Banks is recorded in black-and-white, 8-by-10-inch prints.

A native of Caldwell County, North Carolina, who studied journalism at Columbia University, Brown was stationed at Ocracoke during World War II. He was a civilian intelligence officer with the Navy, charged with the task of removing dead bodies and identifying them after U-boats sank their ships and tankers.

In 1950, he became the first director of the tourist bureau in Manteo. For 20 years, he tirelessly made it his personal mission to make the nation aware of the Outer Banks. He sent out press releases nationwide, always accompanied with his signature photographs of grinning anglers, bathing beauties, and happy families at play. Columnist Lawrence Maddry once wrote, "An editor would look at one with Aycock Brown's name on it and tell the desk man to run it. 'It's not that good,' he would say, 'but Aycock's going to raise hell if I don't print it or else fill my mailbox with shipments of those Dare County figs. I don't know which is worse.'"

Perhaps the most famous photograph of the estimated 100,000 that Brown took was of the lighted Wright Memorial at night with the moon above. With a portable radio in hand, he snapped the shot at the exact moment when man first set foot on the moon.

Fittingly, Dare County named the welcome center in Kitty Hawk after the man who worked so hard to put the Outer Banks on the map. Brown is pictured here with fellow Manteo residents Mollie Fearing (left) and Cora Mae Basnight (right). (Courtesy of OBHC.)

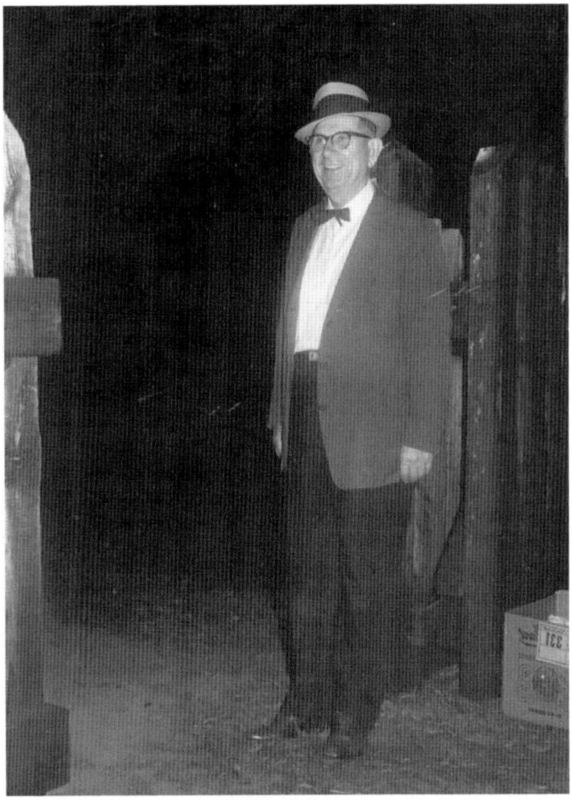

Faithful in 50-Year Segments
Chauncey Meekins walked to his job as Dare County clerk of court and back home every evening for the 52 years that he held his position. He is pictured here in front of *The Lost Colony* Waterside Theatre, where he served as treasurer and worked in the box office. He was also church treasurer and Sunday school superintendent for 50 years at the Methodist church in Wanchese. (Courtesy of OBHC.)

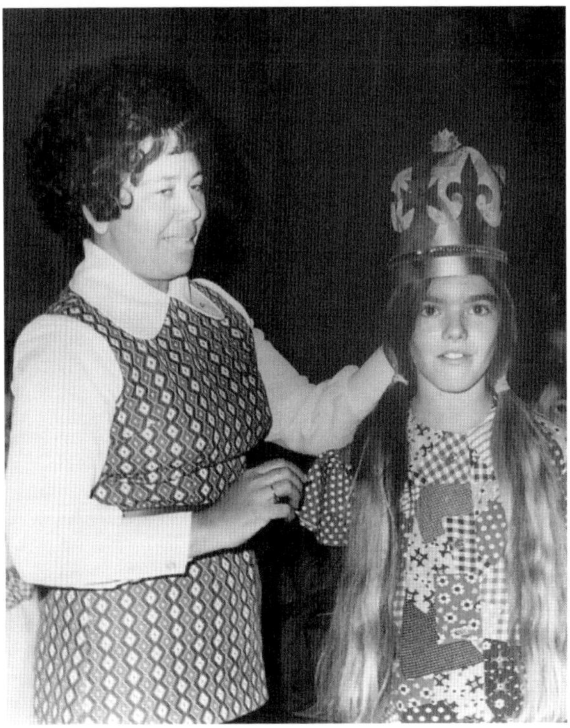

Advocate for the Disenfranchised
Dellerva Collins began her life's work as a social worker when she suddenly became a widow with two children to rear. During her career, she was a tireless advocate for minority children and senior citizens. She became the first woman elected to the Manteo Board of Commissioners and held that office for 25 years. (Courtesy of Aycock Brown Collection; OBHC.)

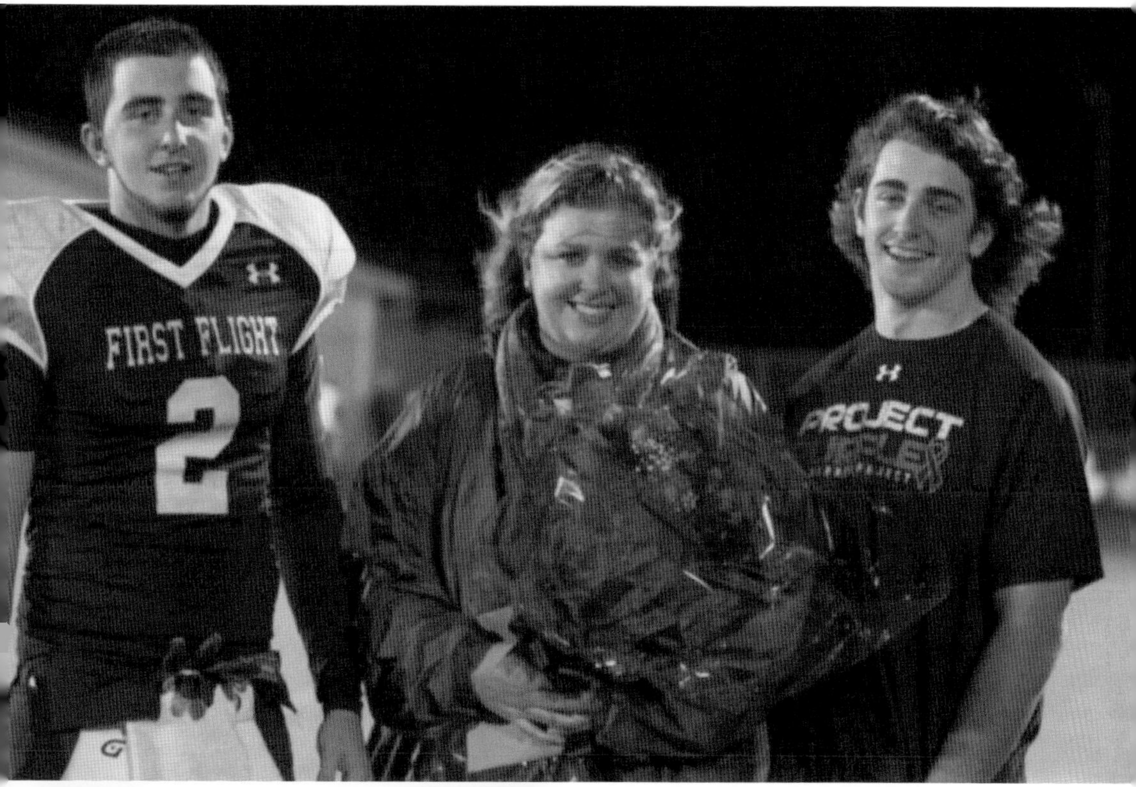

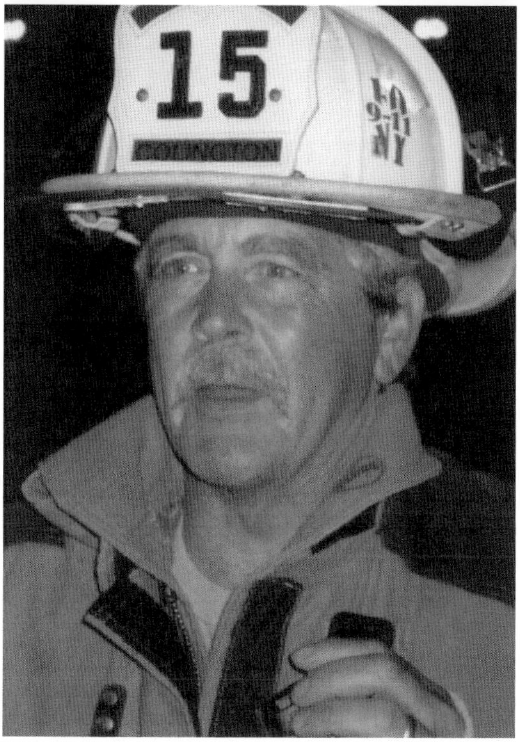

Painting the Outer Banks Purple
Kelly Tobin became aware of Project Purple, an initiative of NBA player Chris Herron, which challenges teens to remain alcohol-free and drug-free. In 2012, Project Purple "took off like crazy" at First Flight High School when 54 athletes took the pledge and wore purple tee shirts, bracelets, and shoelaces to encourage others to join in. Pictured here, Tobin celebrates homecoming with her two sons. (Courtesy of Kelly Ballard.)

A Cool Head
US Air Force veteran Kim Piddington became a volunteer with Colington's fire department and rose through the ranks, becoming the first paid firefighter in 1990 and the first paid chief in 1994. At his 35-year retirement celebration, he was credited for modernizing the department and being the calmest man on a fire scene. (Courtesy of Kim Piddington)

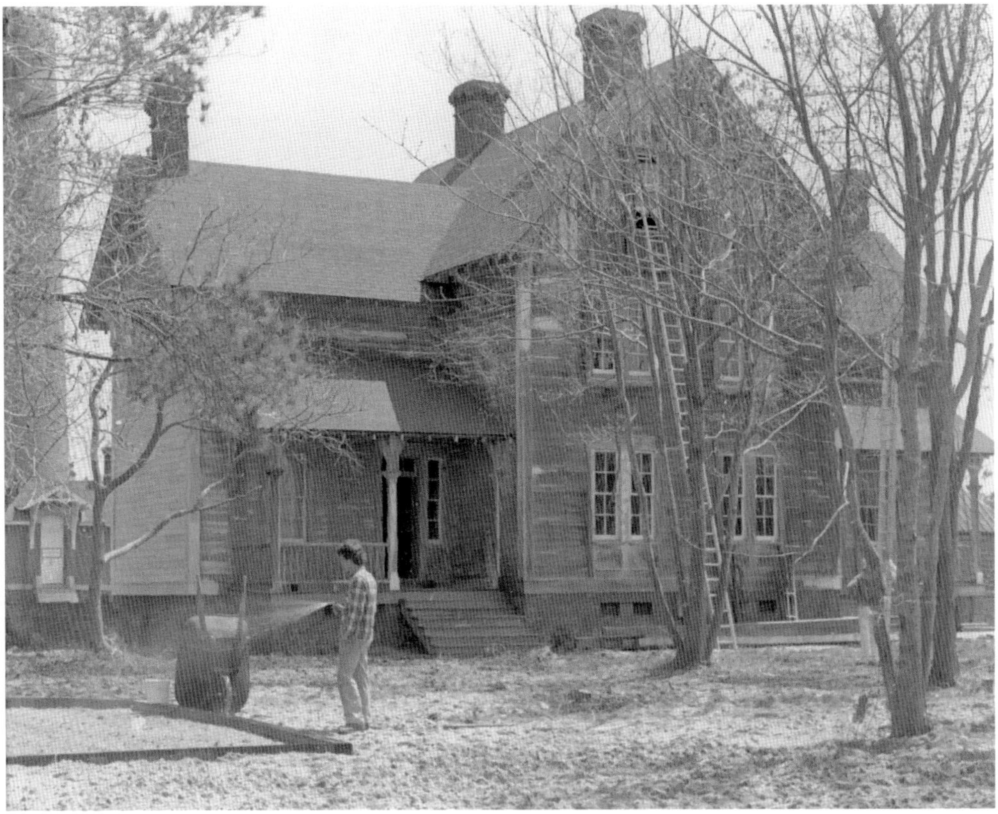

Breathing Life into Historic Structures

Architect John Wilson and landscape architect Billy Parker founded the Outer Banks Conservationists, a nonprofit organization that raised approximately $4 million in private funds to restore the Currituck Beach Light Station. The lighthouse and keeper's house opened to the public in an interpretive educational manner.

In addition to this project, the foundation has supported the Currituck Wildlife Museum, the Old Jarvisburg Colored School, the Currituck Humane Society, the restorations of the Corolla Village Schoolhouse, and two lifesaving stations. The two men have dedicated their lives to maintaining and preserving the natural and cultural resources of the Outer Banks. In these photographs, John Wilson sprays off the wheelbarrow in front of the keeper's house, and Billy Parker inspects the old outhouse. (Both images courtesy of John Wilson.)

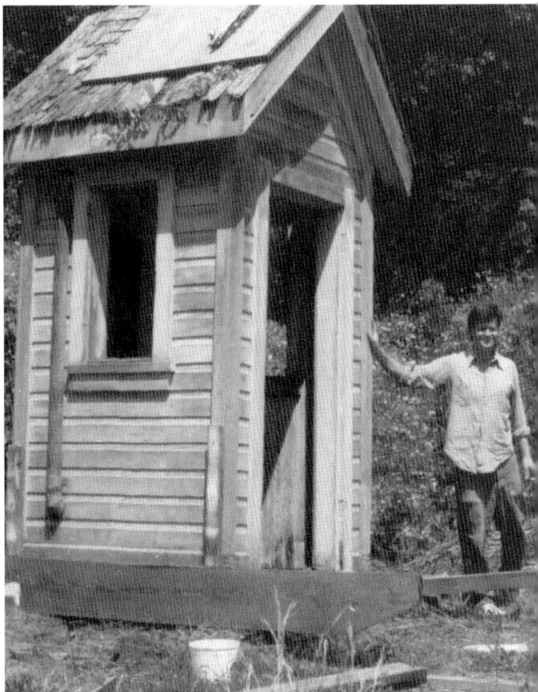

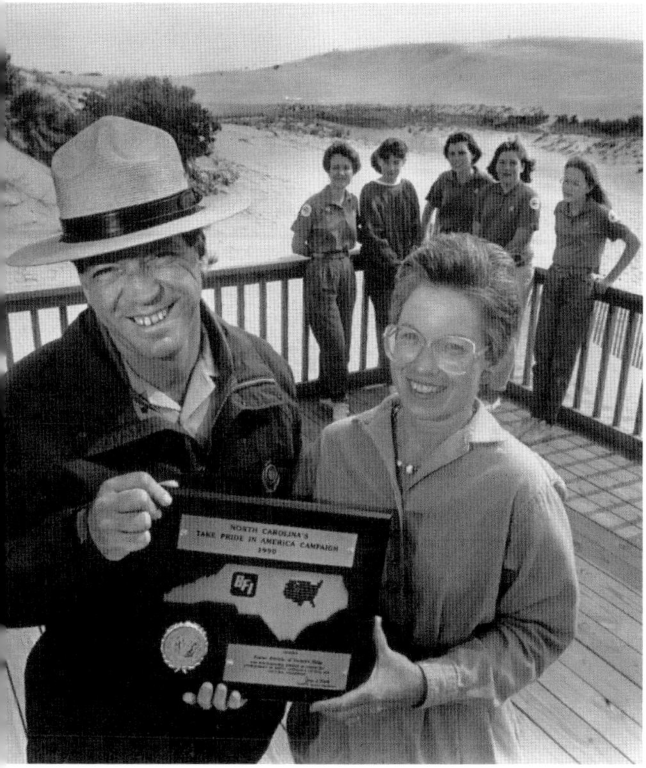

A Full Plate
When Peggy Birkemeier moved to Southern Shores in 1980, she saw "all kinds of things missing" in the simple society of the Outer Banks. She was instrumental in establishing a new Girl Scout service unit and organizing the Junior Friends of Jockey's Ridge. The group was recognized at Jockey's Ridge State Park in 1990 for receiving both the North Carolina and the National Take Pride in America Awards. (Courtesy of Peggy Birkemeier.)

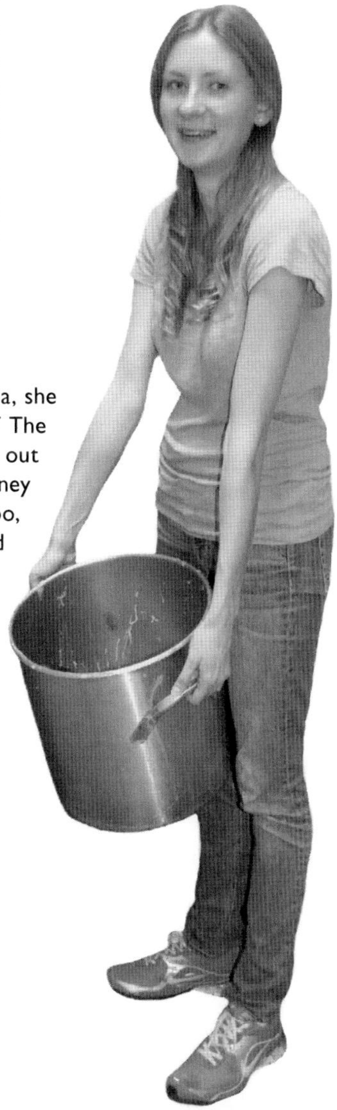

From Russia With Love
The first summer Yulia Vozzhaeva came to Corolla from Siberia, she worked in a bagel shop. After graduating from the College of The Albemarle, she pursued her ultimate American dream by filling out her application to Yale University, knowing that she had no money or resources to go if accepted. Yale must have known that, too, because the school gave her a full scholarship with room and board. (Courtesy of Scott Wheeler.)

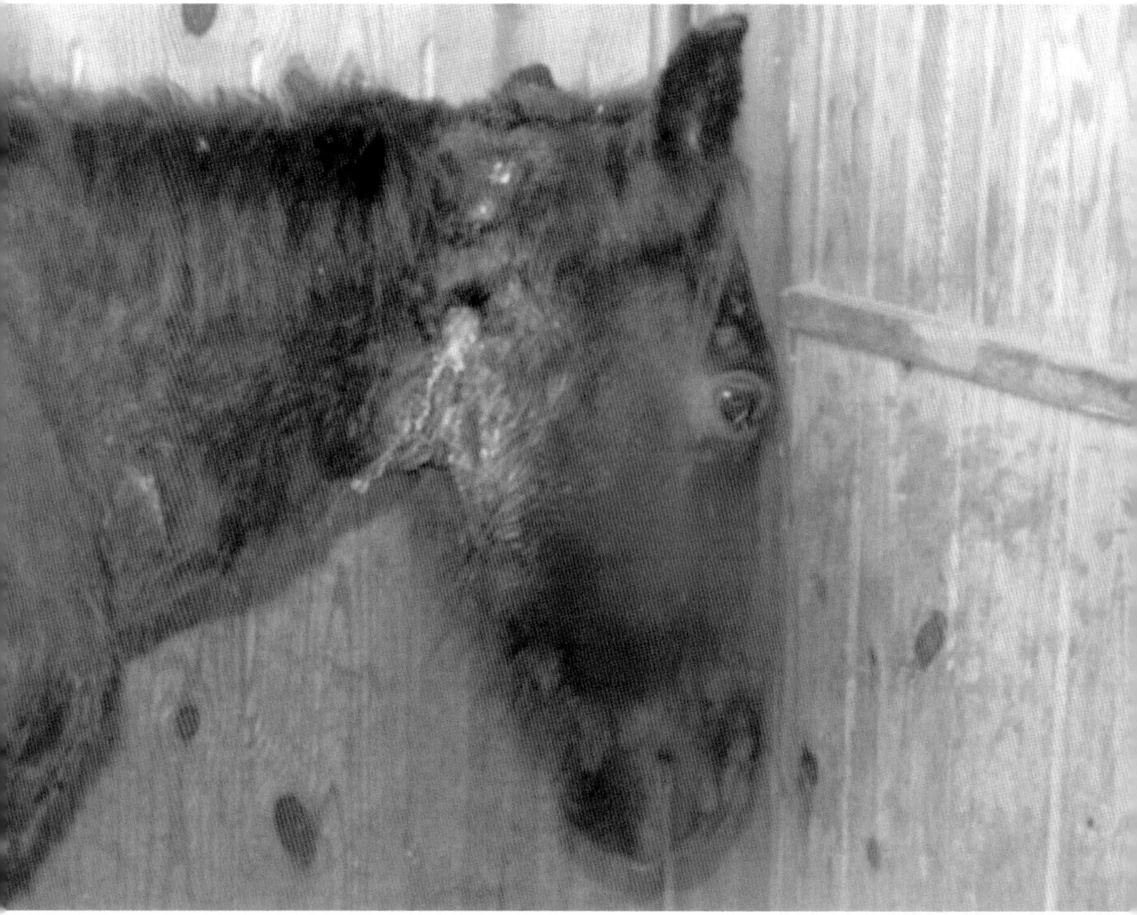

A Local's Second Chance

The nonprofit charity Corolla Wild Horse Fund, Inc., established in 2001, exists to protect, conserve, and responsibly manage the descendants of Colonial Spanish mustangs. A staff of four is on call to respond to emergencies and life-and-death situations like Rainbow found herself in. She was near death when she was rescued on the outskirts of the Corolla National Wildlife Refuge. According to executive director Karen McCalpin, Rainbow had a puncture wound in the center of her chest and two infected abscesses. Rainbow was nursed back to health and then adopted out. She will live out her life at the Island Farm in Manteo where tourists can see a majestic specimen of a unique breed of horse called a "Banker pony." Rainbow's heart-wrenching before image is quite a contrast to her spirited after photograph. (Courtesy of Corolla Wild Horse Fund, Inc.)

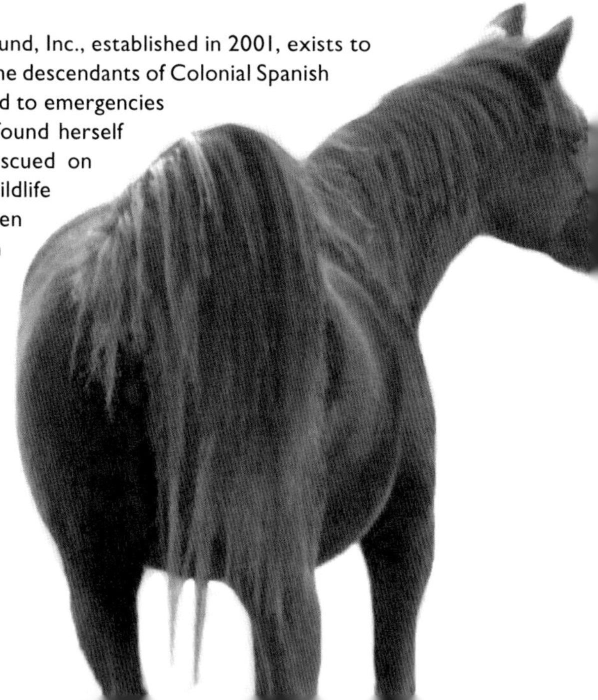

CHAPTER THREE

Businessmen and Watermen

"Shown to bravery and great endeavor."

Businessmen, like watermen, came on the scene early during the making of the Outer Banks. In the 1880s, the small fishing village of Wanchese on the south end of Roanoke Island had 11 general stores to accommodate its community. These stores were meeting places and often stayed open until 11:00 p.m. They were the hub of the various communities, extending credit to customers for a year at a time or until men were paid for their fish. Some stores even gave a 10 percent discount for customers who charged.

The bustling activity at this time was due to unnaturally large catches and shipments of shad fish. Both watermen and businessmen prospered, and a few became wealthy. One businessman reportedly built a mercantile store and a big Victorian home from the proceeds of one fishing season. The first ice plant on the Outer Banks was built on Roanoke Island about this time. It enabled the heavy catches of shad fish to be safely shipped to northern markets.

As the modern age was ushered in, a different breed of businessmen and watermen surfaced. Businessman Steve Brumfield arrived on the scene and began operating a modern bookstore like had never before been seen on the Outer Banks. Mike Kelly, a restaurateur who owns three restaurants, stimulated interest in the Outer Banks through numerous civic contributions such as organizing golf tournaments and helping set up myriad grant and scholarship foundations.

Watermen Britt Shackleford and Dewey Hemilright probably spend more time on land than they do in the ocean, teaching and educating people about preserving and respecting the fishing industry.

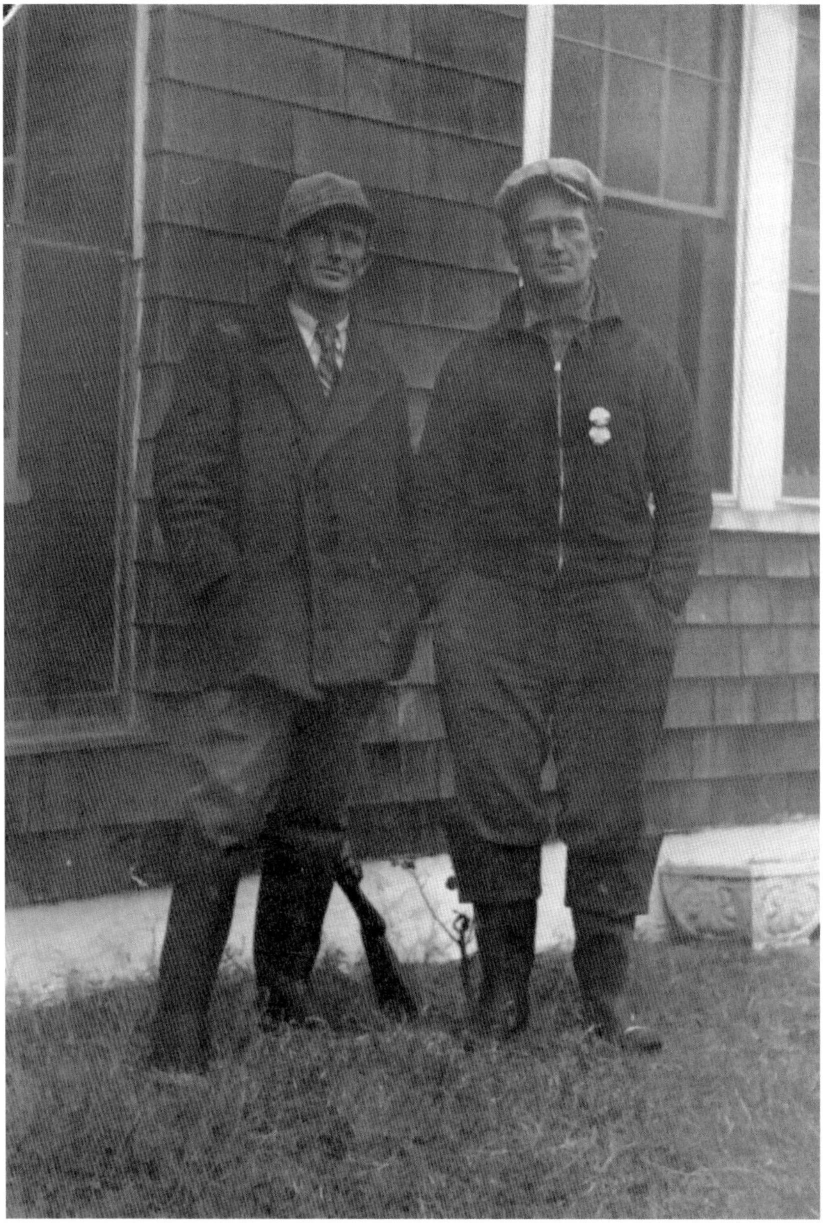

Native Duckers

When Levin Scarborough (left) was born in Duck, it was a minute village accessible only by boat or by vehicles that could travel through soft sand. He and his brother Lewis (right) scratched out a living by fishing and hunting. Lewis was caretaker of the Powder Ridge Hunt Club in the 1930s.

In his golden years, Levin was a sought-after decoy carver. By then he was known as "Pop," and he could be seen daily rocking on his front porch and carving his ducks. His home, situated in the curve entering the town, was one of the last recognizable landmarks from the days before Duck was a developed vacation spot. In her book about Duck, Judith D. Mercier referred to Levin as "the Duck Man." He enjoyed the celebrity status. Like everything else in his life, he took the metamorphosis of Duck in stride. (Courtesy of Jenny Ruth.)

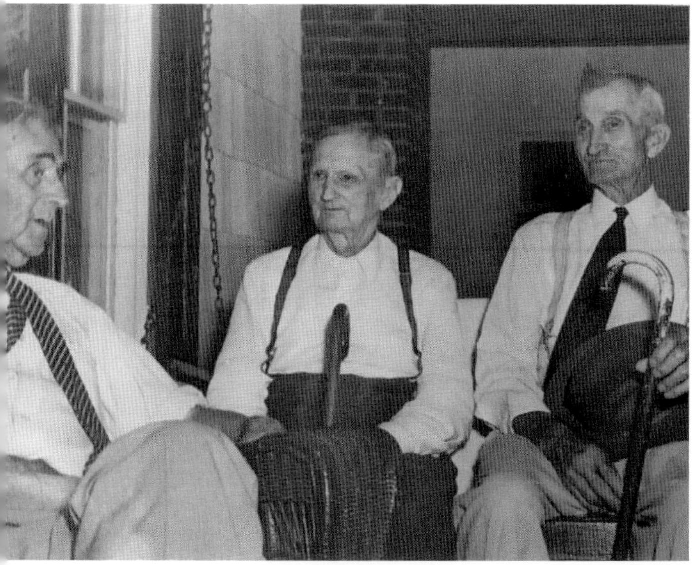

In on the Ground Floor
Will Griffin (center) got his start in business when he ran fish to Elizabeth City in a small sailboat. When the boat sank, instead of being defeated, he became determined to succeed in the area of transportation. He later owned a fleet of delivery boats of which the *Trenton,* a large steamer with lavish accommodations for passengers, was his pride and joy. A side effect of improved transportation was the ingress of ideas and entrepreneurs who helped develop Manteo. (Courtesy of OBHS.)

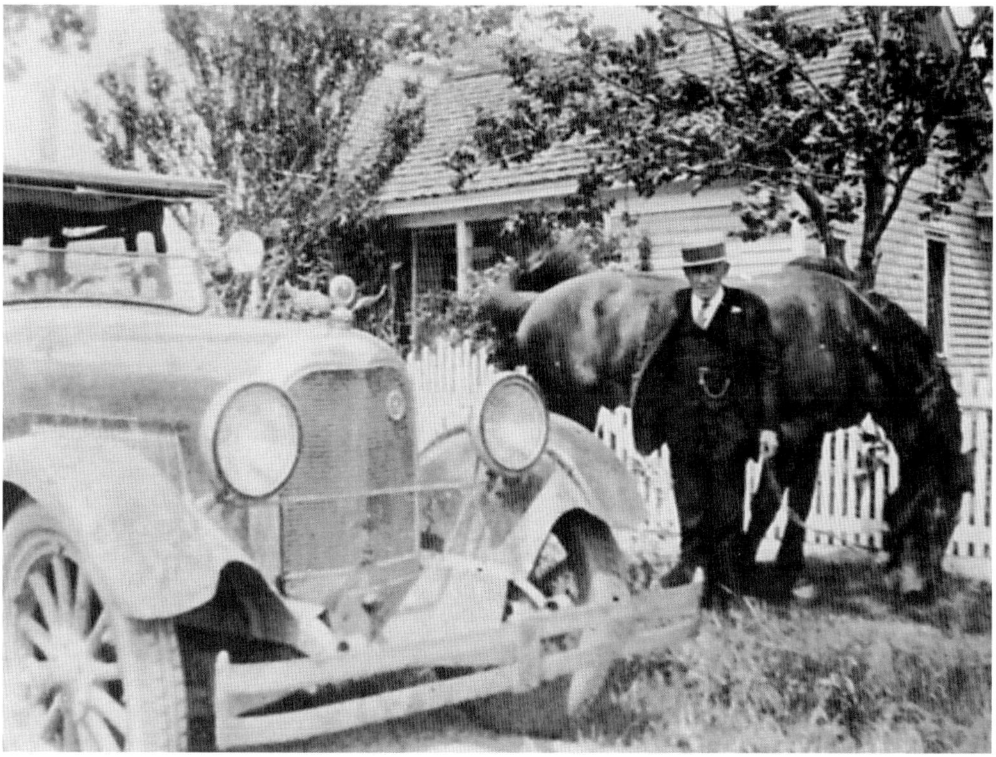

Founding Father of Manteo
Dick Evans was one of four brothers who made Manteo their home around 1870. The brothers were prominent merchants and active in the town's progress. Evans was an early commissioner, postmaster, first president of the Bank of Manteo, and a partner in Hotel Roanoke. He enthusiastically promoted the 1921 silent film, *Lost Colony,* which was the creative endeavor of his daughter Mabel. (Courtesy of OBHC.)

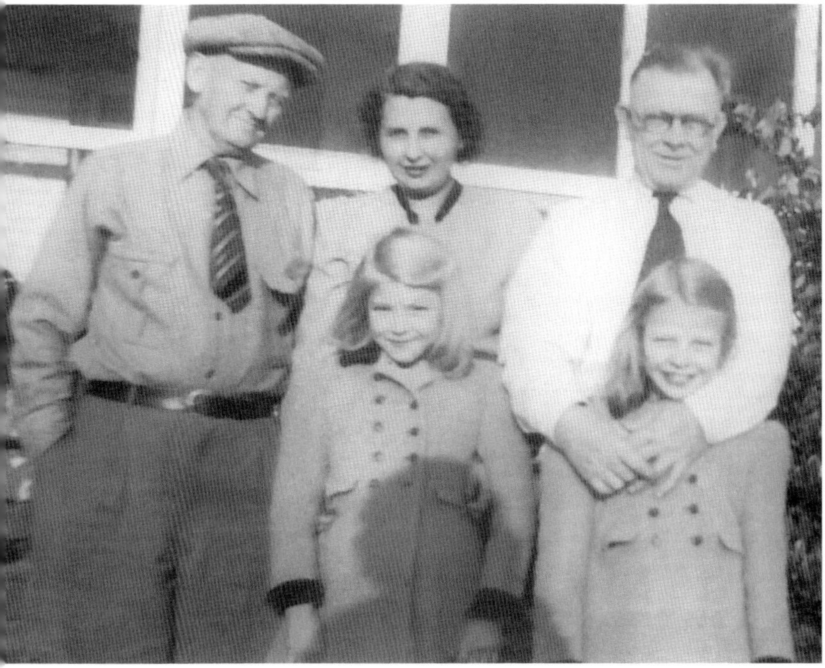

The Ice Man
Alvah Ward (right) knew the availability of ice was critical to the future of Dare's fishing industry. With a background in diesel engineering, he built an ice manufacturing plant dockside at Wanchese Wharf, followed by a more modern plant in Manteo after World War II. He led a 15-year effort to gain public and government support for the initial deepening of Oregon Inlet and construction of navigational channels. (Courtesy of the Ward family.)

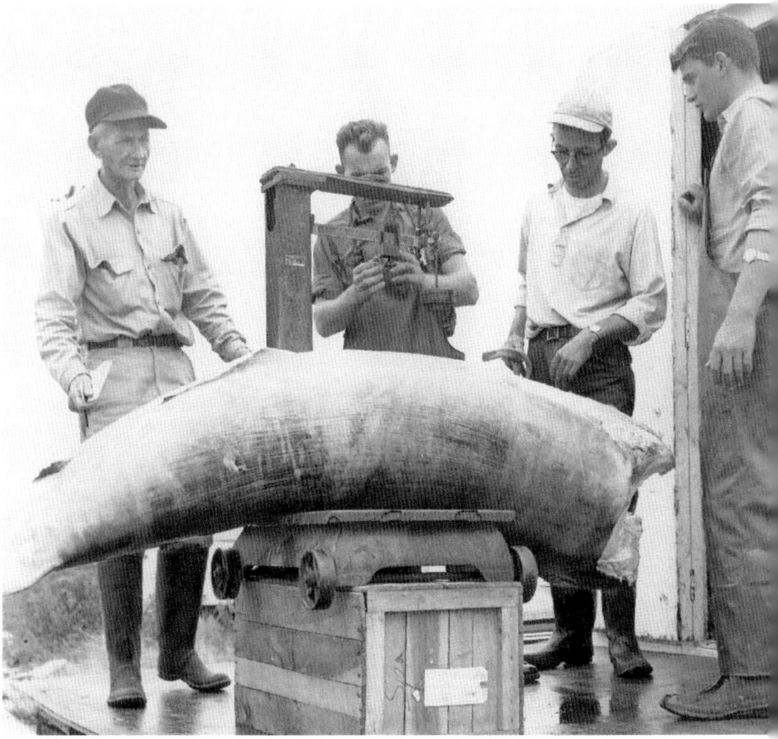

Proponent of the Park
As soon as Ron Tillett (second from right) made a little money, he invested it in another project. He owned the first head boat, a steel-hulled trawler, a crab house, and a fish house. He used his influence as a Dare County Commissioner to obtain funding on the local, state, and federal levels to see the development and construction of the Wanchese Harbor Seafood Industrial Park. (Courtesy of OBHC.)

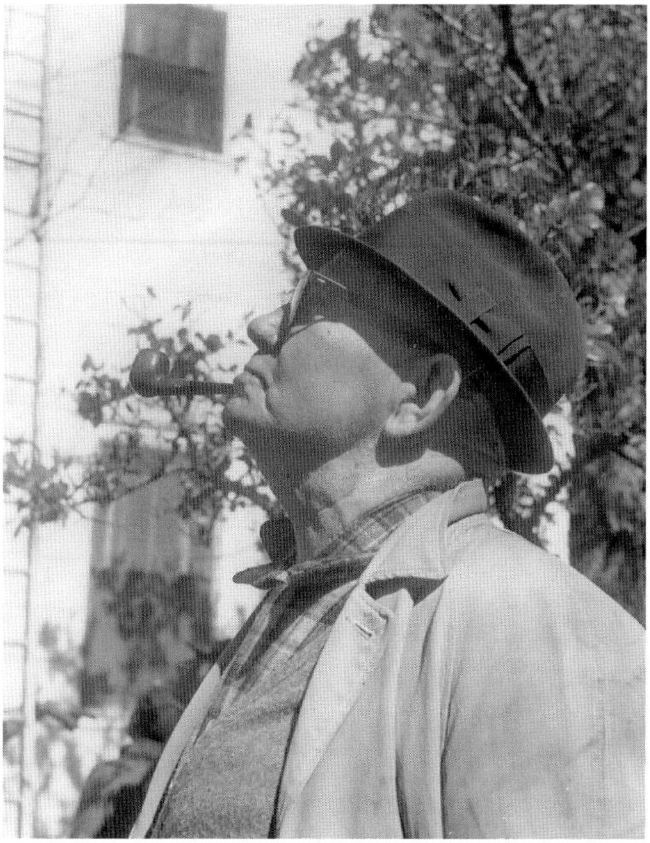

Moving Home Sweet Home

When driving down the beach road with his daughter, John Ferebee pointed to cottage after cottage, saying, "Moved that one, moved that one, moved that one." It seemed to her that he was taking credit for moving almost all of the dwellings.

John got his start in house moving when an airport was needed on the north end of Roanoke Island during World War II. During a committee meeting, the group discussed what they were going to do about the families residing on the land they wanted. John said that it would be no problem to move the small houses, although he had never done any work like that before. He obtained the equipment, did the job, and stuck with the vocation until he was 80 years old.

His can-do attitude spilled over into the financial aspect of his dealings. People would come to him in a frazzled state after a hurricane or other unfortunate circumstances forced them to relocate their home. He would take out his pipe and slowly fill, tamp, and light it. By the time he finished this lengthy process, they had calmed down enough for a discussion. John would loan money in the 1930s when banks were not lending freely. He would take a mortgage on land or other possessions for the loan. (He required this of his daughter when she borrowed money from him.) He also did a lot of trading. He would move a house in exchange for a piece of property. By the time of his death, he was a wealthy landowner.

As a young man, he went out West and became a miner and logger. He bought a mountain in Idaho, and invented a flume that would shoot logs to the river to be floated downstream. There, he acquired enough tales of adventure to tell for a lifetime.

Serving as a Dare County commissioner, he believed in growth and progress and was concerned about the moral fabric of the community. John was known as being thoughtful and kind and, as a result, people who worked with him always tried their best to return the favor. (Courtesy of Aycock Brown Collection; Miriam Ferebee McFadden.)

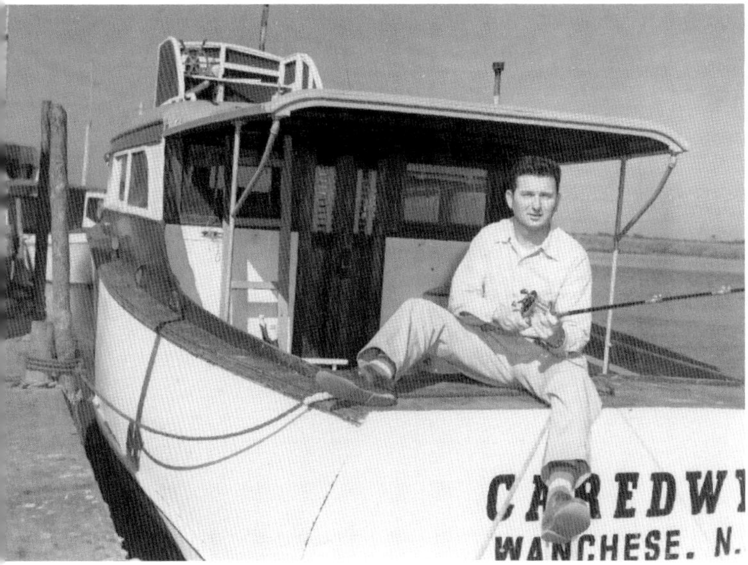

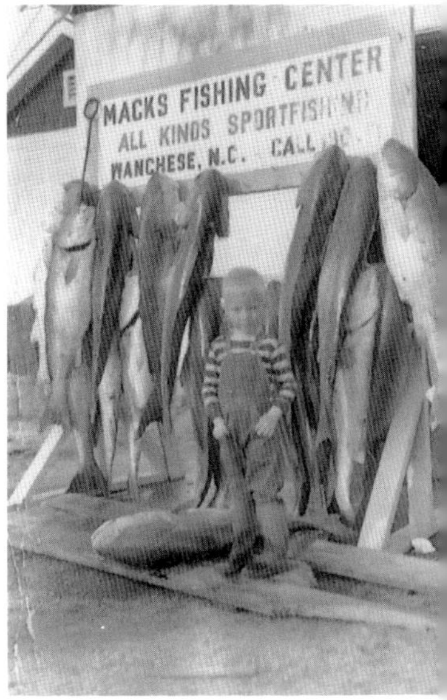

No Fish, No Pay

His name pronounced with a Wanchese twist, McRae "Mac Ray" Etheridge opened his fishing center after returning home from a six-year tour of the world, courtesy of the Coast Guard. He started with a small building on the Mill Landing waterfront where he sold groceries and rented rowboats for $2 and boats with 10-horsepower motors for $5. The 20-foot juniper boats built by Hal Culpepper of Nags Head had etched, metal maps bolted in the inside with Xs marking the best fishing spots.

As young men, Randy O'Neal and Thomas and Walter Baum filled drink boxes, swept floors, painted boats, built duck blinds, and took parties out as fishing and hunting guides. They tacked billets to telephone poles and erected signs in the old Burma-shave style along the causeway, advertising Mac's Fishing Center. Etheridge expanded his business by adding a diner. He extended credit to many commercial fishermen, trusting them to pay the bill when they had a good catch. At one time, he lived in a small room in the back of the fishing center but moved into a pink trailer alongside his building as business grew. Fishing was not only his vocation but also his pleasure, and he fished and hunted in his time off.

The girl that he wanted to wed married another man, so he remained a bachelor. He treated Randy O'Neal like a son, sending him to college for a year and using his political connections to get him the Wanchese postmaster position.

Etheridge was at the forefront of the push to see Oregon Inlet stabilized and the harbor developed. He died from cancer at an early age, but not before he influenced the lives of many young men. (Both images courtesy of Randy O'Neal.)

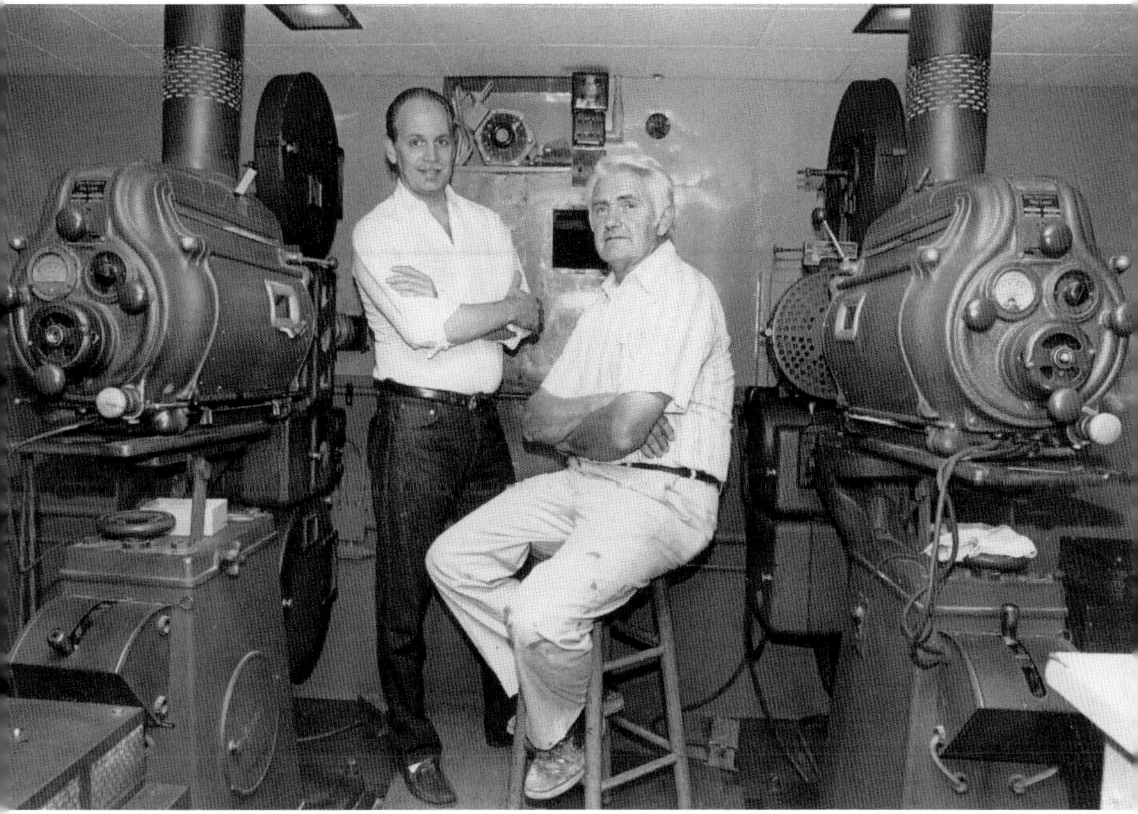

Keepers of the Pioneer Theatre

Boat builder George Washington "Wash" Creef and his wife, Ada, began showing silent "flickers" in a small, wooden Manteo theater behind a doctor's office. In the days before bridges, people from communities across the sound came by boat for an evening of entertainment at the Pioneer Theatre.

When the theater moved one street over in 1934, Wash Creef's son Herbert Augustus took over the duties in the projection room without missing a single night. After World War II, Herbert's son George oversaw the management of the theater, assisted by his Uncle Ben.

A few bright spots in the life of the Pioneer was when Andy Griffith appeared in person on the stage to introduce two of his acclaimed films, *A Face in the Crowd* in 1957 and *No Time for Sergeants* in 1958. The Creef family and Manteo townspeople were proud of their adopted hometown hero who had lived among them for many years when he appeared in *The Lost Colony.*

When George passed away, his brother H.A. (right) took the helm. He was committed to providing his community with low-cost entertainment. Tourists could not believe their eyes when seeing the admission price, let alone the price of the candy, popcorn, and drinks. When H.A. died after decades of working each night, his obituary said that he was the cheapest and most dependable babysitter in the county. All of the young people received his pre-movie speech about how their actions were a reflection on their families. He walked the aisles looking for inappropriate movie behavior, and he certainly did not let anyone leave the theater before the movie ended or their ride had come.

These days, H.A.'s son Buddy is carrying on the legacy. As H.A. espoused, the Pioneer Theatre continues to have "the longest history of one-family ownership of any movie house in the country." (Courtesy of Drew Wilson Collection; OBHC.)

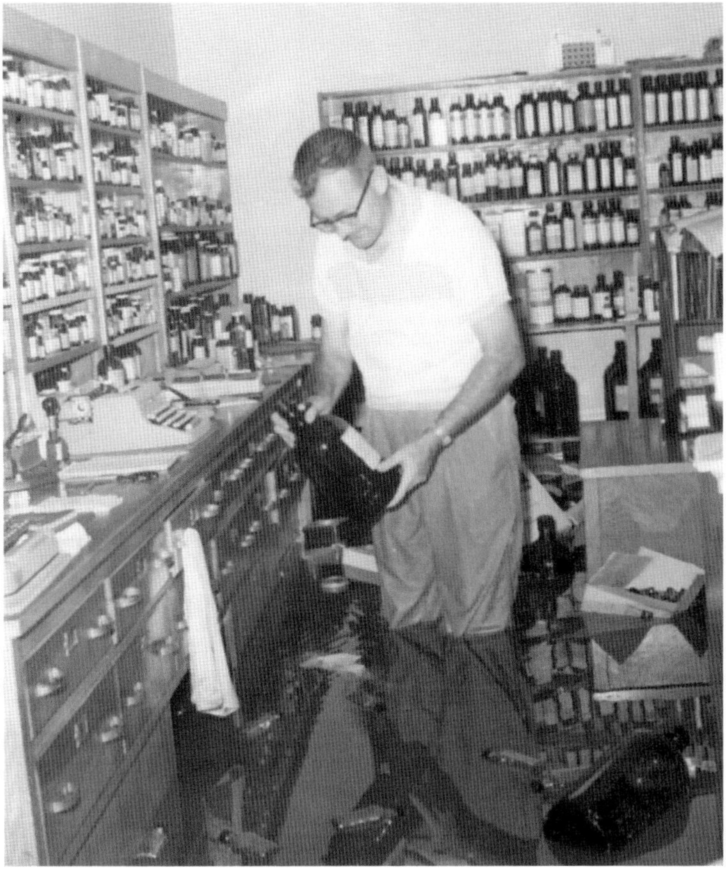

Dare's Pharmacist

As the son of one of Manteo's prominent businessmen, Keith Fearing attended Campbell College, liking the idea of being a doctor, but thinking that medical school would take too long. "I knew I was going into business or I was going into pharmacy," he said. He did both.

The Fearing family already had long-established businesses of a power company, a restaurant, the Fort Raleigh Hotel, a hardware and appliance store, a clothing shop, a general store, and a confectionery. When Keith became the county's first pharmacist in 1947, he added one more venture to the family corporation. The pharmacy was successful, but he still had time to help with other pressing areas in the stores.

His entrepreneurial interests expanded to insurance and real estate. In spite of his heavy schedule, he was a part of almost every organization ever established on the Outer Banks. He served one term in the state legislature and maintained a lifelong interest in politics by supporting and promoting potential candidates.

He was credited with persuading many doctors to come and practice in Dare County. He was often called upon to render aid in the pharmacy and by the fire department in the days before emergency medical service. He was the first one to operate a resuscitator that the firemen bought.

He left the family pharmacy in 1980 and became co-owner of Island Pharmacy from 1981 to 1985. He made the decision to retire when he was chosen as president of the North Carolina Pharmaceutical Association. He was later honored by that professional organization when he was selected as the "Pharmacist of the Year" just 11 months before he died.

In Fearing Drugs, Keith stands knee-deep in sound water brought in by Hurricane Donna in 1960. (Courtesy of Lib Fearing.)

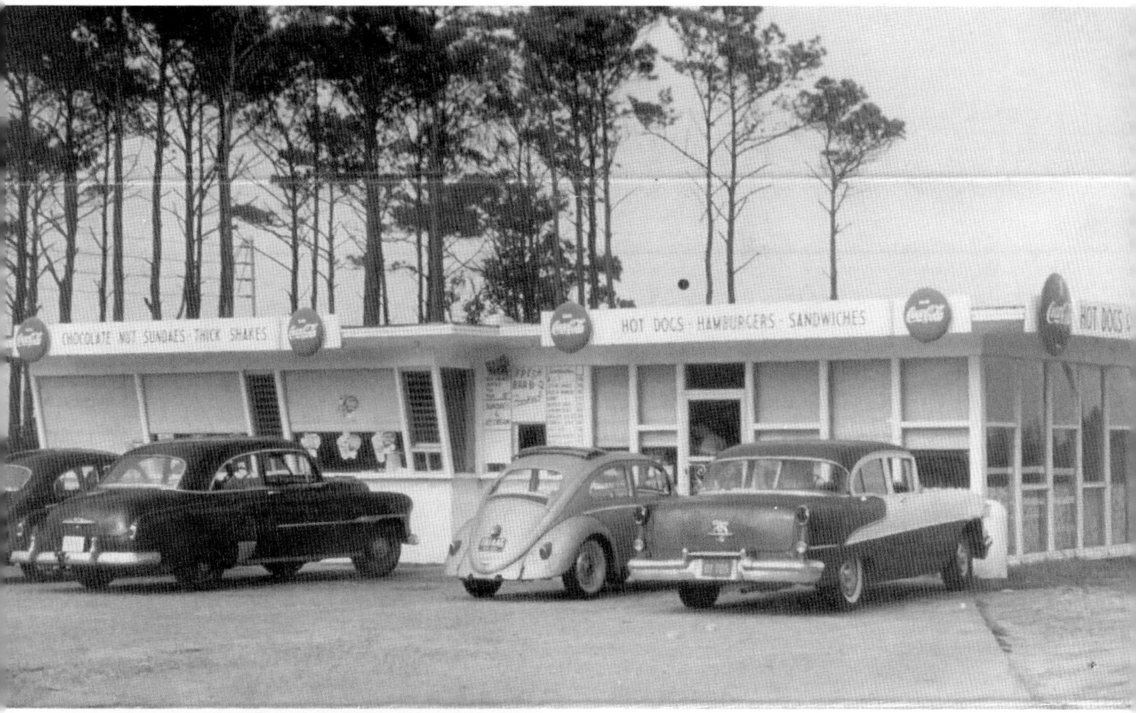

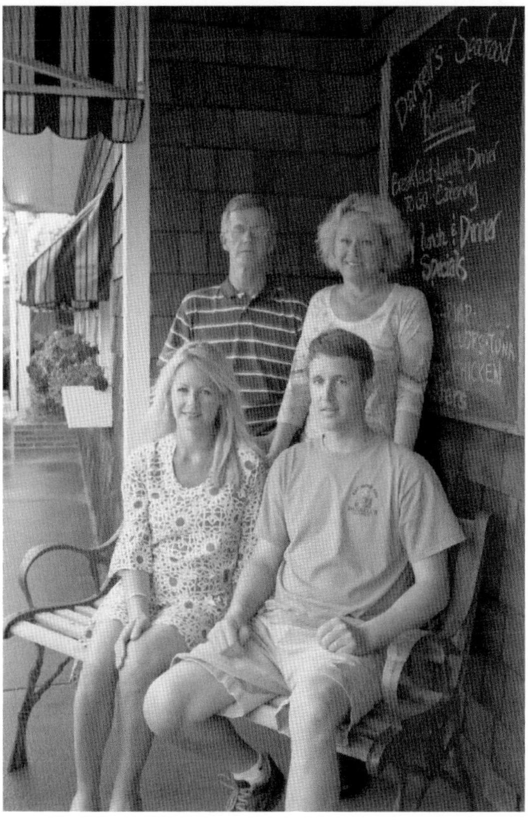

Weathering the Storms

Three generations of the Daniels family have devoted their lives to the day in and day out routine that owning Darrell's Seafood Restaurant demands.

This small-town restaurant on Roanoke Island began in 1960 as the Polar Bear Drive-In. Darrell Daniels lost one of his hands after an accident, but he could do anything with one hand, from tying his shoe to preparing the hotdogs, hamburgers, and other drive-in fare. After years of learning the ropes, Allen and his wife, Lorna, took full control of the business and renamed it Darrell's in1982.

Darrell's has literally weathered many storms and flooded with tidewater from five major hurricanes. Allen and Lorna's son Tanner and daughter Ali are now managing the kitchen and dining room, adding their own signature dishes and leadership skills. They plan to keep the business in the family. And no wonder, they have too much heart invested to let it go. (Both images courtesy of Allen Daniels.)

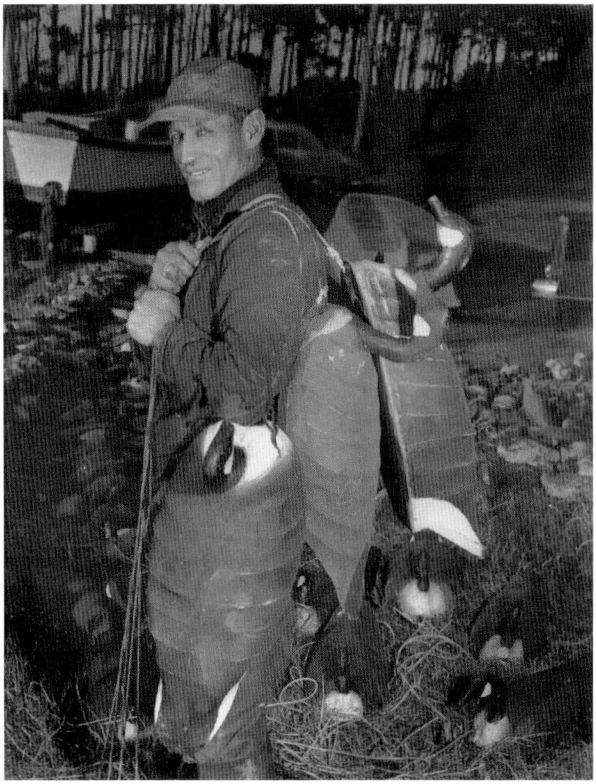

103 Years of Knowledge

After reporting for duty for the churchyard cleanup day, Capt. Wayland Baum, in his 90s, worked circles around the other volunteers half his age. He said that he never had an ache or a pain, but his hands, which were as tough and gnarled as an old cypress knee, gave a different impression.

Wayland worked on the water from the time he was 10 years old. He piloted his father's shad boat for long distances by himself, and he could fix anything that went wrong on the old motor. His first job as a young man was working on an old side-wheel steamer, delivering wood and coal to lighthouses. They would bring the boat in as close to shore as possible and jump overboard in waist-deep water to pull the heavy bags to land.

After stints as a substitute lighthouse keeper and working on a tugboat, he made the decision to come home for good to fish and hunt for a living. Besides acting as a guide, he and his wife, Vivian, boarded people in their home for $1.50 per room and 50¢ per meal. He carved over 700 of his own decoys for duck hunting, and the ones that still exist are prized by serious collectors, partly because many of them were rendered from a single piece of juniper.

At the apex of fishing, he had 13 boats and several crews actively working. He did every kind of commercial fishing from catching shad fish to clamming. He knew every creek, cut, and hammock around Roanoke Island and could run a boat at night anywhere he wanted to go without lights. He carried out fishing parties until he was 82.

He did all of the maintenance work on his home, shingling part of his roof when he was nearly 100. He mowed and picked up his large yard. Once, after a storm, he called his state senator to inform him that all of the blown down limbs were stacked on the side of the road, ready for pickup.

He was a walking encyclopedia of the way life used to be on the Outer Banks. Wayland was an example of a rare man who worked extremely hard all of his life and provided well for his family through sheer will and ingenuity. For those who were fortunate enough to know Captain Wayland, they could see a century of the Outer Banks through his eyes. (Courtesy of Aycock Brown Collection; OBHC.)

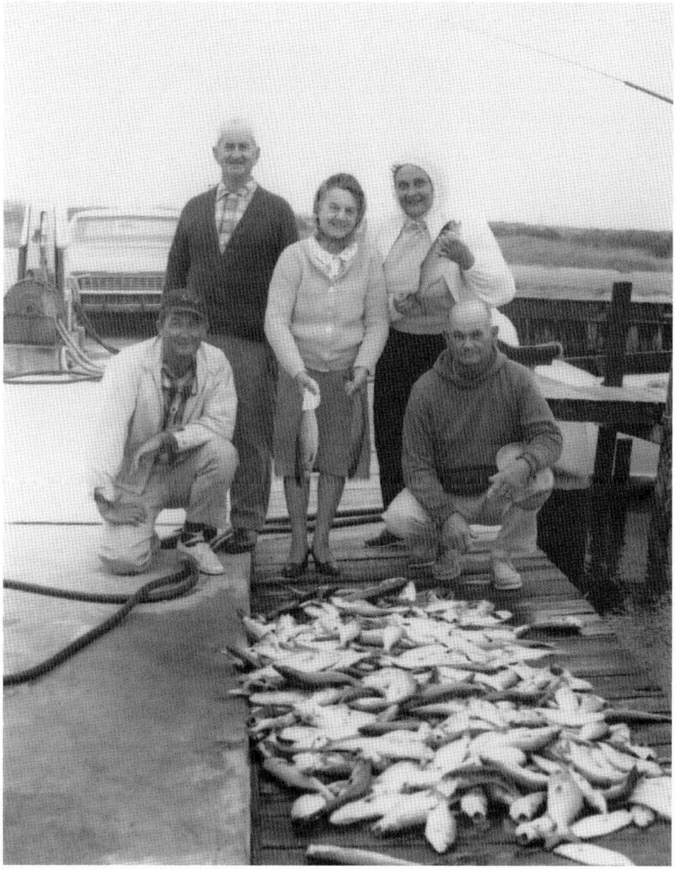

Triple Dose of the Spirit

Anyone who meets Omie Tillett receives a Holy Spirit hug and an exhortation that "Jesus loves you." He loves to talk about fishing, too, yet he would be the last one to tell you that he is a charter sport-fishing pioneer.

Sam Tillett, Omie's father, began taking fishing parties off the Outer Banks in the 1920s. He owned a small restaurant in Nags Head, Sam and Omie's, where anglers booked deep-sea fishing trips and where they could eat a 4:00 a.m. breakfast before their trip. Young Omie began going to the Atlantic's Gulf Stream with his father when he was 10 years old.

He began running his own charter boat, the *Jerry Jr.*, when he was 20 years old. His brother Tony became a renowned fisherman, as well. It was said around the docks that "if you weren't fishing with a Tillett, you weren't fishing."

In the off-season, Omie worked with leading boat builder Warren O'Neal, whose innovative designs made his charter boats most coveted among charter fishermen. Later, Omie built boats for himself and other captains at his own facility, Sportsman Boatworks. Innately understanding how a boat was supposed to handle in Carolina seas, Omie built a number of fine boats that are still operating today. However, he became allergic to resin and glue and had to sell his business.

Each dawn, as the sport-fishing fleet headed out of Oregon Inlet to the ocean, Omie began to pray over the VHF radio for God's blessings for the crews and parties. He received many honors in his lifetime, including the Order of the Long Leaf Pine. His godly influence in the lives of the mates he employed, his fellow charter fishermen, and anyone he hugs is most enduring.

Capt. Omie Tillett, on the left, poses with happy anglers at Oregon Inlet Fishing Center. (Courtesy of OBHC.)

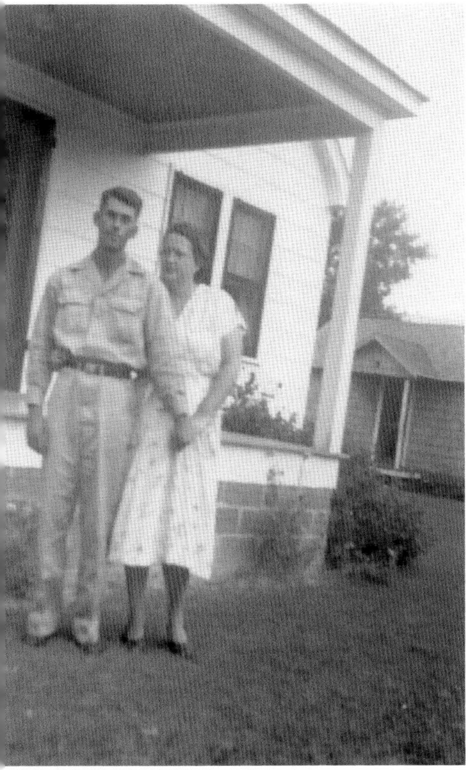

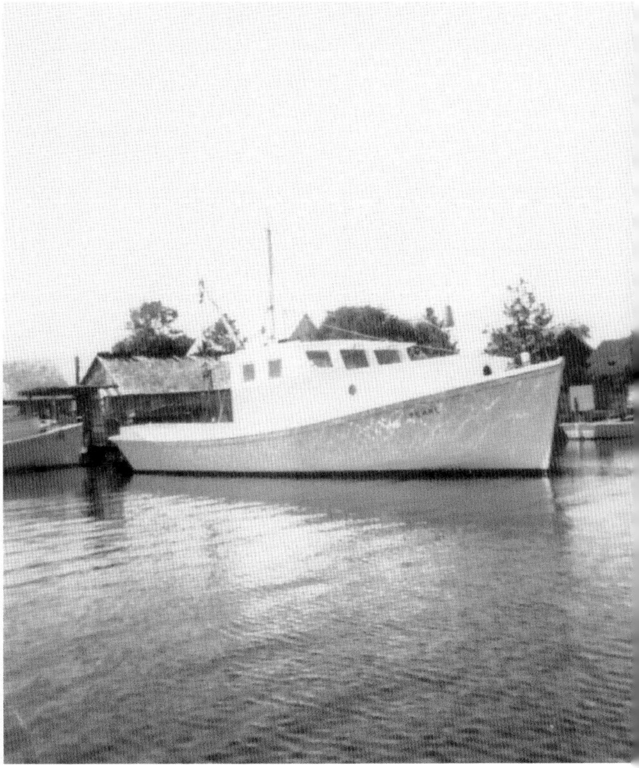

Integrity First
Warren O'Neal was a mentor to the many men who worked with him building boats, and his solid temperament was a role model to all who passed through the doors of his boat shop.

Warren was responsible for launching a new type of sport-fishing boat on the Outer Banks. He worked on the water for the first part of his life and knew what it took to make the boats look sharp and work efficiently. Adapting the design of his charter boats from Rybovich vessels out of Florida, he accentuated the deep-vee on the bow and, in so doing, developed the "Carolina flair." Warren constructed scale models of the hulls he was going to build so he could tell exactly how they were going to appear when finished.

His boat shop, O'Neal's Boatworks, on Dough's Creek, was just down the street from his home in Manteo that he shared with his adored wife, Pearl, for whom his boat was named. (Both images courtesy of Cecelia Bell Smith.)

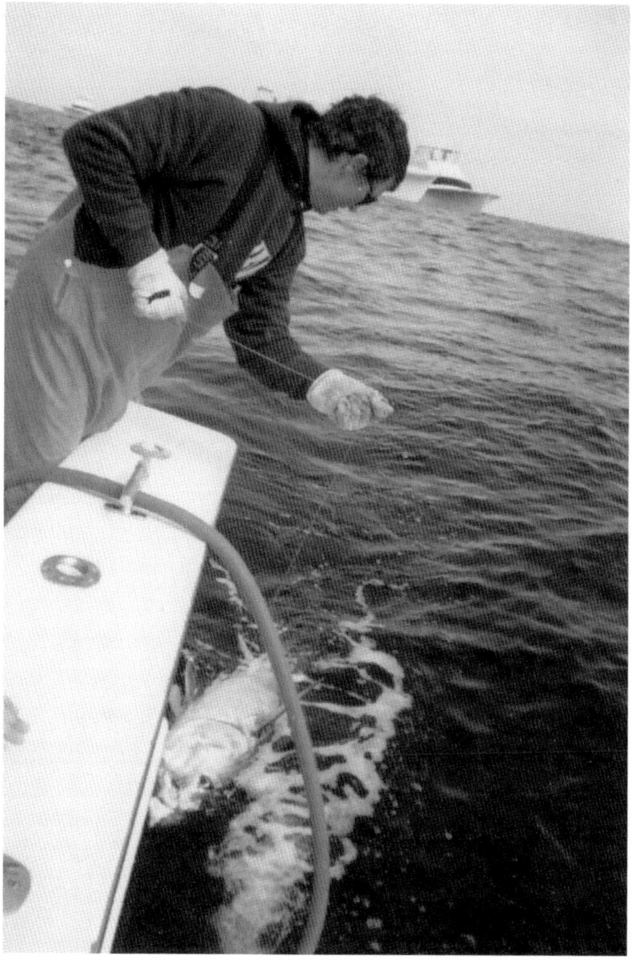

Working Waterman with a Mission

Growing up in Gloucester, Virginia, Britton Shackelford could always be found hanging around the general stores where older fishermen and gentlemen farmers gathered in the evenings to play checkers and talk. From an early age, he was cognizant of the wisdom of his elders. It made him a strange kid.

Coming to the Outer Banks when a friend got a job as a mate, Britton fell right into the world of fishing, learning the ropes by getting out there and doing it.

Britton is accustomed to making a living any way he can. He runs his own 61-foot charter boat *Doghouse*, fishes commercially, and acts as a duck-hunting guide. Through each season, the voices of his old friends ring in his ears, recounting how nature's bounty runs in cycles and how the Creator manages all things well. He became one of the founding members of the North Carolina Watermen United and is currently the acting president. He represents working watermen by attending state and federal meetings in which fishery decisions are discussed and made. He will speak when given a chance, expressing the futility of man trying to manage God's creation when man cannot even manage his own affairs. Knowing that some regulations are needed, he tries to bring a voice of practicality and common sense to the proceedings, but admits that he is looked upon "as a complete oddity."

His boat was recently called upon to be a top competitor in the National Geographic reality television show *Wicked Tuna*, in a North vs. South fishing match.

Not having a television and, therefore, unfamiliar with the show, his main concern was behaving in a way that would not embarrass himself or his Lord. (Courtesy of Audra Shackelford.)

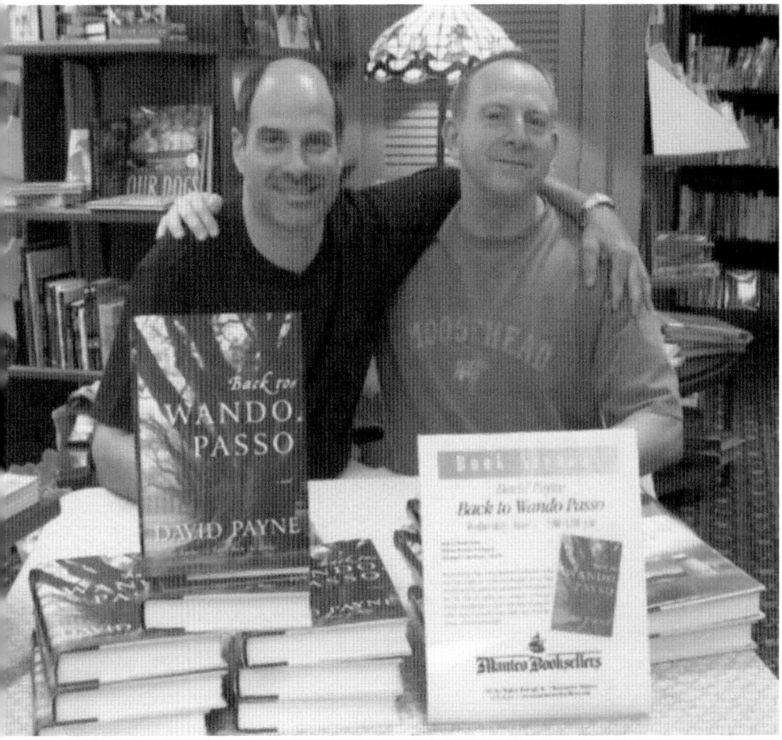

The Bookstore Man

Steve Brumfield was Manteo Booksellers, and Manteo Booksellers was Steve Brumfield. When the business finally succumbed to its 10th and most severe flooding during Hurricane Irene, it was Steve who was left most decimated. Steve's store featured books in every category imaginable. He hosted hundreds of author signings, readings, and events from 1985 to 2011. Steve (right) is pictured with author and frequent guest David Payne. (Courtesy of Steve Brumfield.)

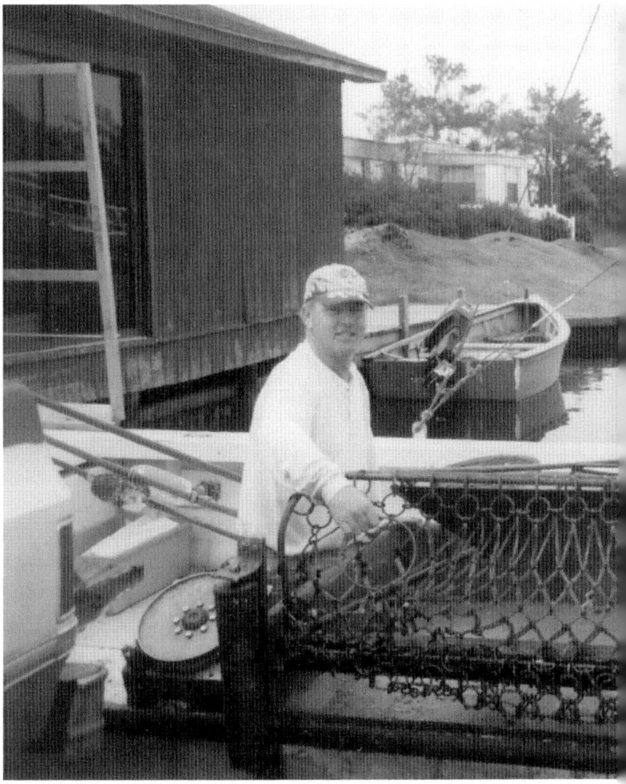

One of a Dying Breed

Georgie Daniels, whose left arm was paralyzed in a childhood accident, has more strength in one side of his body than most men have in their entire bodies. Oddly enough, he has always had physically demanding jobs. An oysterman who learned the trade from his father, he is known for catching "crab slough" oysters, which are considered the premier local shellfish because of their saltiness and the tiny orange pea crab that lives inside. (Courtesy of Georgie Daniels.)

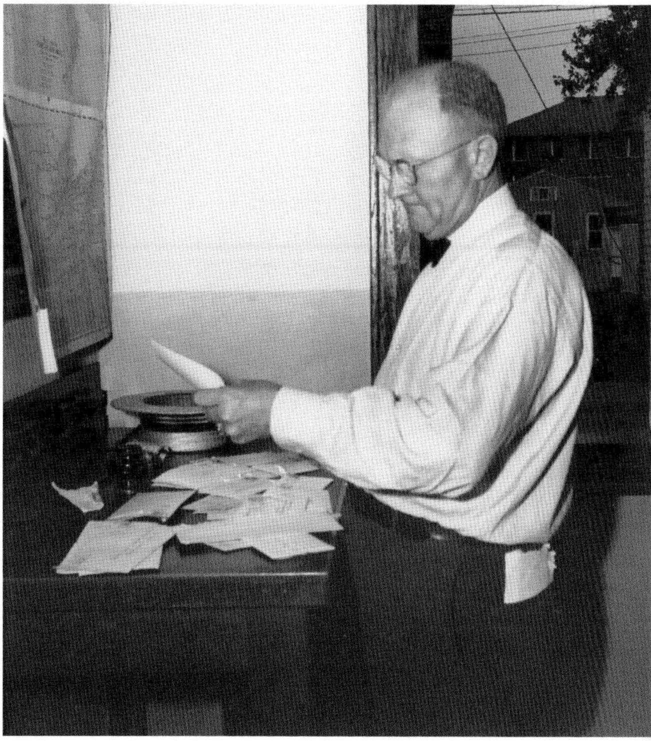

Lobbying for Dare
Bradford Fearing moved from Alabama to Elizabeth City to Manteo all before the age of five, but once ensconced in Dare County, he became a true native. He worked feverishly for his community as a county commissioner. While serving as a senator during three terms of the North Carolina General Assembly, he used his influence to see funds appropriated for starting up *The Lost Colony* symphonic drama, which was first presented in 1937. (Courtesy of Aycock Brown Collection; OBHC.)

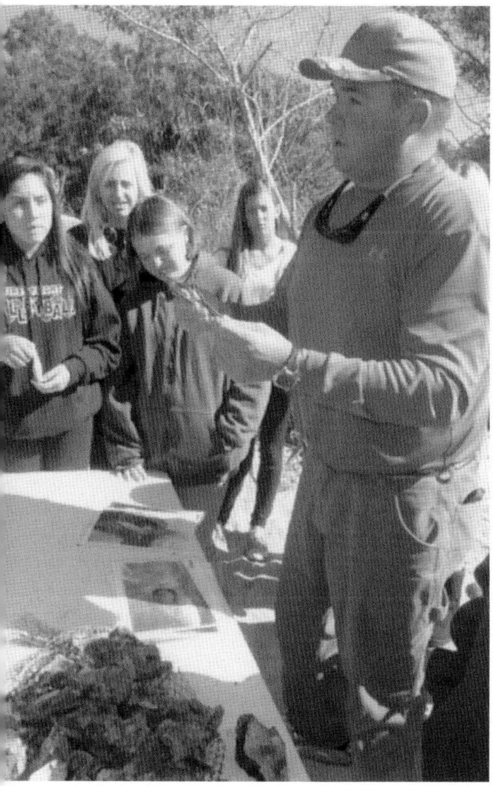

Telling Fishing Stories
As a promoter of the heritage of fishing families, Dewey Hemilwright has become involved with Provider Pals, a program that teaches schoolchildren all over America where their food comes from. He goes into middle and high school assemblies to give a slideshow depicting a day in the life of a fisherman. He is motivated by his passion to see future generations given the chance to make a living from the sea. (Courtesy of Dewey Hemilwright.)

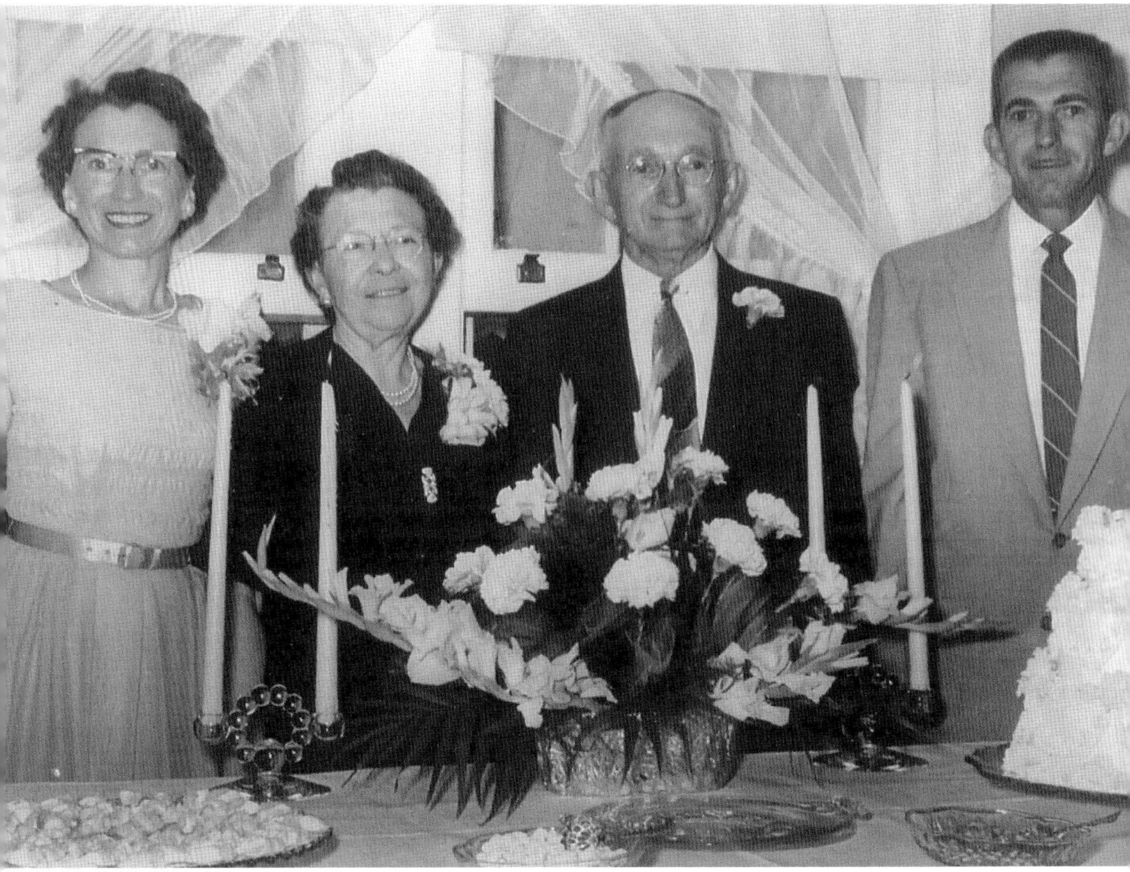

Trusted Counsel of Kitty Hawk

While playing with model sailboats around the edge of the bay as a boy, Elijah Baum (third from left) met a boat bringing in two young men who asked for directions to Bill Tate's home. He showed them the way and refused payment for his good deed. The men were Orville and Wilbur Wright on their first trip to Kitty Hawk. Later, Baum and the other boys would watch from a distance in trees they had climbed as the Wrights conducted their experiments.

A quiet man by nature, probably because of a speech impediment, Baum was one of the more formally educated men in his village. He taught school, ran a general merchandise store, was postmaster, and built homes and cottages all while holding positions in his church and on educational boards.

His family said he rarely spoke of his encounter with the Wrights and missed their historic flight because "he did not think it was worth the walk from Kitty Hawk." (Courtesy of Geneva Harris Ward.)

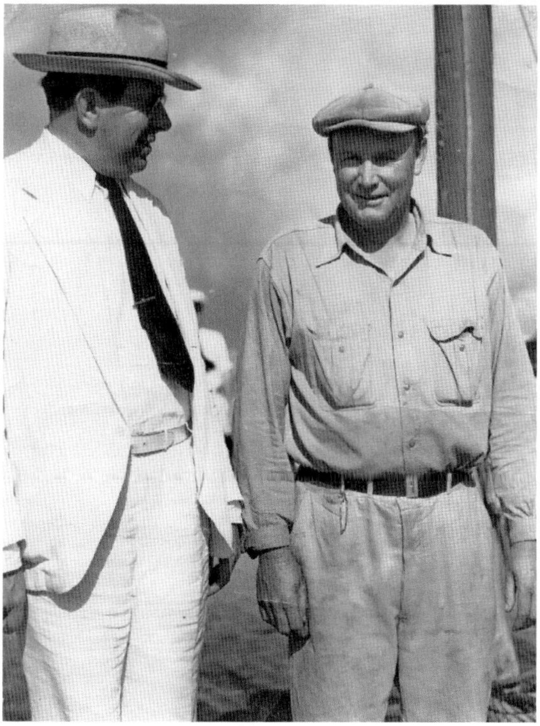

Observing Shifting Shoals

Oregon Inlet has been troublesome to man since it first opened in 1846. Wanchese native Toby Tillett conquered it more than anyone. By the time he sold his ferry service to the state of North Carolina in the 1950s, he was making five round trips and transporting an average of 25 cars daily. In 25 years of running the service, he only missed 14 days, due to severe storms, and never lost an auto overboard.

He took over the ferry service about 1924 from Jack Nelson of Colington, when he and his assistant Pat Miller quit after a few months. They towed a barge that could carry two cars with a motorboat. Needless to say, it was a difficult process to dock the vessel. Tillett later had a 45-foot ferry named *Oregon Inlet* built that was equipped with a motor. In 1938, the *Barcelona* would follow.

Travelers could raise a flag on the south side to tell Tillett to come and take them across. The inlet is a notoriously tricky stretch of water. Tillett had to be an excellent reader of the winds and tides to be able to maneuver his ferry so well and so safely. The flag system was discarded in 1928, and a regular seven-day-a-week schedule began. In 1941, he leased the ferries to the state, and there were no longer any tolls of a $1 or $2 to pay.

With such long hours, the only way for his daughters to see their father was to go to work with him. Tillett's daughter Margaret remembers that he would not leave the south side until the bus operated by Stockton Midgett and his brother would arrive. A vital link to Hatteras Village, the bus carried passengers, packages, and mail. Impatiently, he would climb on top of the wheelhouse, scan the horizon, and say, "Now where are those damn Midgett brothers?"

Tillett went with a coalition to Washington, DC, to discuss with Congressman Herbert C. Bonner the building of a bridge over Oregon Inlet. He was one of the few in the group who did not want to see the bridge built. He told Bonner that the bridge would cause the inlet to close up. Toby had driven stakes in the inlet for years to mark water levels for his ferry, and had observed how sand built up around them. When asked, Tillett told the congressman that the bridge should be built from Wanchese to Rodanthe, North Carolina. If his advice had been heeded, he would have saved the state a lot of money and headaches. Tillett (right) is pictured with governor Melville Broughton. (Courtesy of Aycock Brown Collection; Margaret Tillett Daniels.)

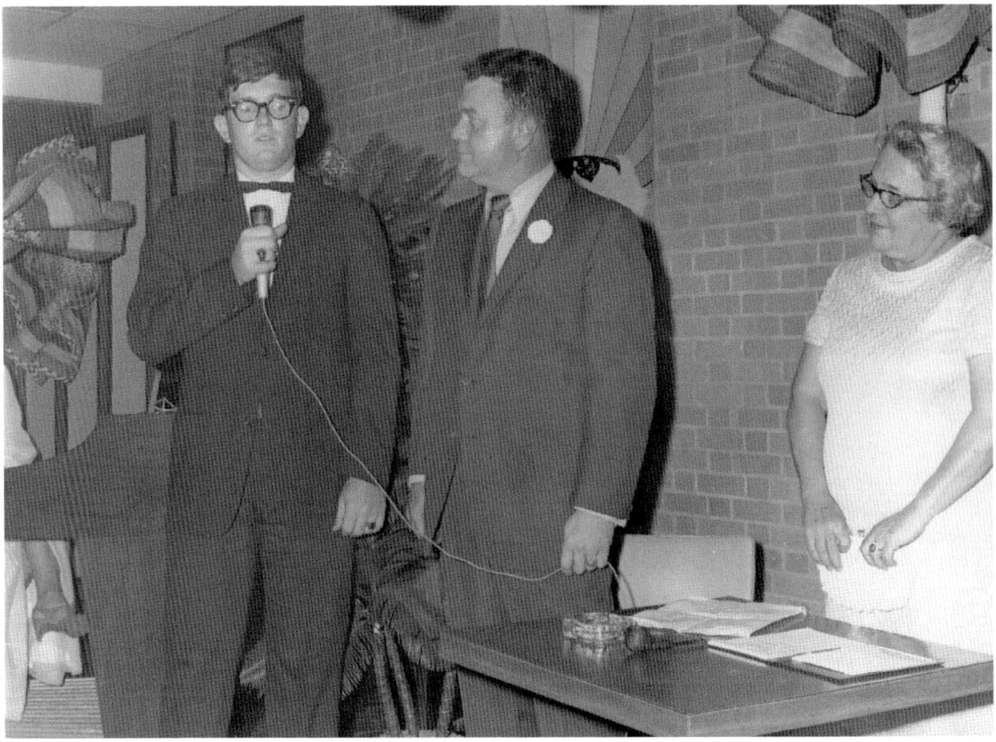

Captain of the Galleon Esplanade

George Crocker (right) came to the Outer Banks in 1953 with a sixth-grade education, a $15,000 loan, and a dream to be an entrepreneur. He built a clothing store called the Galleon Esplanade and a first-class empire of motels, gift shops, restaurants, and an antique car museum. In this photograph, he is presenting a scholarship from his business to a Manteo High School student. (Courtesy of Aycock Brown Collection; OBHC.)

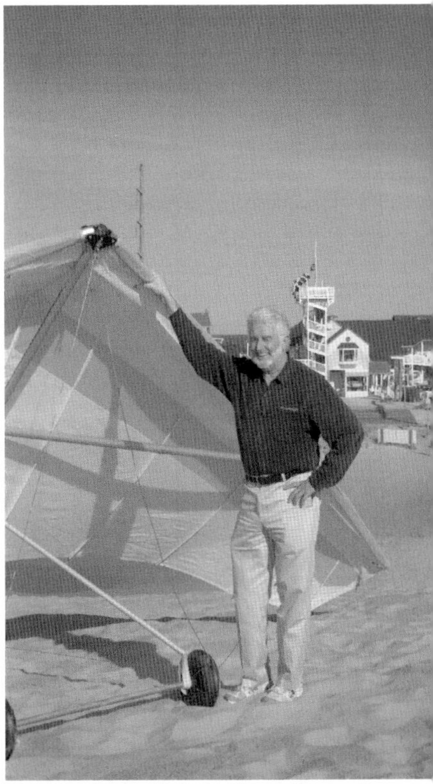

Spectacular Hang Glider

One might expect that after 40 years of being owner and president of Kitty Hawk Kites, John Harris may have lost a little of his enthusiasm for hang gliding. Just the opposite is true. John has stores in North Carolina and Florida and flight schools in North Carolina and New Hampshire. His latest investment is a kite boarding resort in Rodanthe. More than ever, he subscribes to his company's mission statement, "Teaching the world to fly!" (Courtesy of James Seal.)

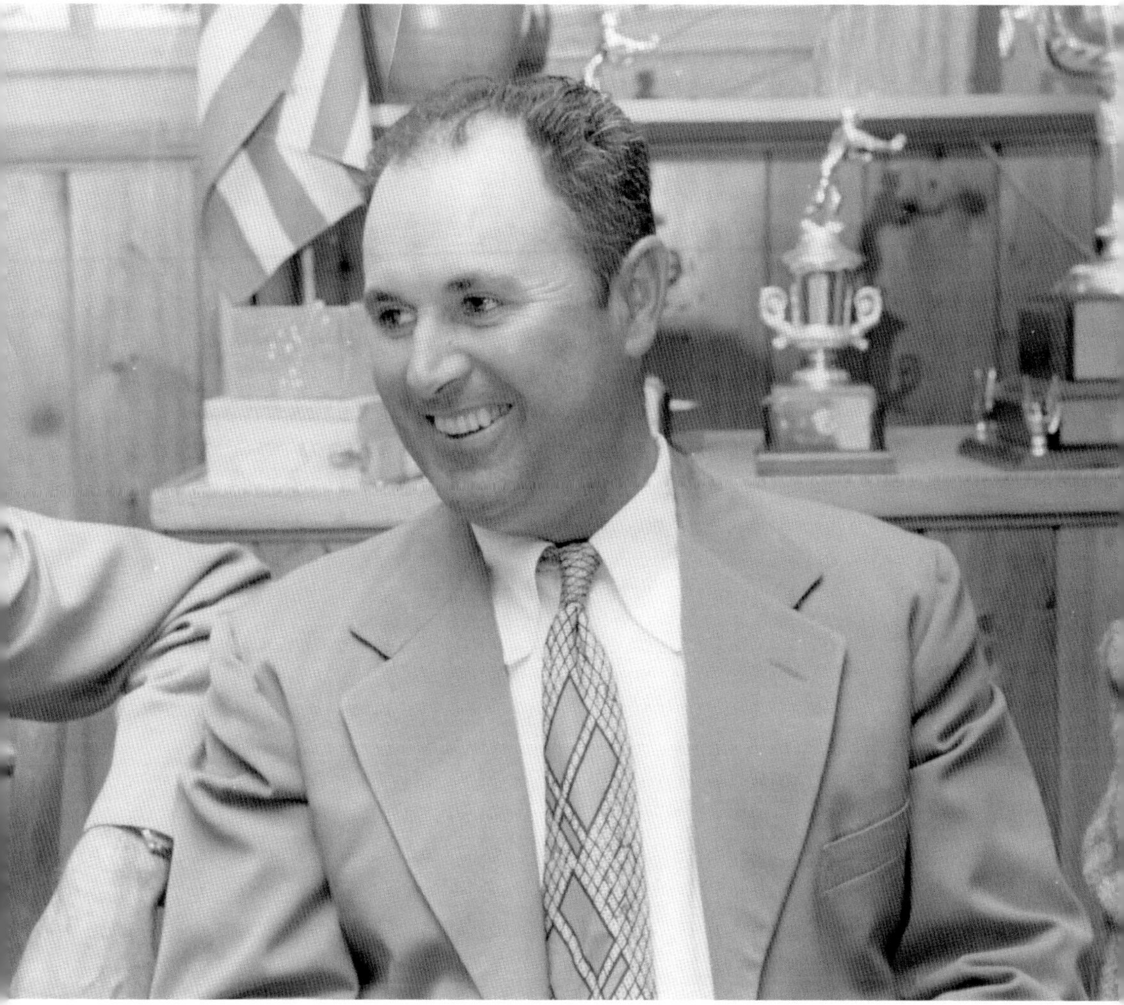

"Holding Court" in a Garage

Jim Scarborough's garage in Nags Head was once the hub of everything happening on the beach. Men would congregate outside his tiny, messy office to shoot the breeze. Their talk was often productive, and it is believed that the ideas for incorporating the town of Nags Head, organizing the Nags Head Fishing Tournament, and promoting the Outer Banks as a vacation destination were born out of these meetings.

Jim sold a little bit of everything: jeeps, cars, gas, appliances, spare parts, and tires. His was the only major auto repair garage on the beach, and for many years he owned the only wrecker. His wife, Jewell, was always by his side, filling any role that was necessary, from bookkeeper to gas attendant. (Courtesy of Karen Whitfield.)

Maestro of Nags Head Casino

When older Outer Bankers talk about the Nags Head Casino, locals under the age of 50 wish that they had been born decades earlier. Ras Wescott turned a building that was originally a boardinghouse into the premier social center for eastern North Carolina. Many couples met and later married after meeting at the casino that was located between the ocean and Jockey's Ridge.

Wescott employed many young people during the 35 or so years he owned and operated the casino. It had 13 bowling alleys that were reset by pin boys. Downstairs were a soda bar, pinball machines, and a snack bar. The upstairs was for the older crowd. There was a bar where beer was available, a bandstand, and a huge wooden dance floor that was buffed and polished daily. Shoes had to be checked before dancers went upstairs, and the patrons danced barefoot or in sock feet. Wescott was very strict about keeping young people downstairs, and he did not tolerate misbehavior.

Wescott lured big bands and big names to the Outer Banks. Whether it was jazz from Louis Armstrong or beach tunes from the Drifters, the sound of their music wafted out of the casino from windows propped up with sticks.

At some point, Dan Davis talked Wescott into sponsoring Wednesday night prizefights that turned out to be very popular. A full-sized ring was set up on the dance floor and a number of locals legitimately boxed there, although they had been fighting in the parking lot for years.

Ras Wescott was a colorful person who would give the shirt off of his back. He was fatherly and generous with his employees and customers, and made sure his business was family-oriented. There was something there for people of all ages.

On the bottom left, Wescott is pictured during his term as Manteo mayor. (Courtesy of Aycock Brown Collection; OBHC.)

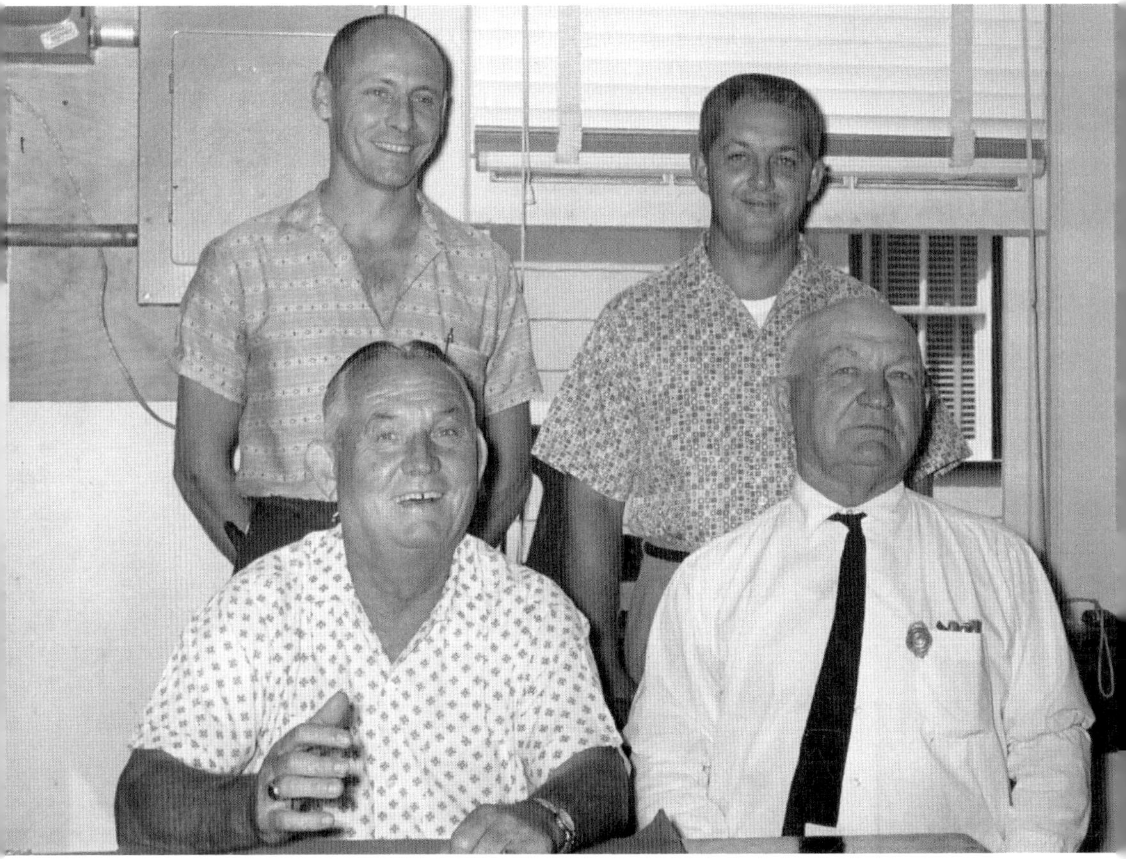

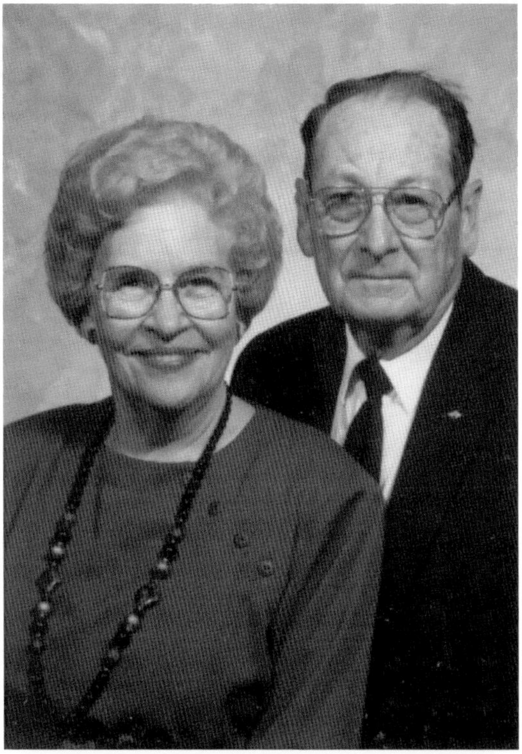

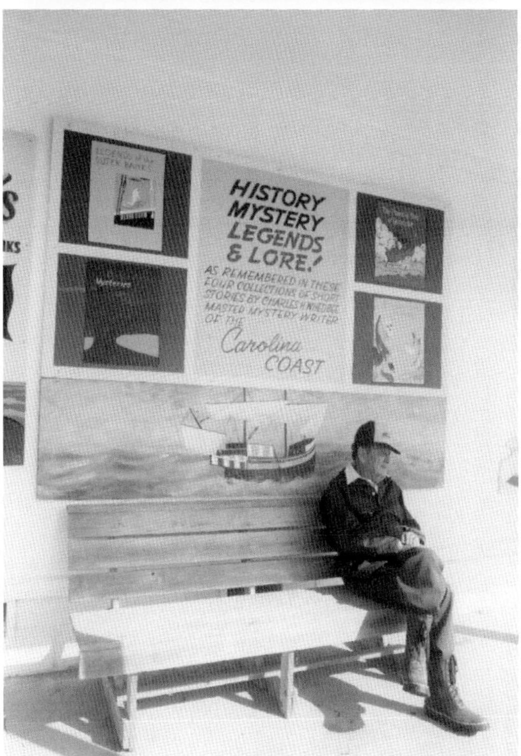

Whalebone's Grocery

When Dot Wheeler married Ray Cahoon, she had picked and chopped enough cotton in Hyde County to know that she did not want to be married to a farmer. The couple ran Ray's father's store in Swan Quarter, North Carolina, and then went out on a precarious limb in 1962 when they purchased Evans' Place at Whalebone Junction in Nags Head. The renamed R.V. Cahoon's Variety Store and Cottages turned out to be a good investment for the Cahoons. It was paid for in 10 years and has sustained three generations of family for over 50 years.

At age 90, Dot explains that she has slowed down a notch or two after a bad fall a few years ago. She still works seven days a week during the tourist season but not quite as many hours. In the lower photograph, Ray Cahoon sits on the store bench in front a mural advertising Charles Whidbee's books. (Above, courtesy of Dot Cahoon; below, photograph by Anna Gartrell, courtesy of Dot Cahoon.)

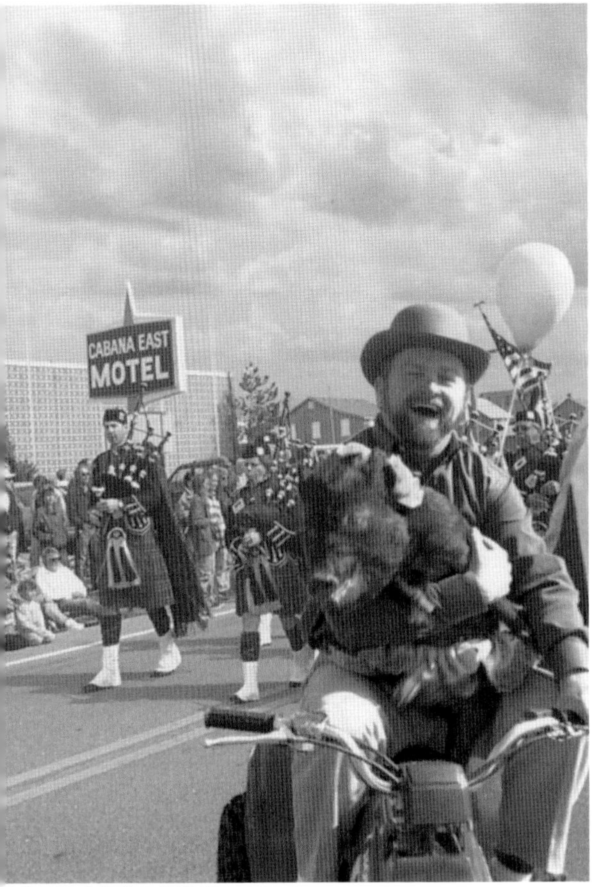

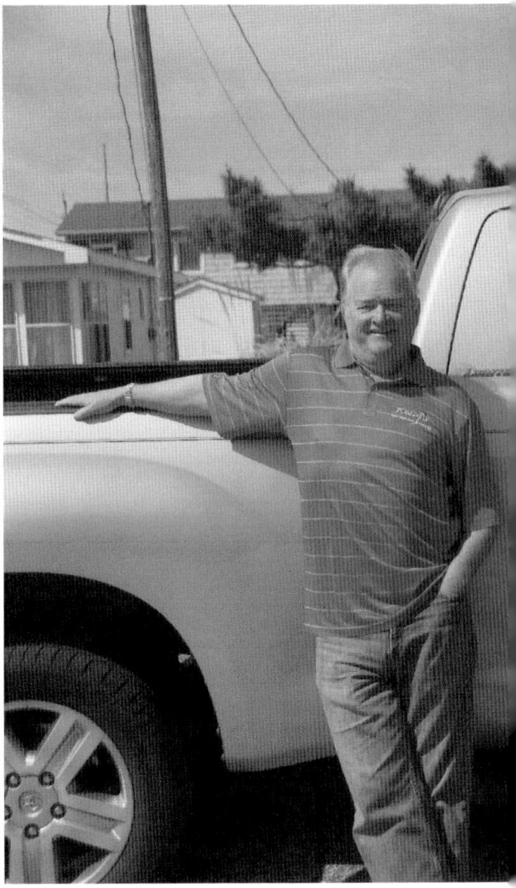

Leading the Parade

Public Outer Banks figure Mike Kelly seems to be everywhere and involved in everything. He is the man behind Kelly's Restaurant and Tavern and Kelly's St. Patrick's Day Parade.

Upon coming to the beach in 1970, his first employer was entrepreneur Mike Hayman of the Seafare Restaurant. Under Hayman's tutelage, he learned a work ethic that helped him rise from salad area worker to full manager by 1976. Mike Kelly also worked as manager at A Restaurant by George, where he was influenced by the very shrewd and imaginative businessman George Crocker. The experience and lessons he obtained from these men inspired him to purchase his own place, the former J. Fleming Mundes, in 1985. (Both photographs courtesy of Mike Kelly.)

CHAPTER FOUR

Pioneers

"Pioneers of a Dream"

Early pioneers on the Outer Banks made learning to live with nature an important part of their lifestyles. Their hard struggles often evolved into creative ways to make earning their livelihood easier. These pioneers set an example of endurance and independence.

Fisherman Malcolm Daniels began a small coastal village fishery using the resources that were available. His example of ingenuity and hard work helped his children take the business to a higher plane: a global fishing industry. Francis Rogallo developed a way for thousands of people to experience personal flight without making a penny in royalties. Whether they were flying the first helicopter like Dave Driskill, selling beach lots like real estate giant Robert Young Sr., or popularizing the Outer Banks through politics like Sen. Marc Basnight, all of the pioneers have set a high bar for others to follow. These pioneers had dreams, and many of their dreams were fulfilled. These pathfinders had a positive impact on the land and its people and laid the foundation for others to build upon.

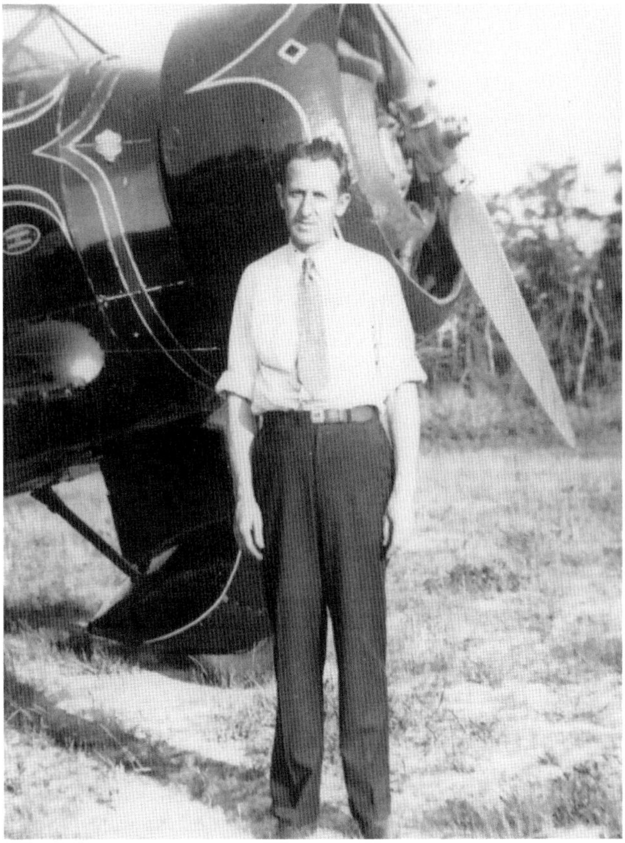

Putting Wings to Isolation

A 1930s journalist described the Outer Banks as remote and inaccessible as any place this side of the Arctic Circle. In that era, Dave Driskill and his airplane connected the small villages in a way that seemed almost miraculous.

Before the Depression, wealthy sportsmen wanted to get to Hatteras, North Carolina in a grander manner than a jarring Model-T ride down sand trails or an endless boat trip. They sent for Driskill, a young barnstormer, and gave him $60,000 to buy an airplane. He chose a Bellanca.

He flew the businessmen in style until the Depression hit. Driskill then took a job with the National Park Service, transporting groceries, payroll, and mail to the 1,000 men stationed in five CCC camps ranging from the Currituck Light to Ocracoke. The men who were stabilizing sand dunes and building the National Seashore were grateful for the fresh vegetables and meat that Driskill delivered in his Fairchild freighter.

In 1938, a group of local men started the first commercial air service in the area, the Roanoke Island Flying Service. Driskill gave rides in his Taylor Cub for as little as $1. He undertook more serious missions also, flying over 500 patients from Cape Hatteras to the hospital in Norfolk, Virginia. Driskill's logbook told of an improbable tale of tonnage and flying hours with no record of any minor disasters. There may have been forced landings, but the whole strip of banks provided a safe landing field.

After living in Manteo for six years, Driskill accepted a position as test pilot for Kellett Autogiro in Philadelphia, Pennsylvania. The autogiro was one of the first rotating wing aircraft. He died in a crash while testing one of these early helicopters.

Driskill and other pilots who flew over the Outer Banks would wiggle their wings as they passed over each village in a friendly greeting. It was also a tradition to salute the Wright Brothers Monument for good luck by dipping their wing as they passed. (Courtesy of OBHC.)

The Lost Colony's Miracle Worker

An immigrant from Yorkshire, England, Albert "Skipper" Bell must have felt a kinship with Sir Walter Raleigh's colonists who inhabited Roanoke Island. Upon first coming to the United States in 1920, he worked on the restoration of Jamestown, Virginia, and built ships in Elizabeth City. He said that he came to the island because "I thought the bloody place was tropical."

He created and built *The Lost Colony* Waterside Theatre for the first production. His contemporary, Ben Dixon MacNeill, wrote, "Albert Bell has always been a poet. It was a poet who dreamed the restoration of the site of the first settlers on Roanoke Island." He did prove to be a literary poet when he wrote and published *Actors in the Colony,* a book of essays and poems about people involved in the production.

Skipper, a nickname given to him by the *Colony* cast, rebuilt the theater twice; once after a fire in 1947, and once after Hurricane Donna completely destroyed it in 1960. When the fire occurred, this man of few spoken words was remembered as saying, "Give me some men and some lumber, and I will rebuild the theater in five to six days." No one believed that it was possible, but with the help of the cast, he did just that.

Bell had a penchant for growing things, and he and his wife founded a nursery.

He was tasked with helping to establish the Elizabethan Gardens in 1951, doing the site work and preparing the elevations so that masons from Fayetteville, North Carolina, could fashion the garden walls and gatehouse. The azaleas, camellias, hydrangeas, and magnolias came from the Bell nursery.

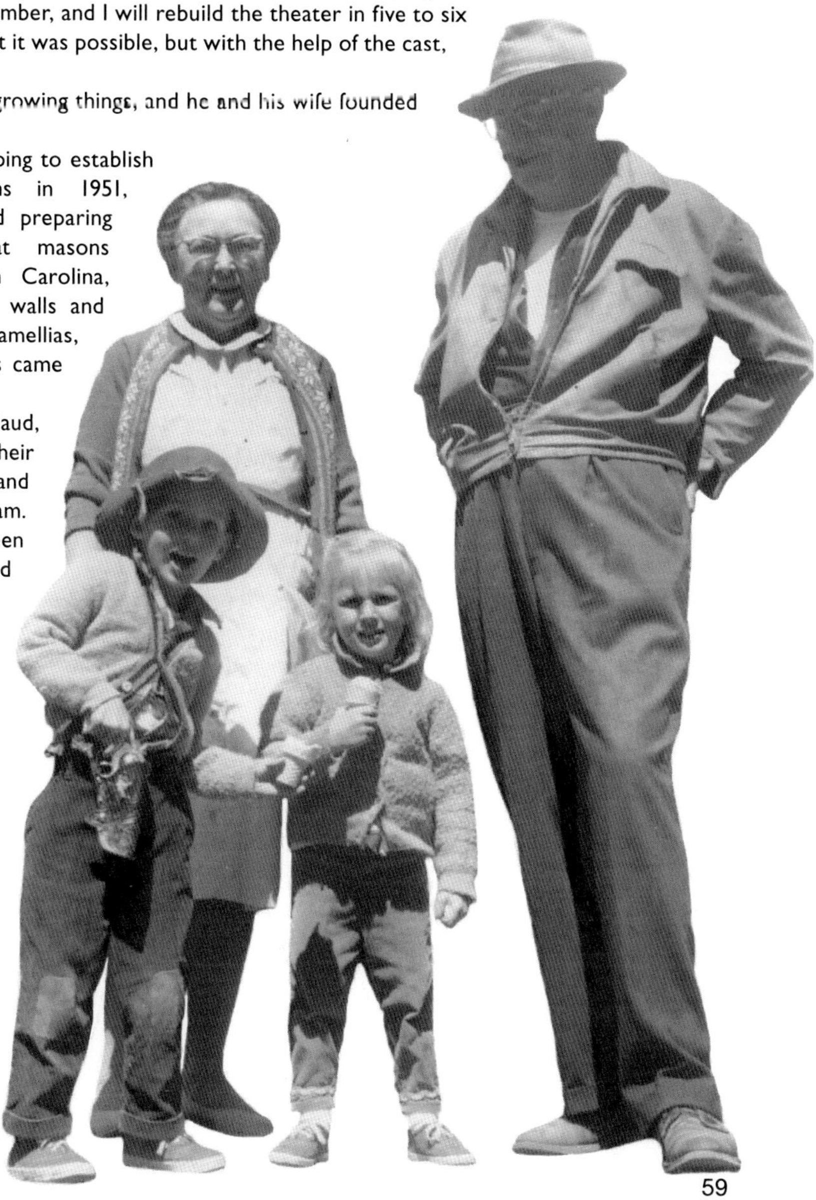

Skipper and his wife, Maud, are pictured here having their grandchildren Stewart and Cecelia over for ice cream. Skipper was rarely seen without his slouch hat and cigar. (Courtesy of Cecelia Bell Smith.)

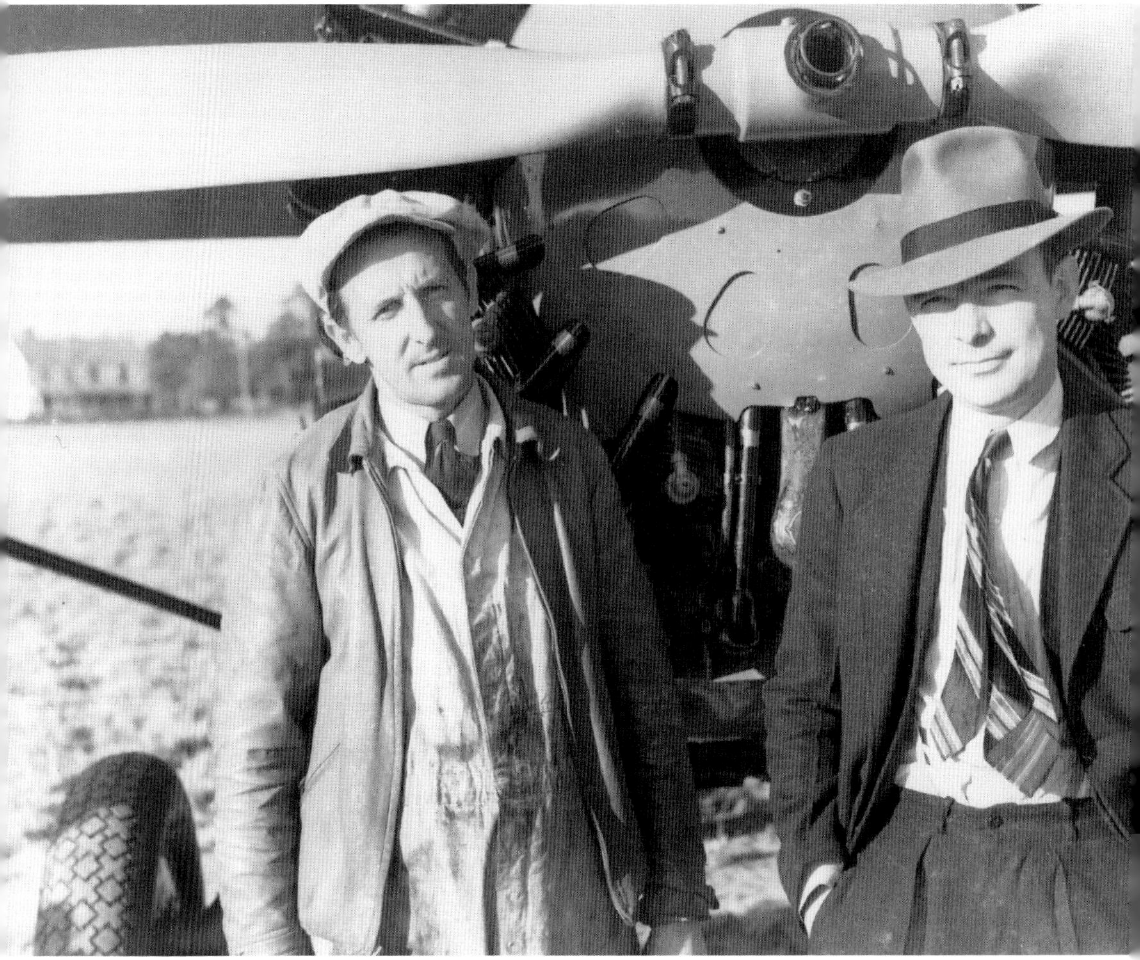

Meticulous Attention to Detail
Martin Kellogg Jr. (on right with Dave Driskill) received his law degree from UNC-Chapel Hill and moved to Manteo to set up a practice, becoming Dare County's first resident attorney at 23 years of age.

Energized with a strong sense of community, Kellogg recruited the first coach for local school sports, became a charter member of the Manteo Rotary Club, was instrumental in consolidating the county's one-room schools, helped develop the regional airport, and guided the incorporation of Nags Head.

The Lost Colony was special to Kellogg. During the first four seasons of the show, he played the role of Ananias Dare. For over 50 years, he served as general counsel for the producers. Roanoke Island Historical Association (RIHA) gave him the Distinguished Service Award in 1983, and it is now named in his honor. (Courtesy of RIHA.)

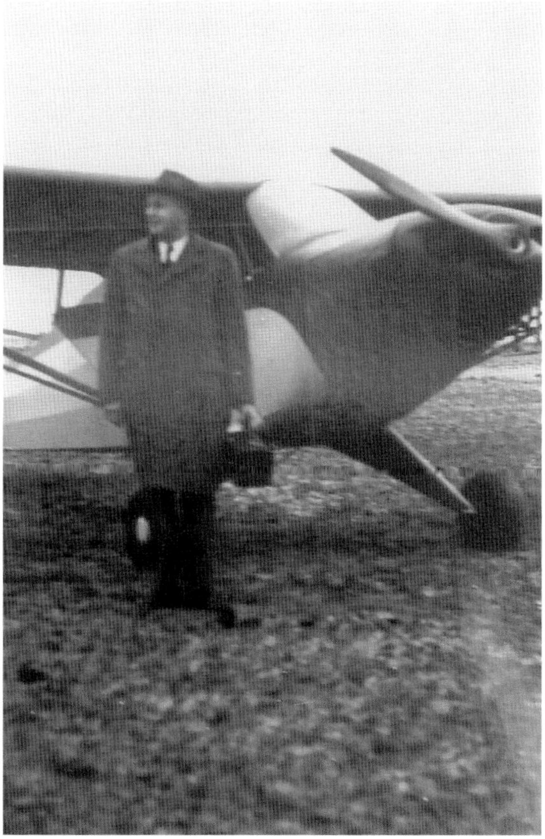

Have Medical Bag Will Travel

Coming to Roanoke Island with his nurse wife from Winston-Salem, North Carolina, Dr. Wiley Johnston joined the established practice of Dr. Franklin Gates. He fell in love with the area, partly because of his fondness of fishing and hunting. He stayed on to practice medicine for over 40 years and also served as director of health departments for Dare, Currituck, and Hyde Counties for 25 years.

In those days, doctors did whatever was needed: from treating minor injuries due to a drunken fight, to managing trauma from a logging accident. Toothaches and snakebites were standard calls. Bonnie Agliardo interviewed his daughter, Laura Johnston Tillett, who remembered people coming to their home at all hours of the day and night where her father sewed up head wounds on the back porch and her mother assisted him with deliveries. He was even known to take a look at the family dog when it was brought to him.

Since there was no pharmacy on the island, Dr. Johnston dispensed his own medicine. His basic fee for a visit was $2, but even at that rate some people did not have the cash to pay him. Some would pay him in fish, wild game, and firewood.

When people in other villages on the Outer Banks that were separated by bodies of water needed treatment, he would rely on the Coast Guard to take him back and forth from Roanoke to Hatteras Island. Once the news got out that the doctor was "down the banks," everyone who had an ailment would come. After World War II, pilots like Dave Driskill and Roger Meekins would fly him to wherever he needed to go to attend the sick.

When Dr. Johnston retired, there was still a tremendous amount of money that was owed to him. One man, however, sent a check for $25, explaining that he did not believe he ever paid for his child's delivery. Laura said, "My dad was surprised but rather pleased that he had remembered." (Courtesy of Laura Tillett.)

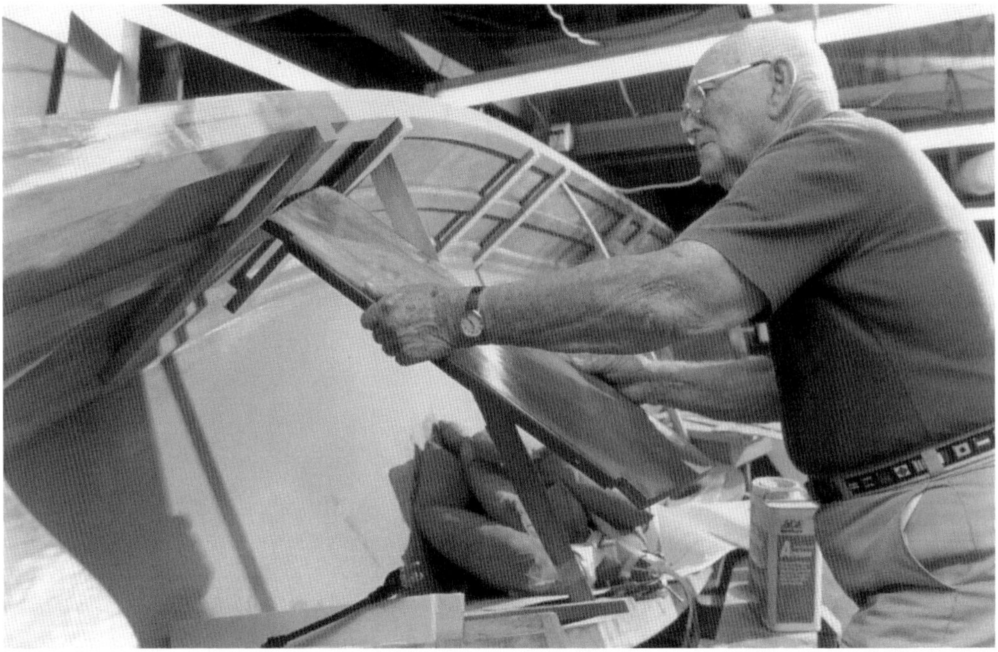

Brothers with a Need for Speed

It seemed as if Vernon (above) and Ralph Davis had boat building in their blood. Without any formal training, these brothers developed an innovative hull design for runabouts that they raced competitively. Their *Miss Manteo* held a 1940 world record for speed in its class. It had a flat stern designed with rounded corners on the rear to keep the racing boat from "tripping" on sharp turns.

During World War II, the brothers were two of 12 stockholders in a business called Manteo Boat Building Company, Inc. that made small vessels, lifesaving rafts, and 112-foot-long aircraft rescue boats until the war's end.

The brothers were also partners in a clothing store. Visitors to the Outer Banks knew they were getting close to their destination when they saw the billboards that said, "Davis Wants to See You—Everything to Wear." (Above, courtesy of *Manteo, A Roanoke Island Town* Collection, OBHC; below, courtesy of Manteo Boatbuilding Co. Collection, OBHC.)

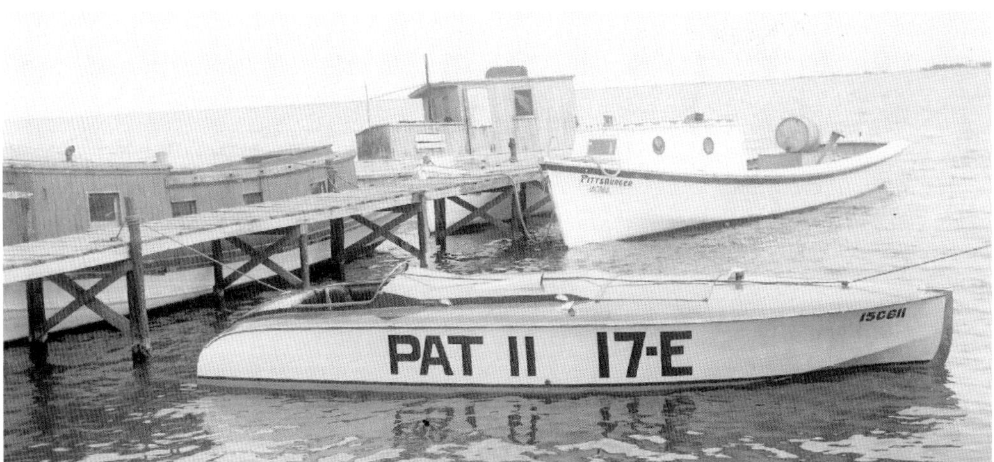

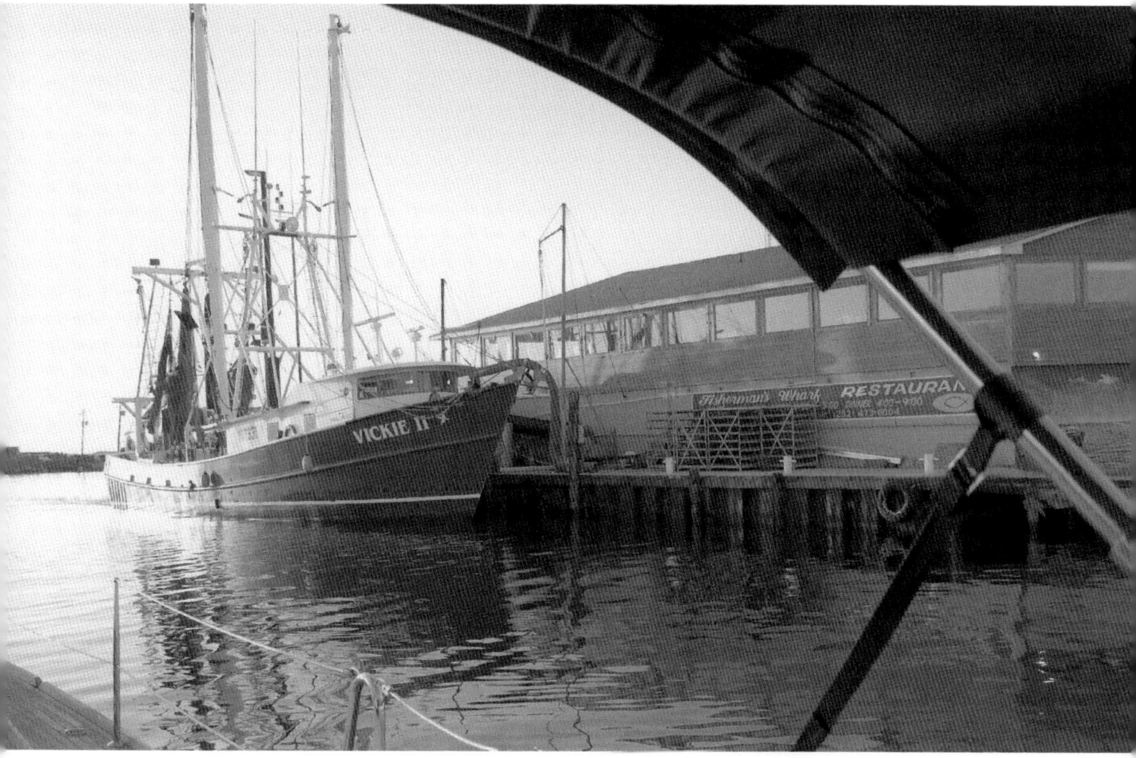

Turning Trash into Treasure

One fisherman who had a mindset way before his time was Malcolm Daniels, according to college writer Daisy Pearce. He founded Wanchese Fish Company in the 1940s and caught, bought, sold, and transported fish in previously unheard of ways. He had a penchant for transforming old equipment into something useful, recycling and repurposing before it was a fad.

Wanchese Fish Company currently has a business office in France that handles the sales of millions of pounds of scallops that originate in Argentina, caught by two 180-foot-long factory trawlers. What started as a ramshackle building on the edge of Roanoke Island is now a multimillion-dollar global company.

Malcolm and Maude Daniels were devout Christians who had 15 children who all worked hard in all aspects of the business. The family today is reaping the benefits of their parents' gumption, commitment, and prayers. (Above, courtesy of Dallas Daniels; below, courtesy of Barbara Tillett.)

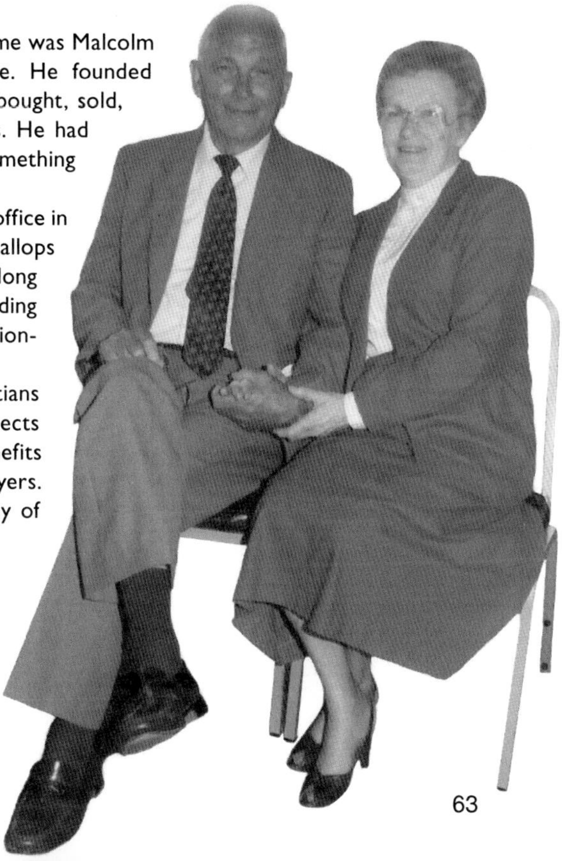

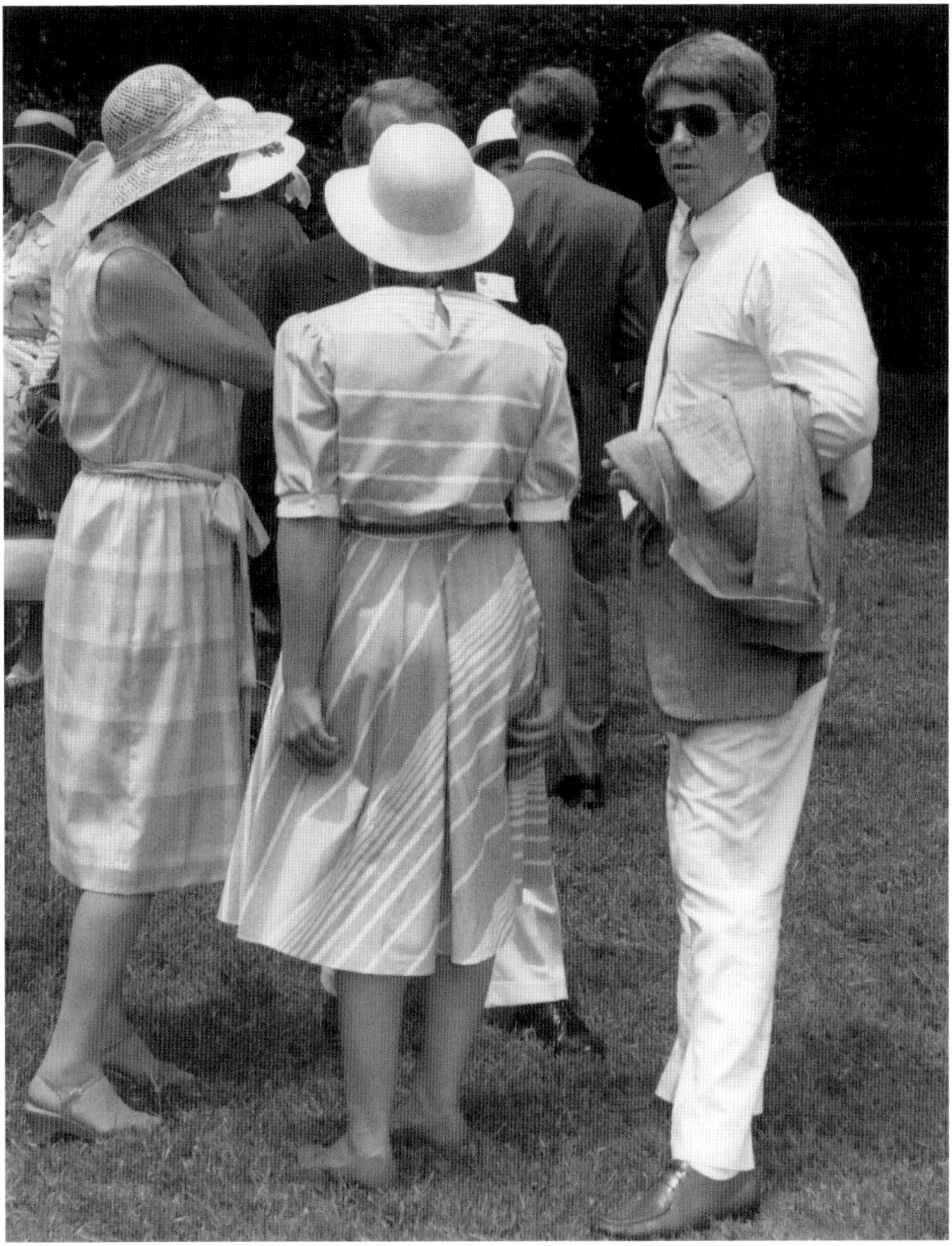

Beloved Senator

Democrat Marc Basnight, known for speaking his mind and cutting through red tape, was beloved by his constituents for being accessible and promoting the eastern part of the state. Basnight was elected to the North Carolina Senate in 1984 and served the first district for 26 years, the last 17 as president pro tempore. He was often referred to as having more power and clout than the governor. His intellectual curiosity helped him to become fully familiar with issues, and he became increasingly supportive of educational and environmental causes. Although elected for a 14th term, he stepped down when the disease ALS affected his speech and endurance. He still works daily at Basnight's Lone Cedar Café, where he warmly greets and visits with the people who love his Outer Banks. (Courtesy of OBHC.)

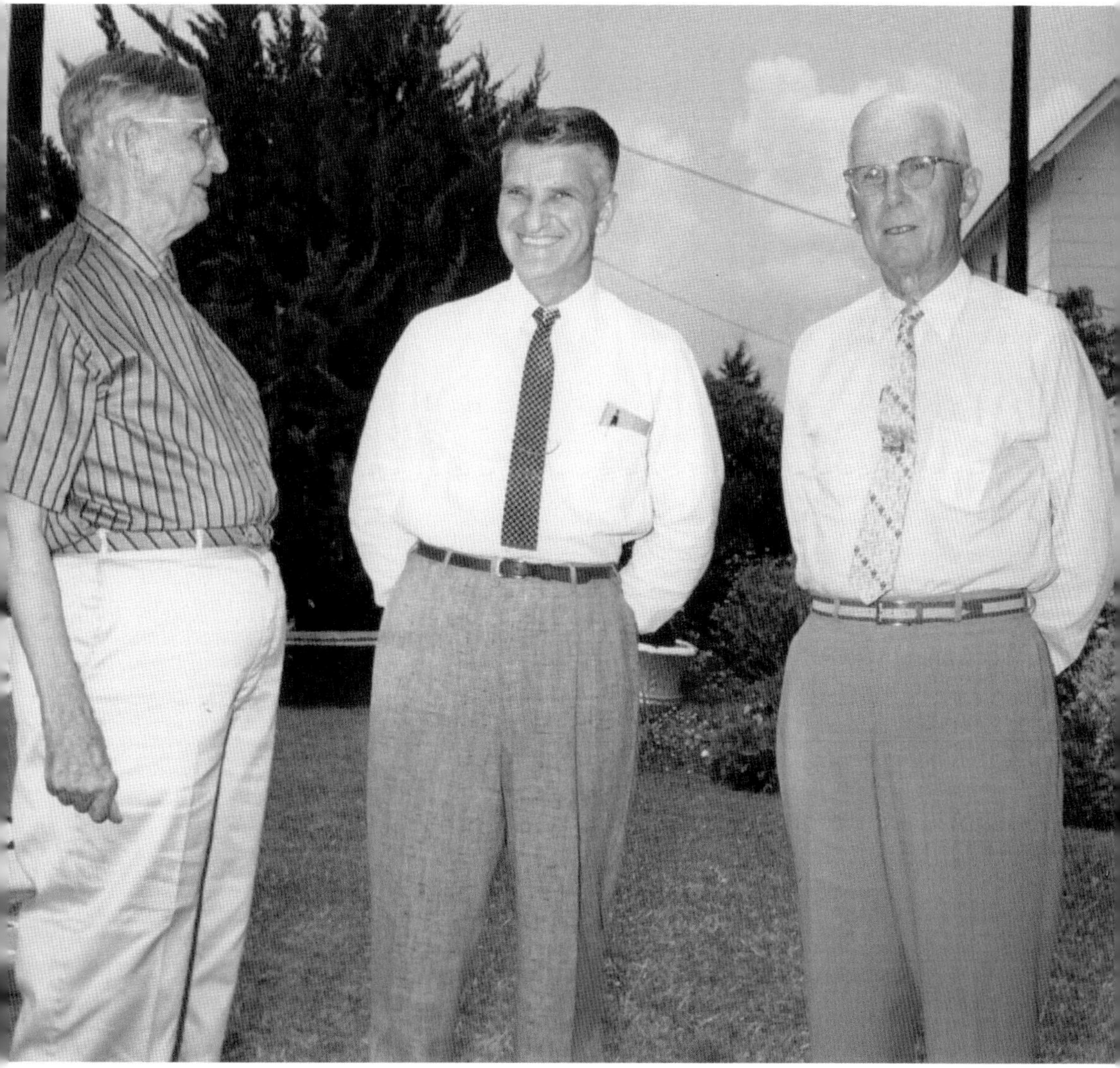

Publicizing the Wright's Flight

Telegraph operator Alf Drinkwater (left with Sheriff Frank Cahoon and Rep. R. Bruce Etheridge) knew a good story when he saw it. When *Moccasin,* a small submarine, wallowed ashore on Currituck Beach, he rushed to the site to report on it until it was pulled off the sandbar a week later. However, Alf missed the biggest story of his life: 30 miles south of his camp, the Wright brothers achieved the first powered flight, and he had been invited to attend.

He said that he "patched in" a telegraph about the flight, but that claim was negligible. Joe Dosher at the weather bureau in Kitty Hawk was credited for that communiqué. In the ensuing years, Alf sent in many creative tales about his association with the Wrights, to the point that publishers from leading papers sent their finest reporters to the area to substantiate his embellishments. When the reporters wrote their stories about Kitty Hawk, Alf inadvertently put the Outer Banks on the map. (Courtesy of OBHC.)

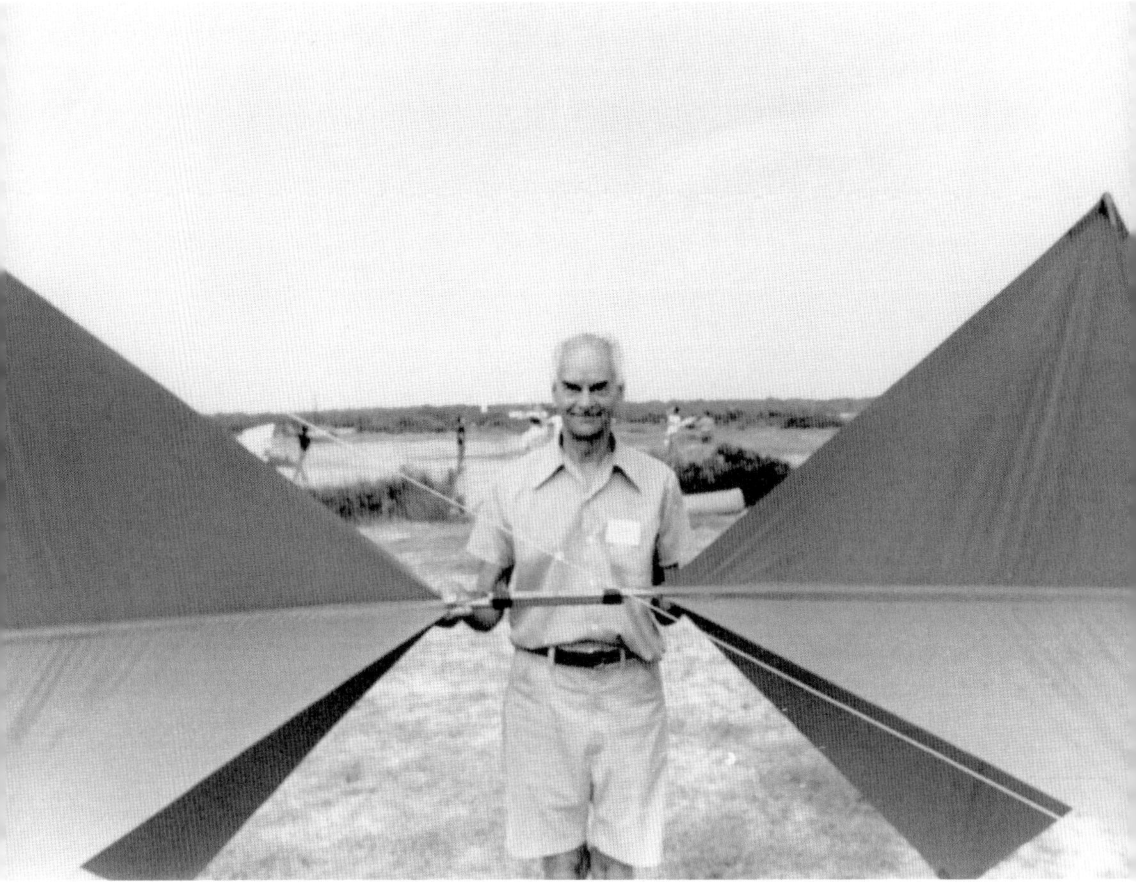

The Father of Hang Gliding

Francis Rogallo's obsession with flight was very similar to the Wright brothers' preoccupation. He patented a kite called the "flexible wing" that he flew as a glider. His hang glider made it possible for hundreds of thousands of people to experience personal flight. Like the Wrights, he sewed his own early prototype (more accurately, his wife, Gertrude, did the sewing, using her old kitchen curtains for material). And, like the Wrights, he came to the Outer Banks to test his invention, which received more attention in Europe than it did at home.

Rogallo, a NASA career man, actually met Orville Wright and talked with him in 1939. The military tested Rogallo's design in the mid-1950s to use for space capsules returning to the Earth. They decided on using parachutes instead, because his design had not "proven itself."

He and his wife worked on the "Rogallo wing" for 10 years. In the 1960s and 1970s, he could be seen flying over Jockey's Ridge in a red and white hang glider, just five miles from where the Wrights first flew. In 1967, the Rogallos gave their patent to the government. He never collected any royalties from his invention, letting others make millions. He was not interested in making money, joking that he would just give it away.

He and his wife retired to live in their oceanfront Southern Shores home in 1972. Rogallo flew until he was 80 and lived to be 97. He once said that hang gliding "is like a dream. It's like a fast run on skis or the short but exciting ride by a surfer." He must have had that feeling all 700 times that he flew off of Jockey's Ridge. (Courtesy of the Aycock Brown Collection; OBHC.)

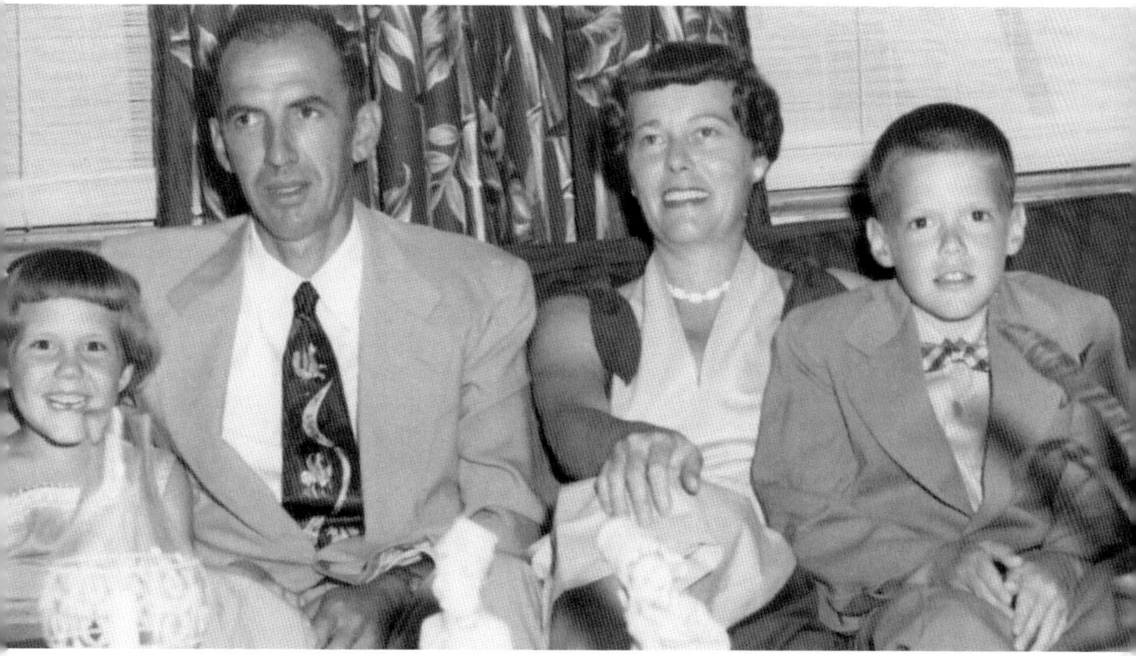

Under the Umbrella

In the 1950s, Robert Young Sr. began to sell lots in Avalon Beach, a neighborhood that went from ocean to sound in what is now Kill Devil Hills. He would sit on the beach under an umbrella since there was no office for his real estate venture. He took flyers to the Tidewater Virginia area and placed them on the windshields of cars belonging to shipyard workers and employees of the Ford Motor Plant.

He would accept a down payment of $50 and then finance the rest of the cost of the lot. Once the lot was paid for, he would suggest that the owner build a small two-bedroom stucco cottage that he would rent to summer vacationers and, in so doing, provide income for the owner and a commission for himself. This allowed an average, middle-income worker to realize a dream of owning a vacation home at the beach and supporting it with weekly rental income. (Courtesy of Tanya Young.)

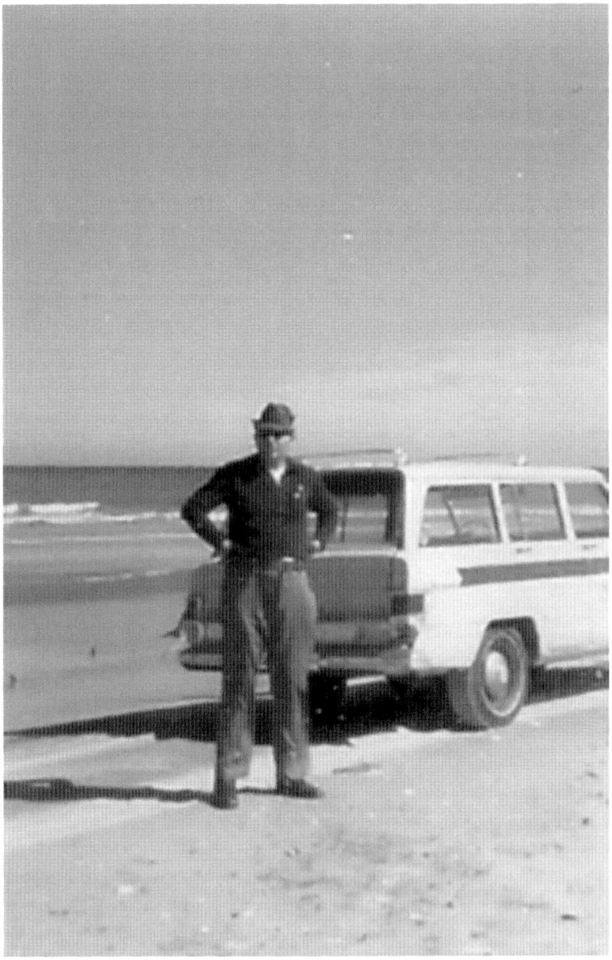

Hunting in His Blood
Travis Morris's great-grandfather thought the northern Outer Banks was good for nothing but raising cattle. He would sail across the sound from Currituck to feed them, putting runners on the bottom of his boat to slide along when the sound froze over.

In the 1970s, Morris had a different opinion of the undeveloped Currituck Banks. He got into real estate and established Currituck Realty, which still operates out of its original trailer along the Currituck highway. He took prospective buyers to Corolla in an old boat and then took them touring in an ancient Corvair with "Currituck Realty" written on the door in white shoe polish. He would sell them a dream for $12,000. He kept on selling and sold several miles of beachfront when it was going for $1 million a mile. Also credited for developing Corolla Village, Travis promoted the sale of lots for Elizabeth City investors.

His true passion, however, lies in hunting and fishing. He started hunting at age six and working as a guide at 15. He began recording stories and writing about his own hunting adventures, preserving a portion of Currituck history. Owning 43 hunting blinds at one time, Travis hobnobbed with rich, powerful, and prominent men when they came to Currituck to shoot their limit of waterfowl.

Travis ran the Monkey Island Hunt Club for the Penn family, one of the founders of the American Tobacco Company. He received a windfall when he later sold it for $3 million.

He once wrote, "The ducks have opened a lot of doors that otherwise would be closed to us Currituckers." (Courtesy of Travis Morris.)

CHAPTER FIVE

Educators, Ministers, and Writers

"Roanoke! Thou hast made a man of me."

In the early days of the Outer Banks, education and ministry jobs were often part-time professions. There were almost no writers living in the area. Teachers came to the area in the 1880s and lived with prominent families. Those families and other community members often built small schoolhouses. Early ministers were circuit riders who shared the gospel in homes and in the open air until churches could be built. In many instances, schoolhouses also served as churches. Natives living in the area were too busy trying to make a living to record events in writing. Writers passing through like John Lawson are credited with preserving the area's history. Journalists sent from *National Geographic* and *Harper's Weekly* wrote lasting and valuable accounts of our culture and events.

As commerce prospered, great strides were made by people in these three areas. Professionals emerged as villages grew into towns. Prominent educators like Mabel Evans Jones brought a new awareness of educational needs. Missionary couples such as Craig and Chetty Parker and Mark and Cathy Daniels have bridged their ministries from Roanoke Island to Haiti and India. Modern writers like Angel Ellis Khoury, Jan DeBlieu, and Molly Harrison have promoted the Outer Banks and continue to record its history for future generations.

Today's Outer Banks is a thriving community. Its many schools have a combined multimillion-dollar yearly budget. Many graduates go on to receive higher degrees and recognition as professionals worldwide. The churches are strong in local and global outreach. The region also boasts a myriad of authors, from feature writers for newspapers and magazines to nationally known novelists.

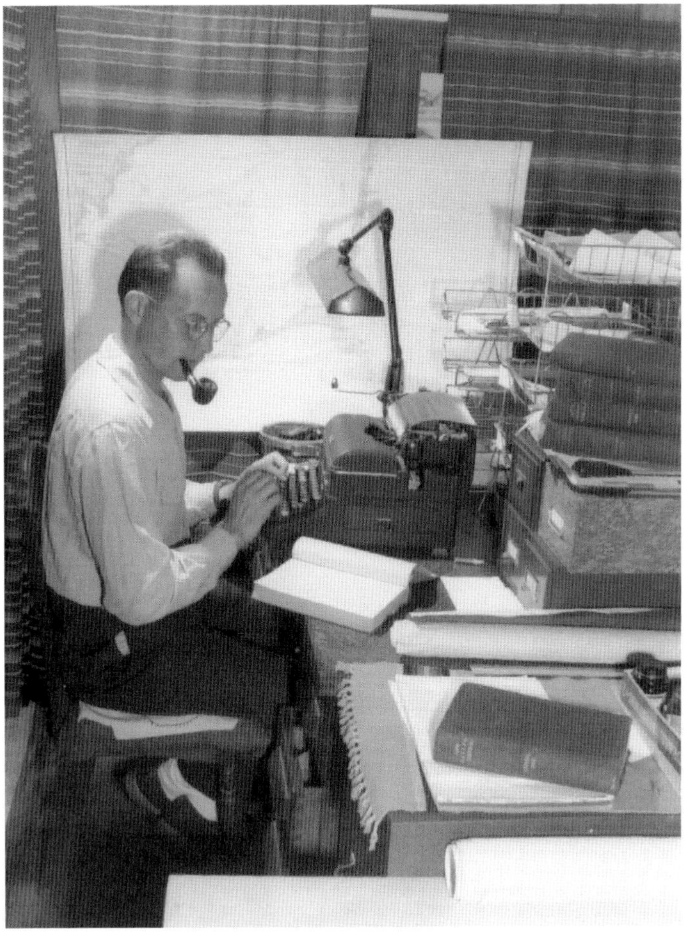

Working the Hatteras Beat

Ben Dixon MacNeill came to Manteo in 1937 as a journalist for the Raleigh *News and Observer*, assigned to write about the opening of the new outdoor drama *The Lost Colony*. At the end of his short visit, he decided to stay and work as publicity director for the pageant. He was tireless in producing manifold articles promoting the drama, so much so that he was credited with saving the play when it was about to go under.

His love for his adopted home prompted him to campaign to save another Outer Banks symbol, the Cape Hatteras Lighthouse. After seeing it abandoned because of beach erosion, Ben led a one-man march to have CCC men plant grass and erect sand fences in front of the lighthouse. Their efforts resulted in the light being reactivated after it was deemed safe.

After serving in the Navy during World War II, MacNeill retired and moved to a small cottage a short distance from the Cape Hatteras Lighthouse. His training under the bigger-than-life owner of the *News and Observer*, Josepheus Daniels, was put back to use when he became a correspondent for the newspaper again. There were hundreds of articles about the lighthouse, the Coast Guardsmen, German U-boats, the paving of Highway 12, Old Christmas, Billy Mitchell, the Marconi Wireless Telegraph Tower, and all things Hatteras. He wrote two books about the Outer Banks, *The Hatterasman* and *Sand Roots*, which explored the history, folklore, and lives of the people of Hatteras whom he loved.

He was considered by many to be an eccentric and a loner, but he had the ability to win people over to whatever cause he was promoting. He died alone in 1960 in his cottage on his beloved Hatteras Island, and his ashes were spread over the nearby Atlantic Ocean. (Courtesy of OBHC.)

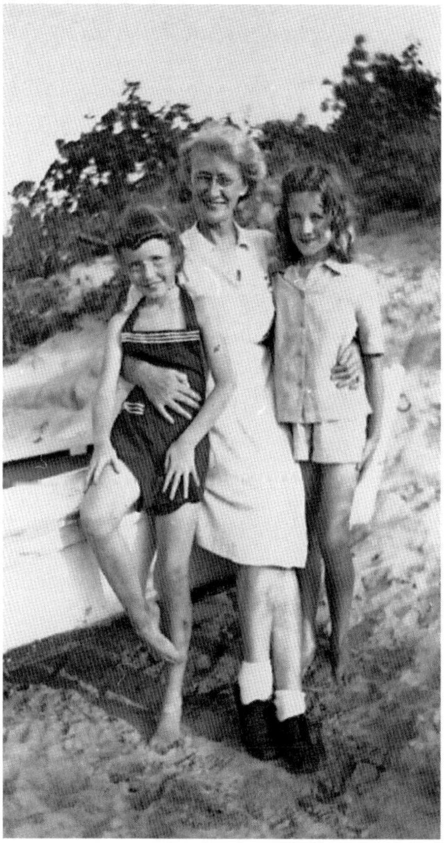

Ahead of Her Time

Mabel Evans Jones was a beautiful, talented, intelligent woman who also had a knack for getting people to work together. At age 17, she left Roanoke Island to earn a certificate from Greensboro College and teach in Alabama for a decade. When she returned to her home in 1920, she was elected the first superintendent of schools for Dare County. She remembered, "At the time there were no bridges to the Outer Banks, and I traveled to the schools by way of the mail boat. The Coast Guard was a great help in my travels to the county schools, and I got a grand kick out of it all."

When she heard that the North Carolina State Board of Education was going to do a film on North Carolina history, she convinced the state superintendent that Roanoke Island was where the state's history began. She was primarily responsible for the production, writing the script, recruiting 125 local people to act, and playing Eleanor Dare's role herself. A Chicago company was awarded a contract to do the filming and provide a director. The whole summer of 1921 was devoted to sewing costumes and making wigs from untwisted hemp rope. The motion picture, titled *Lost Colony*, was filmed on the north end of the island near Fort Raleigh. It was shown throughout the state by the board of education, and, for many viewers, it was the first movie they ever saw.

Mabel married for the first time when she was in her 40s. She acquired a tract of land with sound beachfront, designed buildings herself, and started Camp Seatone, a summer camp for boys and girls. The camp offered an array of fun things to do: water sports, horseback riding, crabbing, and arts and crafts, as well as training in dance and rhythm. She published a children's book, *A Rascal, Oh No,* about a dog rescued by the lifesaving service in 1889 and the boy who became his master.

Despite many disabilities in her later years, she wrote, painted, lectured, played the organ, and served in organizations that, according to a cousin, "made her interesting and delightful to be with." (Courtesy of Edna Evans Bell Collection; OBHC.)

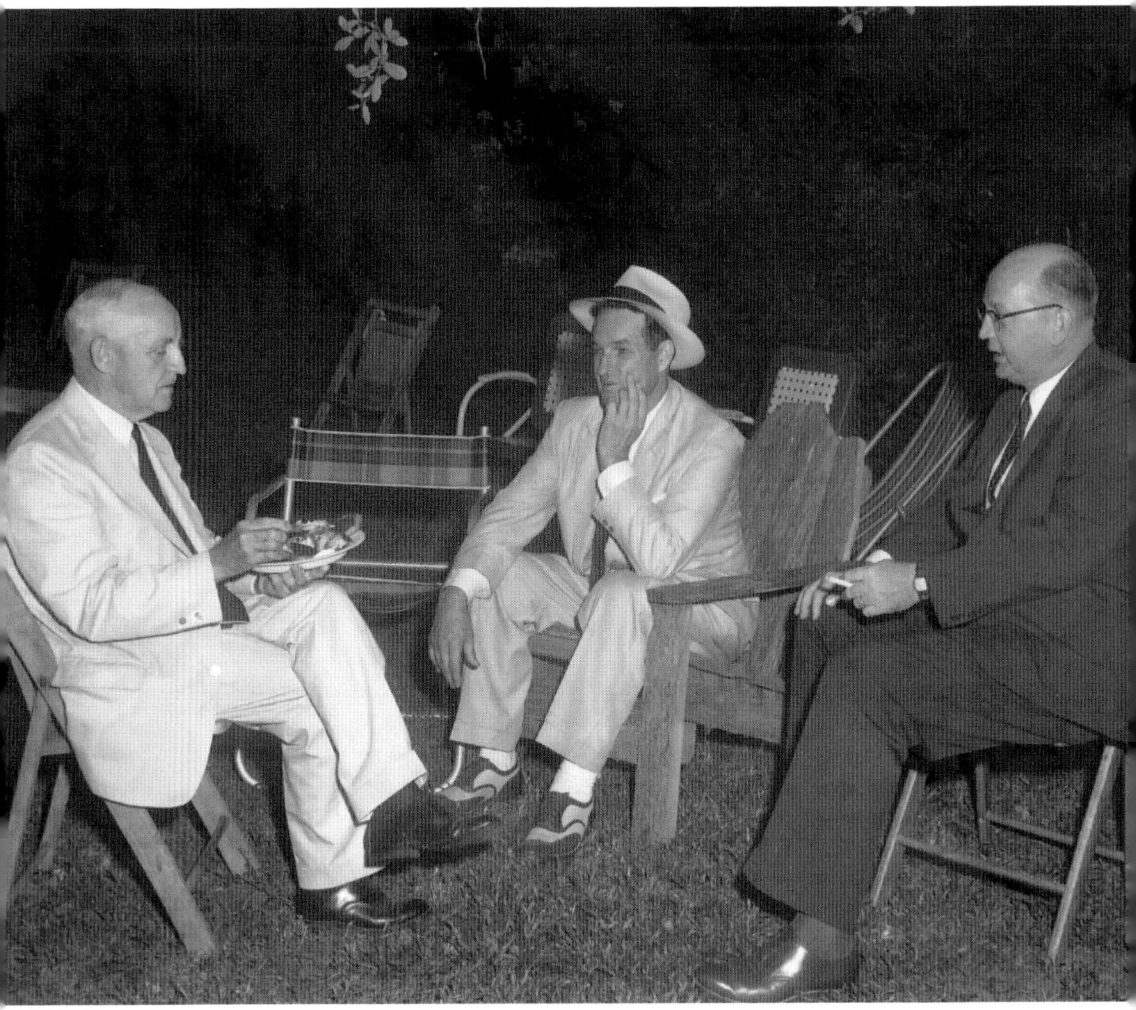

Creator of the Symphonic Drama
Paul Green (center) created the formula for outdoor plays in America. In Europe, he studied different drama types and combined pantomime, poetic dialogue, music, dance, pageantry, light, sound, colorful costumes, and factual history. He called his experimental effort symphonic drama. The set would always be on the very site of the story.

Having recently won the Pulitzer Prize for *In Abraham's Bosom*, Green was considered by Bradford Fearing, one of Manteo's visionaries, the logical choice to write *The Lost Colony*. Green visited Manteo and agreed to write the pageant.

In 1937, Green's outdoor drama was played in the Fort Raleigh natural waterside amphitheater in Manteo for the first time. Pres. Franklin D. Roosevelt was in the audience. The play tells the story of Sir Walter Raleigh's colonists who established the first nonpermanent colony in America. (Courtesy of OBHC.)

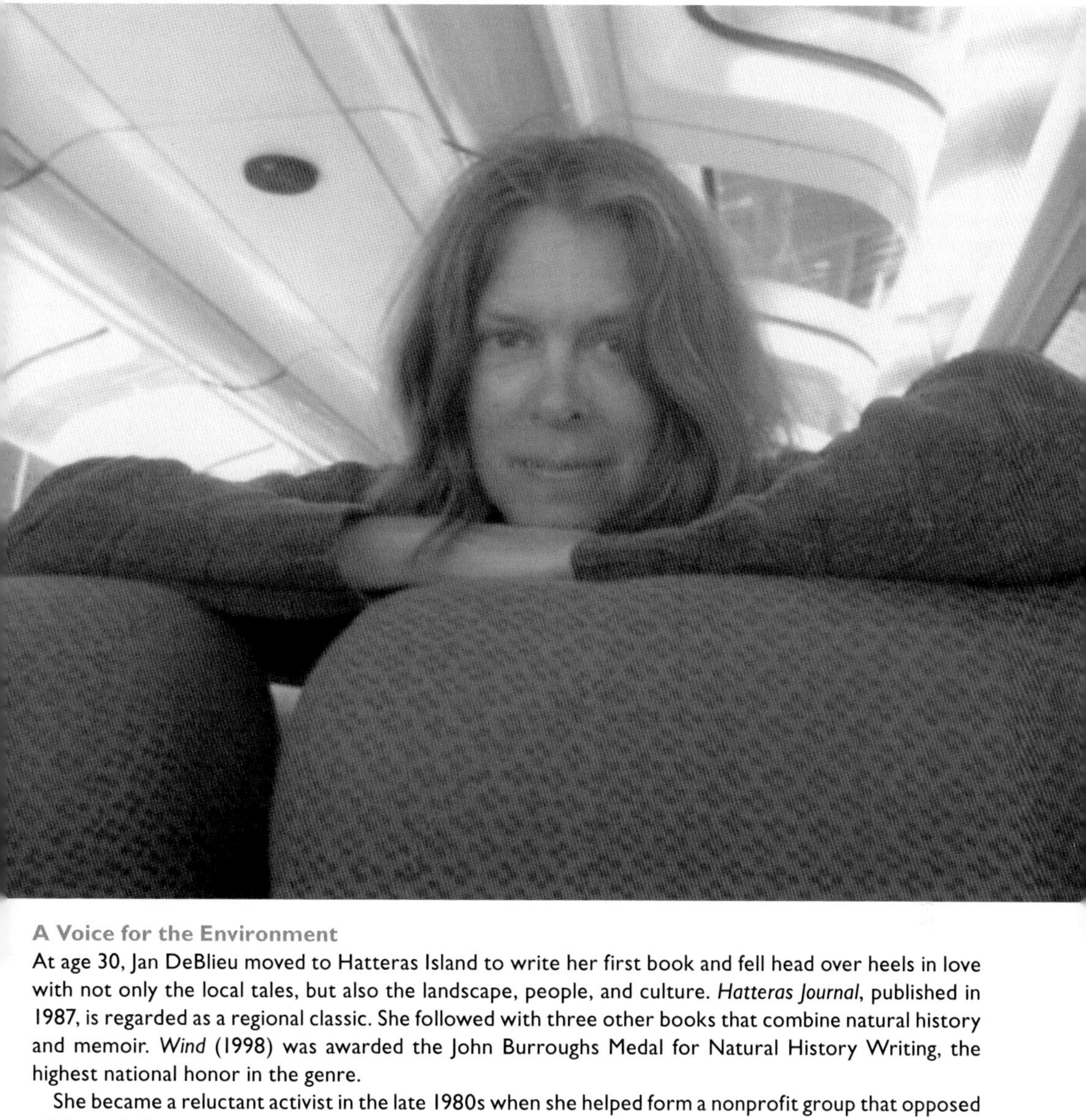

A Voice for the Environment

At age 30, Jan DeBlieu moved to Hatteras Island to write her first book and fell head over heels in love with not only the local tales, but also the landscape, people, and culture. *Hatteras Journal*, published in 1987, is regarded as a regional classic. She followed with three other books that combine natural history and memoir. *Wind* (1998) was awarded the John Burroughs Medal for Natural History Writing, the highest national honor in the genre.

She became a reluctant activist in the late 1980s when she helped form a nonprofit group that opposed offshore drilling in the Graveyard of the Atlantic. In 2000, Mobil Oil and its partners abandoned their leases without sinking a single well.

From 2003 through 2011, DeBlieu served as a coastal advocate for the North Carolina Coastal Federation, safeguarding wetlands and working to promote policies that protect coastal waters from pollution. In 2012, she returned to full-time writing. (Courtesy of Jan DeBlieu.)

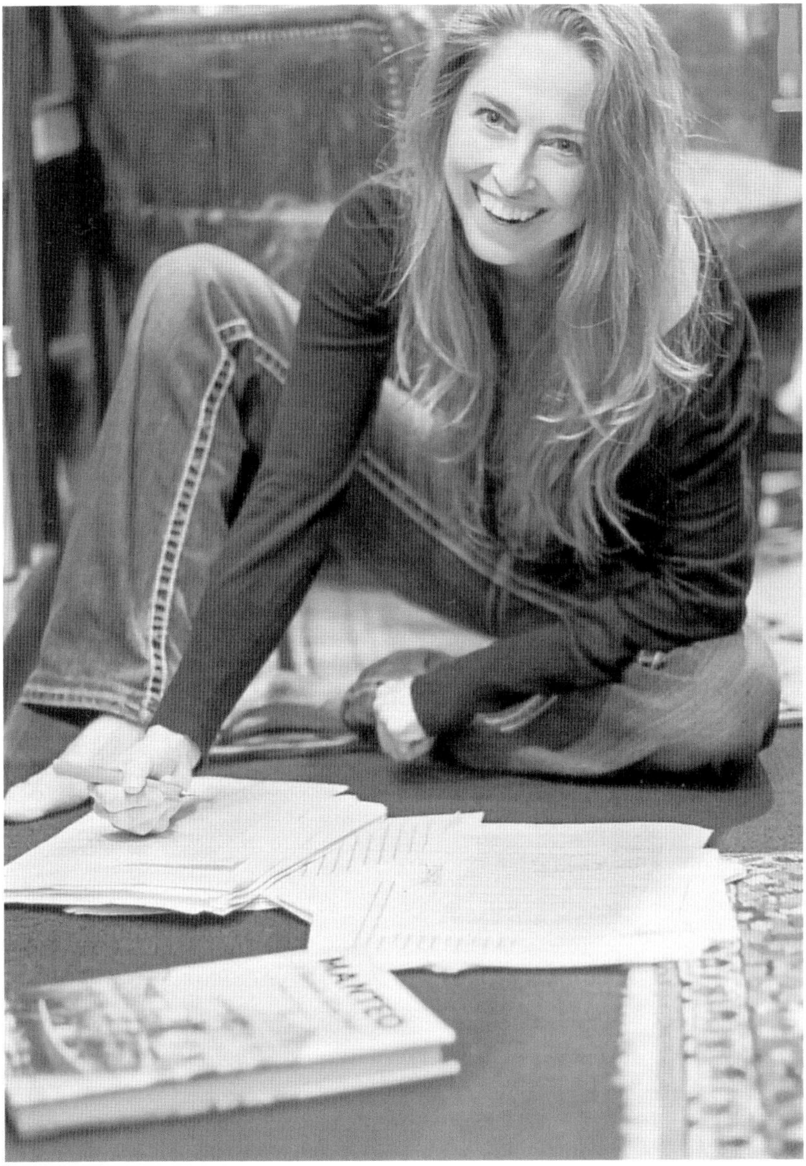

Recording the History of Manteo

Angel Ellis Khoury first dreamed of writing about the Outer Banks in 1979. Elbow-deep in suds as a dishwasher at the Avalon Fishing Pier, she watched the waves foam below through cracks in the floor while reading her water-stained copy of MacNeill's *The Hatterasman*. She has been writing about the place and its people ever since.

Her first love is writing, but her passion has been giving voice to other writers—and those they write about. As associate editor of the *Coastland Times*, and editor and publisher of *Outer Banks Magazine*, she worked with dozens of writers, photographers, and artists, regionally and nationally known, to create an Outer Banks vernacular through story, fiction, poetry, art, and design.

In *Manteo: A Roanoke Island Town*, she invokes the words and deeds of five generations in what David Stick called the definitive history of the Outer Banks' first incorporated town. (Courtesy of Angel Ellis Khoury.)

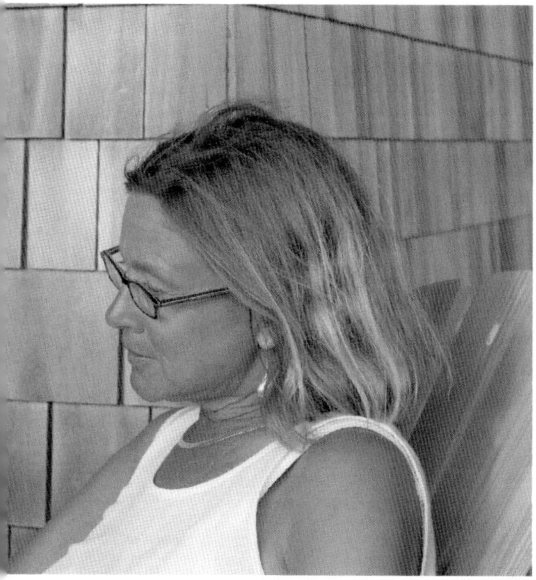

Looking up the Answers
Norfolk native Sarah Downing has immersed herself in Outer Banks history. As assistant curator at the Outer Banks History Center in Manteo for the last 15 years, she can respond to most questions posed to her. Currently working on her fifth book for North Carolina History Press, she also writes a history column for the *Outer Banks Sentinel* newspaper. (Courtesy of Becky "Shells" Ballou.)

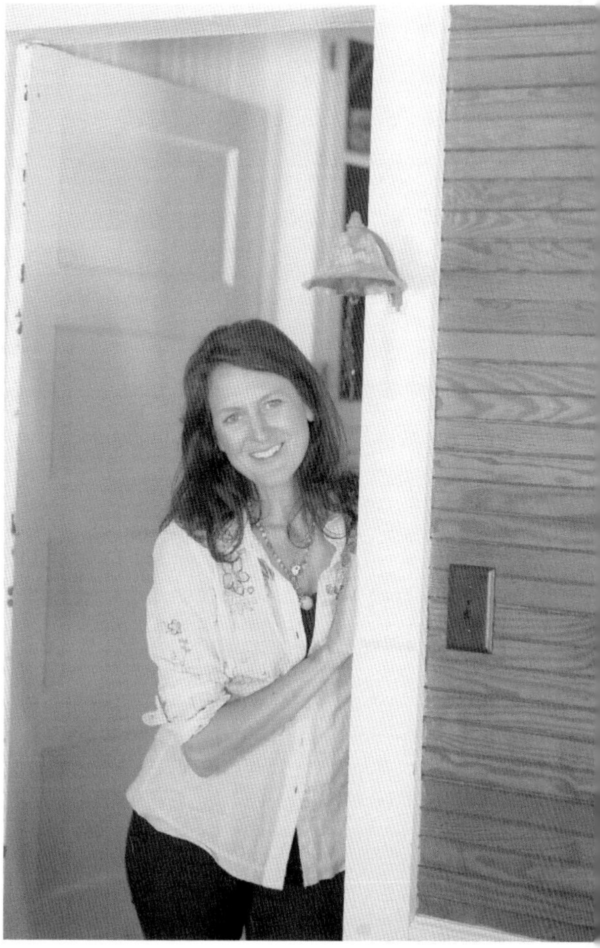

Weaving Stories
In 1994, working as a cub reporter for the *Coastland Times* seemed like a simple summer job for recent English major graduate Molly Harrison. It turned out to lead to a career in writing about the Outer Banks in over 50 articles published in *Our State* magazine, four tour books, and a collection of nonfiction stories. Currently, Molly is the editor of *Outer Banks Magazine* and the weekly entertainment publication the *Coast,* both published by Pilot Media. (Courtesy of Julie Dreelin.)

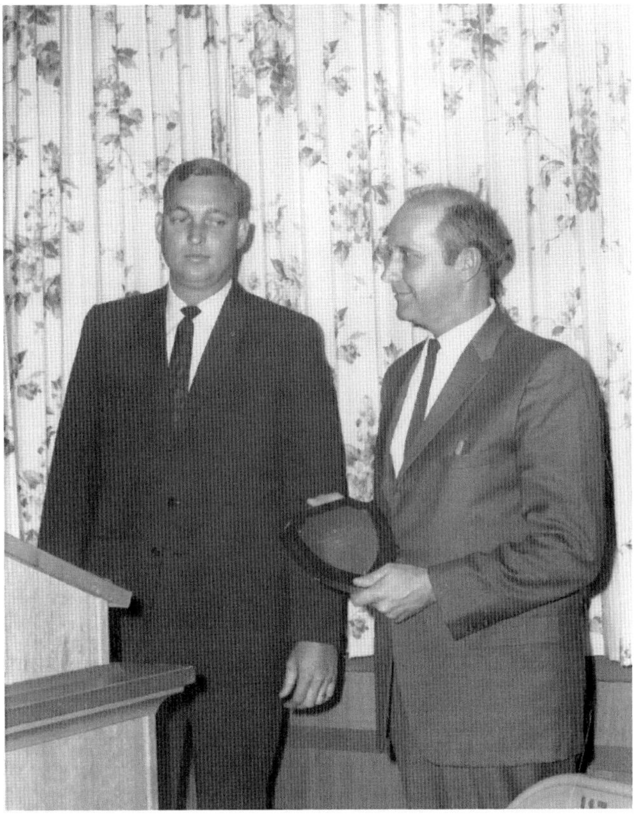

Getting the Facts Straight

Outer Banks inhabitants can thank David Stick (right) for accurately recording their history as far back as when the explorer Giovanni da Verrazzano first laid eyes on what he thought was a great isthmus. An avid student of history, Stick often had to heed the very advice he gave novice writers: "At some point you have to stop researching and start writing."

Stick came to his beloved new homeland at age nine when his father, Frank Stick, moved the family from New Jersey to Skyco. He lived a little boy's paradise on the sound side, riding his horse, playing with neighbors, and going fishing with Marshall Collins, the patriarch of a prominent local African American family. As a young man, he developed an interest in diving on shipwrecks and spear fishing in the ocean.

He learned his writing skills working for newspapers out of Elizabeth City and Raleigh. He put out his own paper, *Nags Head News and Notes,* for a year. Over the course of his life, he wrote 12 books and countless articles and pamphlets on his favorite subject. *The Outer Banks of North Carolina* was his most popular book, and it is still in circulation.

Stick was a bookstore owner for a while, but he was perhaps more interested in the buying side of the business. He amassed an impressive collection of rare maps and a library of books about North Carolina.

He became concerned with changes to beach communities that he felt were brought about by lack of planning. He joined with his father in his real estate venture, Southern Shores, and practiced careful development of land. He became involved in local politics to see if he could make a difference and served as a Dare County commissioner.

Before his death, Stick gave his tremendous library to the state and later helped form the Outer Banks History Center where his collection resides. Now others can continue on David Stick's path of research and writing. (Courtesy of Aycock Brown Collection; OBHC.)

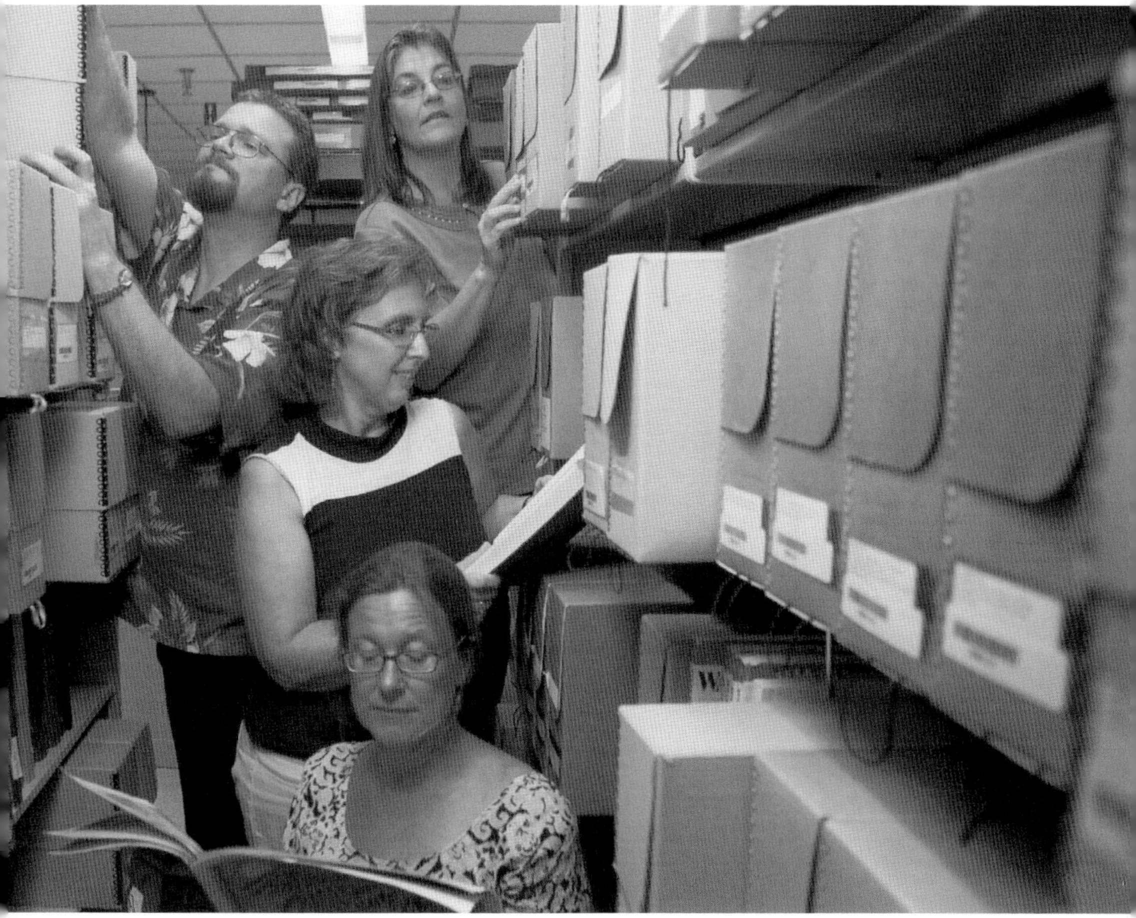

Best Resource is the Staff

The Outer Banks History Center is a regional archives and research library of the state archives of North Carolina. The collection, housed in Manteo, is made up of books, maps, periodicals, microfilm, photographs, oral history recordings, and works of art. The center was founded in 1989 after noted author and historian David Stick donated his personal library to the North Carolina Department of Cultural Resources.

The current staff is made up of four unique and talented individuals who each bring special strengths to their jobs. Ohio-born KaeLi Schurr (center) is the curator and site manager. During her tenure, she has proven herself to be a community resource and collaborator. She is always willing to share her passion for Wright brothers and African American history. Sarah Downing (bottom) serves as assistant curator and enjoys researching, writing, and sharing stories about the Outer Banks. As certified public librarian and published author, her enthusiasm for reference is evident. Archivist Stuart R. Parks II uses his unrivaled skills to design exhibits that time after time conjure praise from individuals from all positions in society. Parks also handles the scanning of photographs and digitizing of collections. Archivist Tama N. Creef (top, right) enlists her superior organizational skills to keep the center running smoothly and draws on her background in museum education to shepherd outreach activities to teachers and students. (Courtesy of Chris Bickford.)

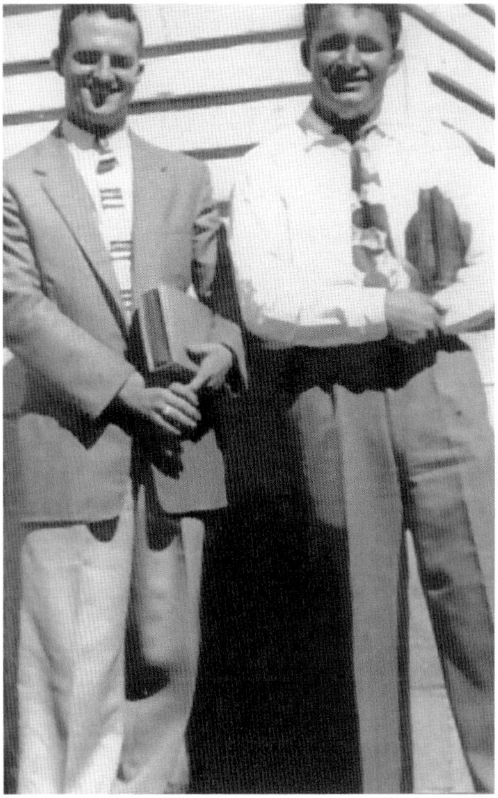

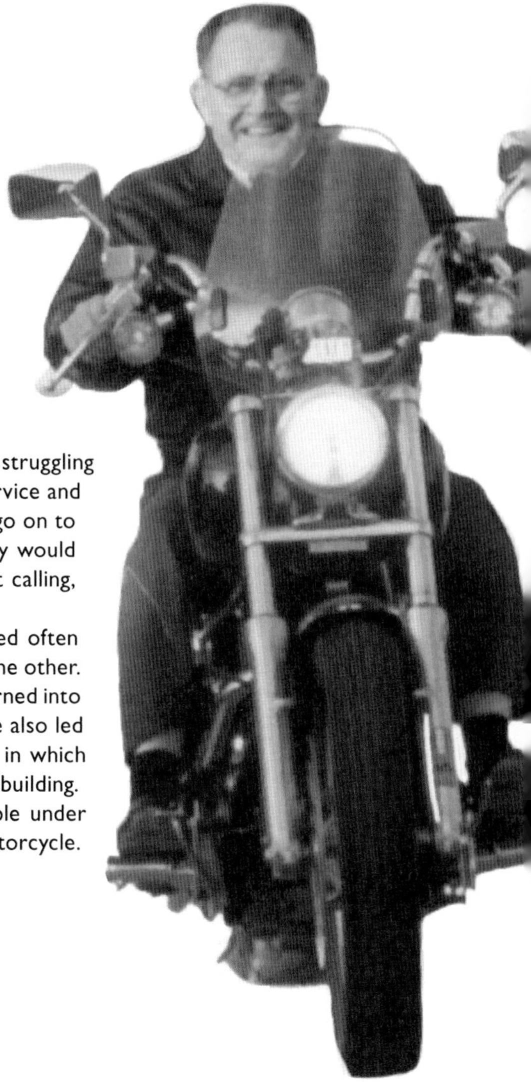

Build up and Move on

A preacher in the Assemblies of God denomination, Carroll Daniels had a lifetime ministry of taking on a struggling church, providing them with a dynamic worship service and an attractive building, and giving them strength to go on to the next level. When the first wind of controversy would blow, Brother Carroll would move on to the next calling, often resigning with nowhere to go.

He and his wife, Evelena, and five children moved often and served churches from one side of the state to the other. He came back to Wanchese to hold a revival that turned into a full-time pastorate when 75 souls were saved. He also led the Manteo congregation during a time of growth in which they constructed a large sanctuary and educational building.

Young Pastor Daniels is on the right with a Bible under his arm. Older Pastor Daniels enjoyed riding his motorcycle. (Both images courtesy of the Daniels family.)

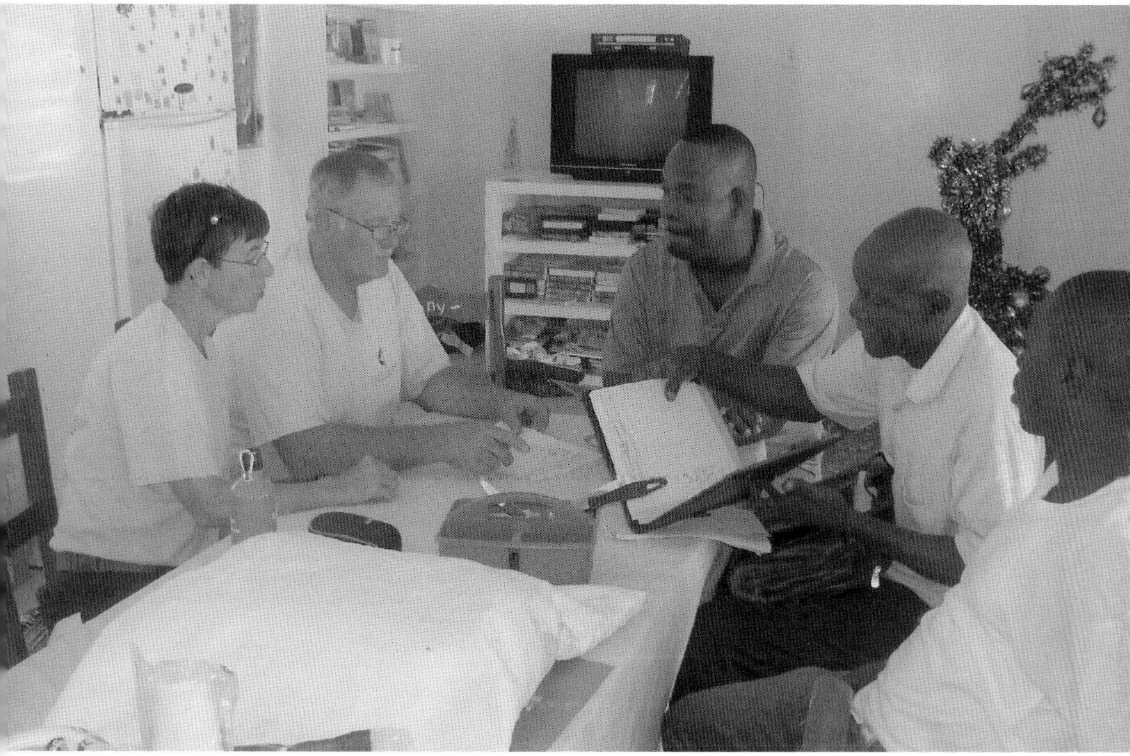

Unlikely Missionaries to Haiti

When their only son Craig Jr., or "Boo," as his family nicknamed him, died over a decade ago, Craig and Chetty Parker were understandably devastated. Just out of high school, Boo was electrocuted in the garage of their home while working on his truck. Both parents were equally paralyzed with sorrow, but the toll of the grief was particularly apparent in Chetty. She seemed to be sleepwalking. The months turned into years, and the grief seemed just as raw as it was when Boo first died.

Craig was invited on a mission trip to Haiti by Helen Little, an octogenarian with a heart for the poorest country in the world. He went somewhat reluctantly but immediately fell in love with the people of Haiti. He used his practical skills to help construct buildings at an orphanage sponsored by the Methodist Church. Soon he was part of the team that regularly went to Haiti. His home church became involved by raising money and gathering clothing. Craig kept asking Chetty to go along, but she always declined.

One day, Chetty finally agreed to go on the next trip, and the transformation in her was miraculous. Chetty woke up. In every photograph they sent home, Chetty had a child on her lap. The children sought her out, and she responded with love and tenderness.

Little approached Craig with another project. Would he be willing to help build a church that had been destroyed in the earthquake? He accepted the challenge. Craig and Chetty's faith has grown by leaps and bounds as they share the Gospel in Haiti. What they would have formerly labeled as coincidence, they now see as the movement of the hand of God.

Craig and Chetty meet with Pastor Augustin and his son to discuss plans for the new church. Pastor Yvon Pierre, in the center, acts as interpreter. (Courtesy of Caroline Stetson.)

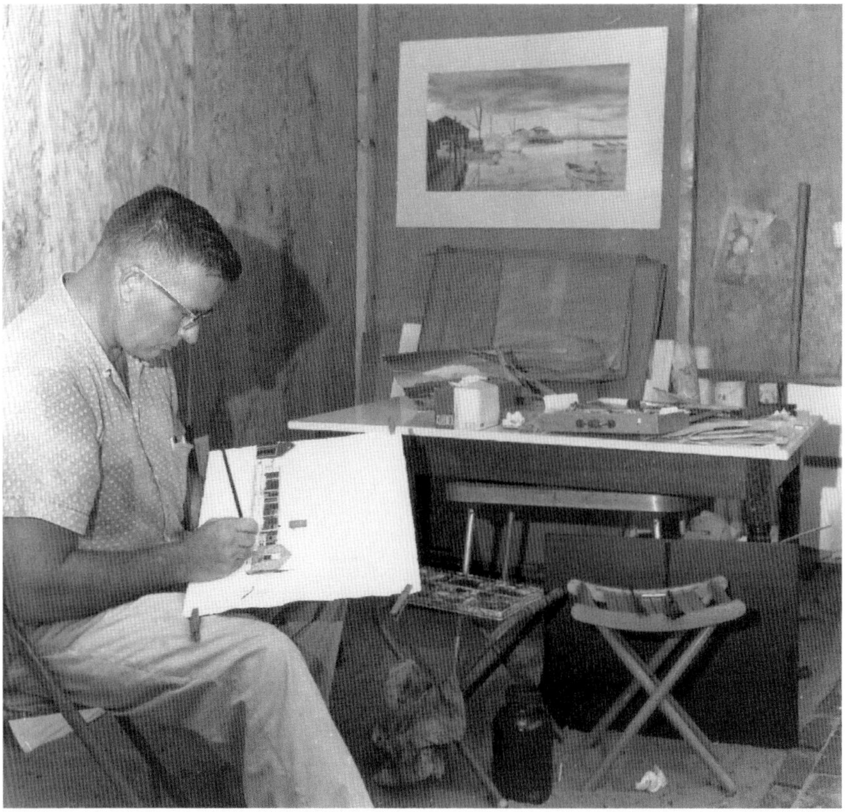

Renaissance Man

As a summer student pastor at the Manteo Baptist Church on Roanoke Island, Frank Dinwiddie met with a beach group of believers who envisioned a Baptist mission church in Nags Head. After he was ordained, the plan began to take on life, and this diversified man of God drew up the plans and helped to build a one-room church that sat at the southern base of Jockey's Ridge on Jigsaw Road. He had to complete the front steps of the church so that his wedding to Dr. Wiley Johnston's daughter Laura could take place in 1951.

His demeanor was usually unassuming and nonconfrontational, but he was unswerving in his convictions. He wrote to Governor Broughton in 1942 about what he believed to be a U-boat attack and explosion offshore. The sunken vessel was the SS *Byron D. Benson*, an oil tanker, and Dinwiddie was correct in what he surmised. He also rightly theorized that the U-boat captain was able to get off a perfect shot because of the back lighting of the bright lights of the Nags Head Casino and the automobile headlights in the parking lot.

Reverend Dinwiddie was a man who liked to dabble in many areas. He was an official weather observer, keeping daily records on wind direction and cloud formation. In addition to architectural renderings, he was a master of watercolor. He painted beach scenes that depicted the hardworking seine fishermen who were his neighbors. A very large and strong figure, he rowed dories to sea when an extra man was needed on the fishing crew.

He used his love of art in ministry when he developed what he called "chalk talks." He held the attention of the most unruly Vacation Bible School attendees as he spoke of Bible principles while simultaneously illustrating in pastels.

Reverend Dinwiddie introduced young boys in his congregation to a forerunner of surfing. Cutting large ironing board shapes from wood and varnishing them, he taught the teenagers to bodyboard in the waves just across the road from the church. (Courtesy of Ginny Zdanski.)

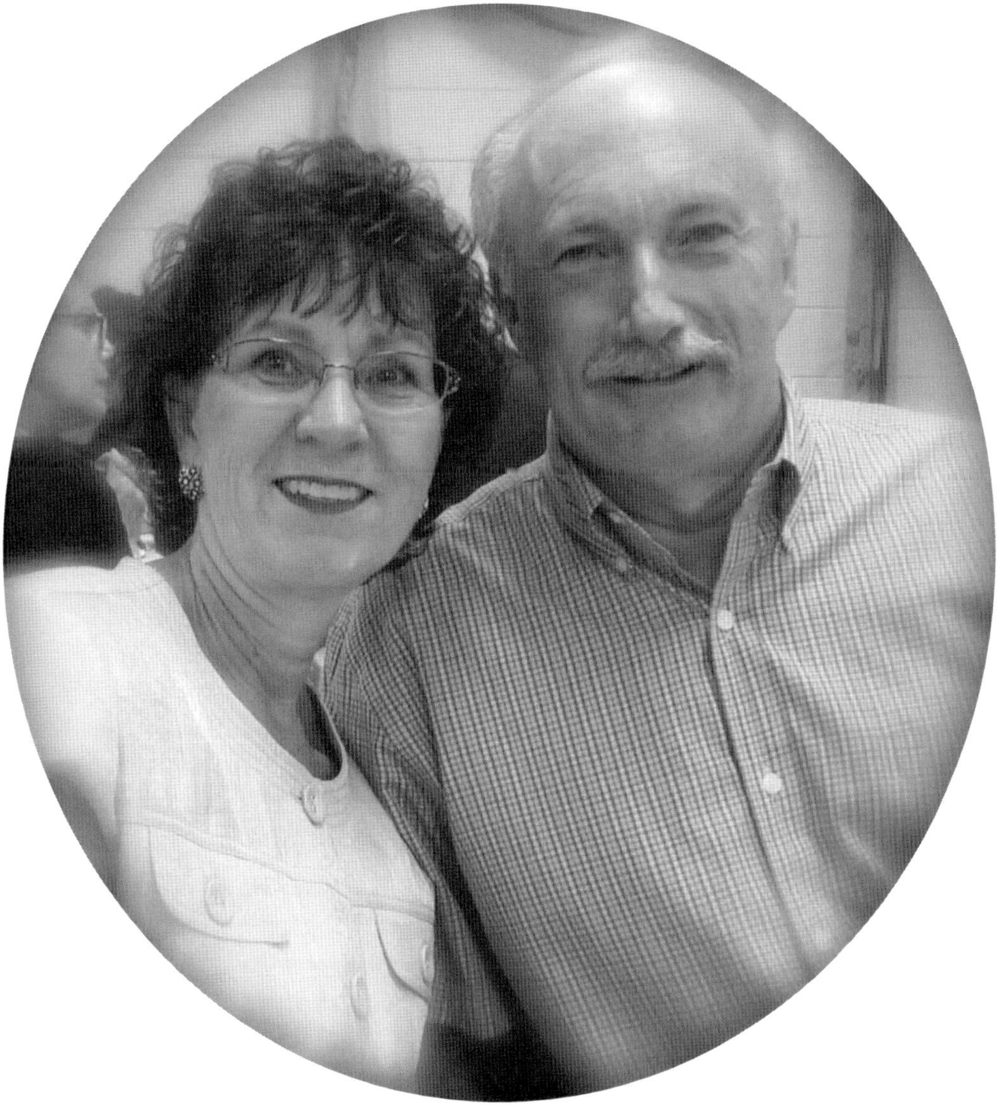

It Takes a Village . . .
Knowing he would never be a missionary, Mark Daniels took what he thought would be an easy elective called "Introduction to Missions." The college course sparked a calling that would take his family to Israel for 10 years and India for 12 years. Mark and Cathy Daniels now live in Lakeland, Florida, where Mark is on the staff of the 3,000-member independent Family Worship Center.

Mark and Cathy both grew up in Wanchese. They can list an astounding number of kinsmen and neighbors who have either become pastors or missionaries, all growing up in the confines of the little fishing village. He commented, "It is amazing the influence and impact that a little Christian community has had by sending out its people to go around the world with the Gospel." And, by the way, the senior pastor at the Lakeland church where Mark works happens to be Wanchester Reginald Scarborough. (Courtesy of Cathy Daniels.)

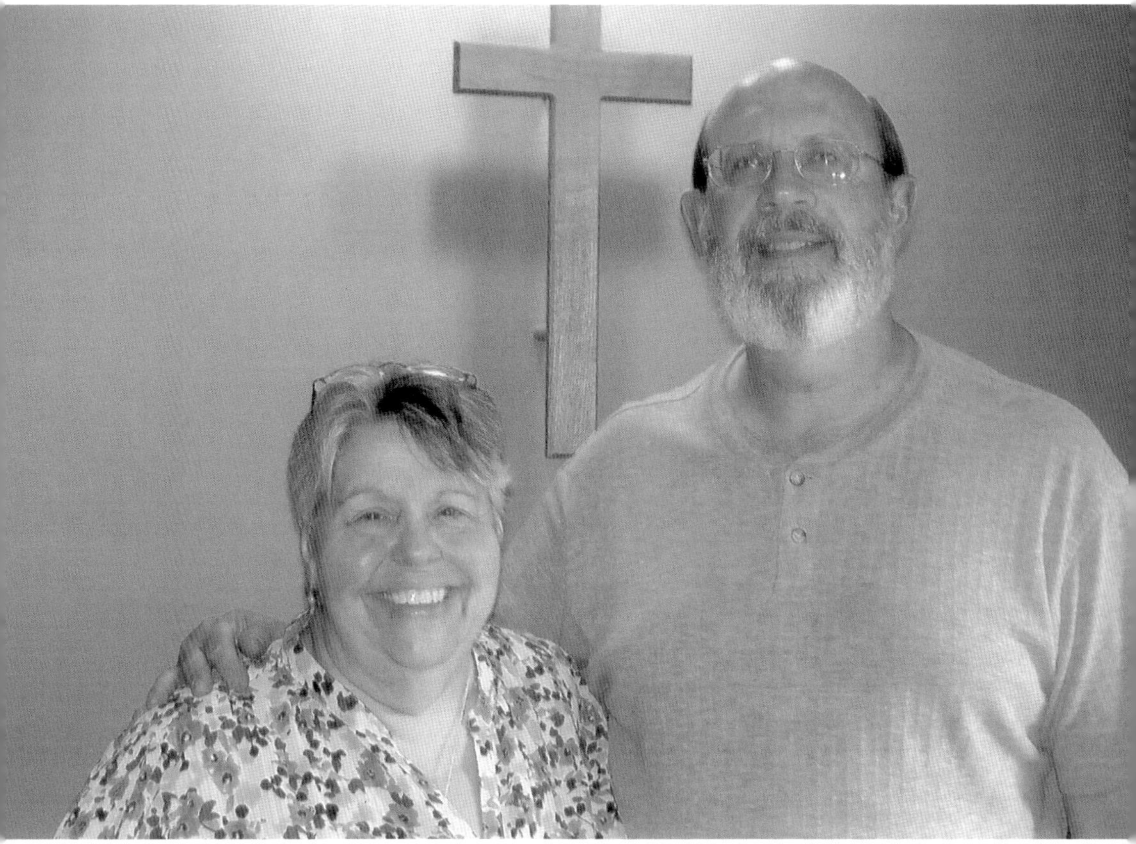

Waiting on the Lord

After moving to the Outer Banks from Ohio, artist Cheryl Glover volunteered at the local crisis pregnancy center, counseling young women. She felt that the women could be taught to care for their babies, handle finances, and learn other skills for life. Thus, the idea of the Hosea House was born.

Moving, renovating, and furnishing a house that was given to them has taken seven years, but Jefferson and Cheryl Glover have learned to wait on the Lord for His timing. Now they are waiting for the right inhabitants for the recovery home for women and their infants. The women must commit to staying one year, and often they would rather return to a crisis situation than give up a part of their self-will. The Glovers are not worried. They will continue to wait upon the Lord. (Courtesy of R. Wayne Gray.)

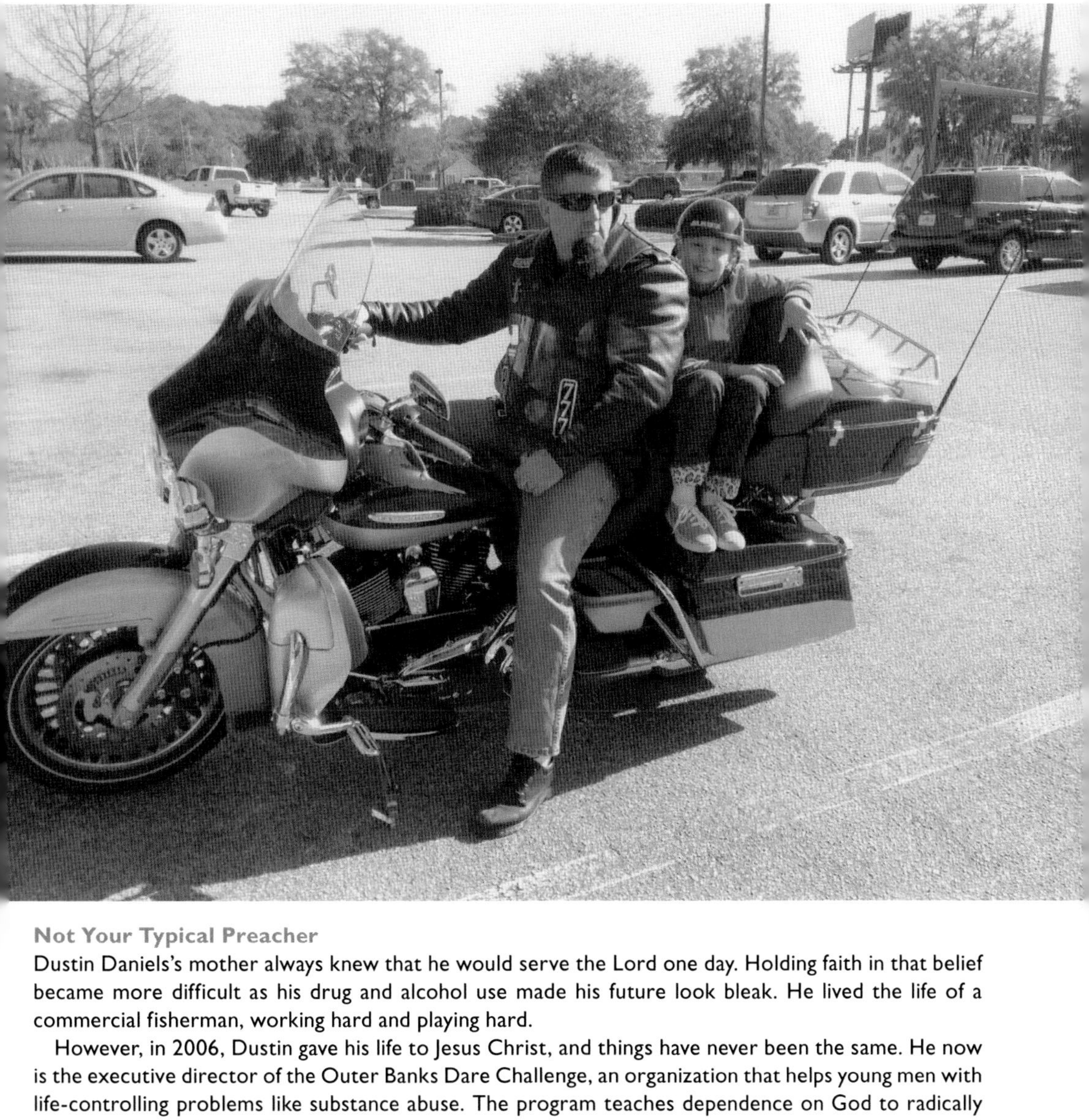

Not Your Typical Preacher
Dustin Daniels's mother always knew that he would serve the Lord one day. Holding faith in that belief became more difficult as his drug and alcohol use made his future look bleak. He lived the life of a commercial fisherman, working hard and playing hard.

However, in 2006, Dustin gave his life to Jesus Christ, and things have never been the same. He now is the executive director of the Outer Banks Dare Challenge, an organization that helps young men with life-controlling problems like substance abuse. The program teaches dependence on God to radically change and transform a life.

Dustin is also senior pastor at Lifeboat Community Church in Salvo, North Carolina. He is pictured here preparing to take his daughter Breeze on a motorcycle ride. (Courtesy of Heather Daniels.)

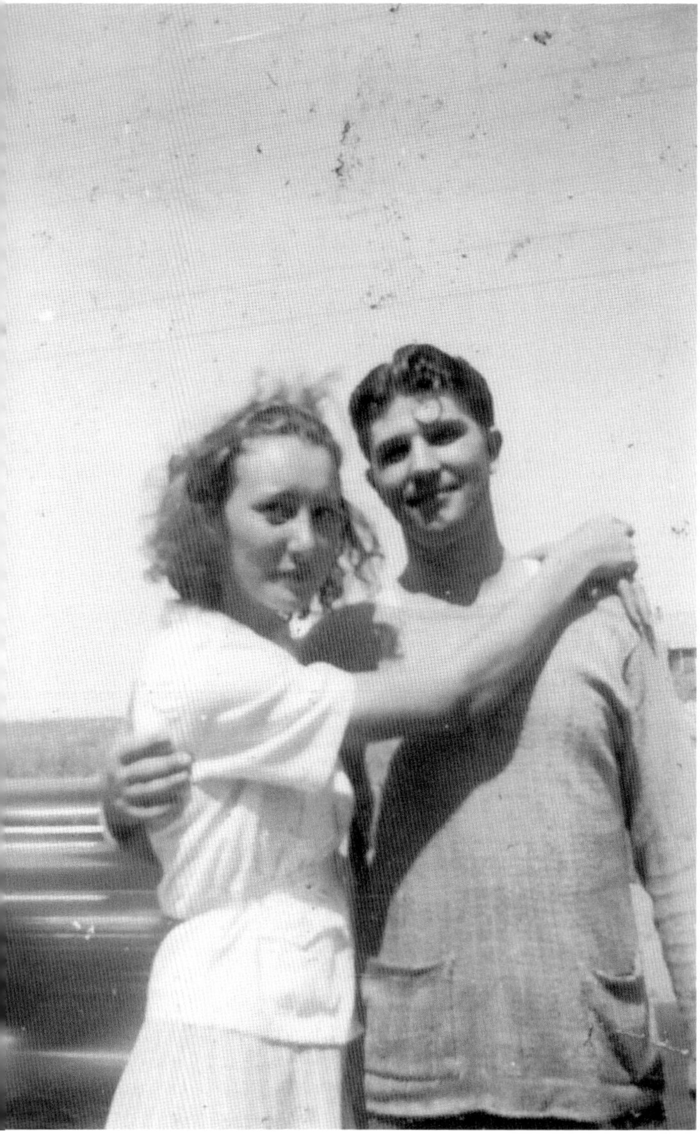

Preferring Beaches to People

One way to tell if someone is a longstanding resident of Nags Head is if he or she remembers Nellie Myrtle. Although no last name was needed for this legendary beachcomber, Nellie Myrtle Pridgen walked her "beat" of beach in front of the "Unpainted Aristocracy," the beautiful one-mile stretch of cedar-shaked historic cottages, with a vengeance. She would walk, patrol, and run off any trespassers on cottage properties even though she did not necessarily get along with the cottage owners.

She was obsessive about collecting items that had washed ashore. Anything was fair game, from shells and worn bricks to artifacts deposited on the beach by torpedoed German and Allied ships during World War II.

She lived in a home behind her parents' beach road store. As a young woman, she worked as a hydraulic mechanic at the Norfolk Air Station, catching the bus back and forth on the weekends. Her mother played a big part in raising her children.

As an older woman, beachcombing became her job. Nellie Myrtle was a well-read person who knew a lot about the weather and the sea by observation and extensive reading. She was a fierce supporter for the environment and its creatures.

She fought a lifelong battle against tourists and patrons of the casino nightclub who blocked her driveway with the cars they tried to keep out of the sand. She often cried foul on county and state officials who made decisions about Dare County contrary to what she felt was right. She ruffled a lot of feathers, but she was often correct in her assessments.

Her huge collection of sea glass, fulgarite (glass tubes formed from lightning strikes), shells, and all manner of flotsam and jetsam is now displayed in her parents' old store. By the efforts of her daughter Carmen Gray, Chaz Winkler, and Dorothy Hope, the Beachcombers' Museum is on the National Register of Historic Places. (Courtesy of Jeffrey Midgett.)

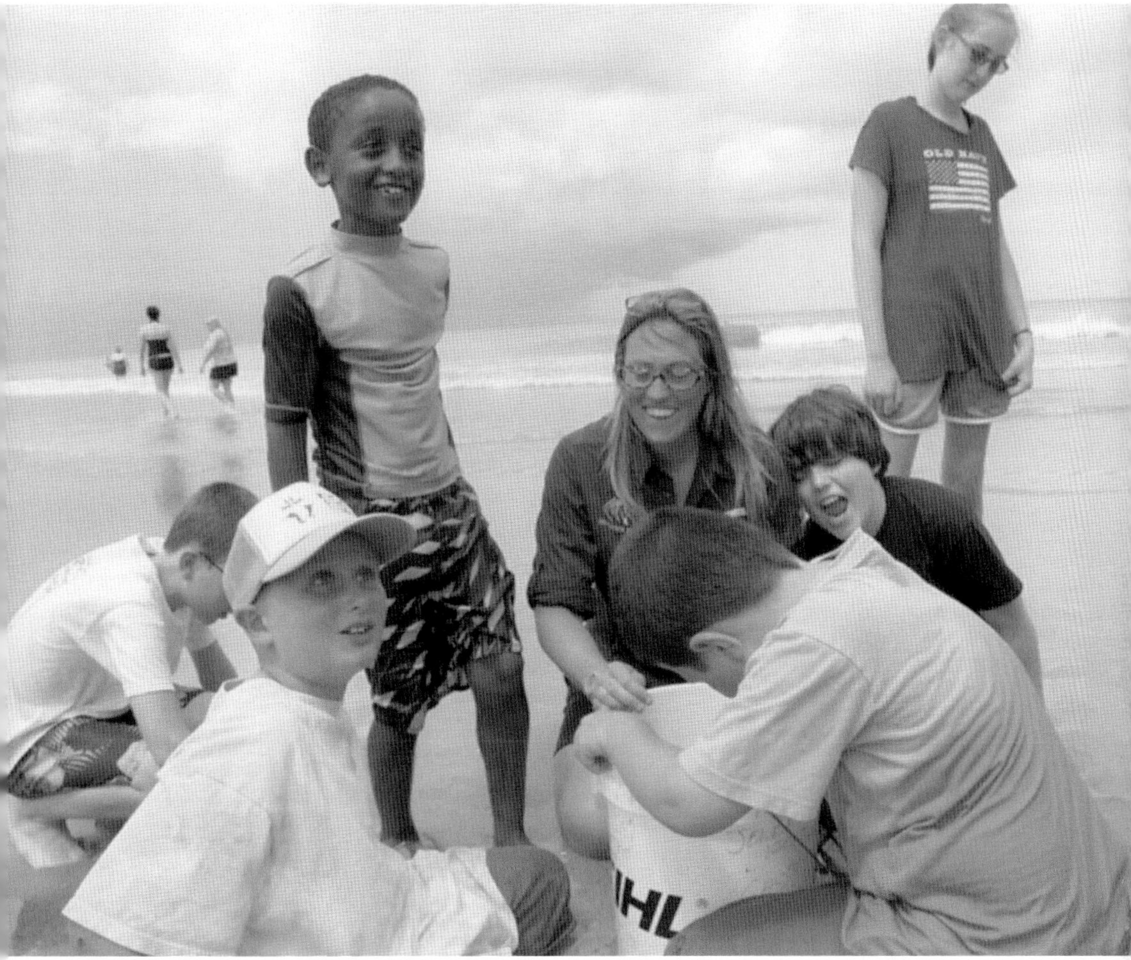

Teaching in a Big Classroom

Known for making learning fun, the education curator at Jennette's Pier in Nags Head, Christin Brown, works hard to keep her reputation up. Before landing the job with the North Carolina Aquariums, Brown held a position as public educator at Cape Hatteras Secondary School of Coastal Studies, where she gained experience and developed a coastal-themed curriculum for three years.

The original 1939 wooden pier was battered and beaten by storms and replaced by the state-of-the-art award-winning green facility in 2011. Christin and her small, but busy staff teach people about wind and solar energy and sea life as well as just how to fish. "We offer great opportunities for school groups to learn about science without realizing they are learning," she says. (Courtesy of Jennette's Pier.)

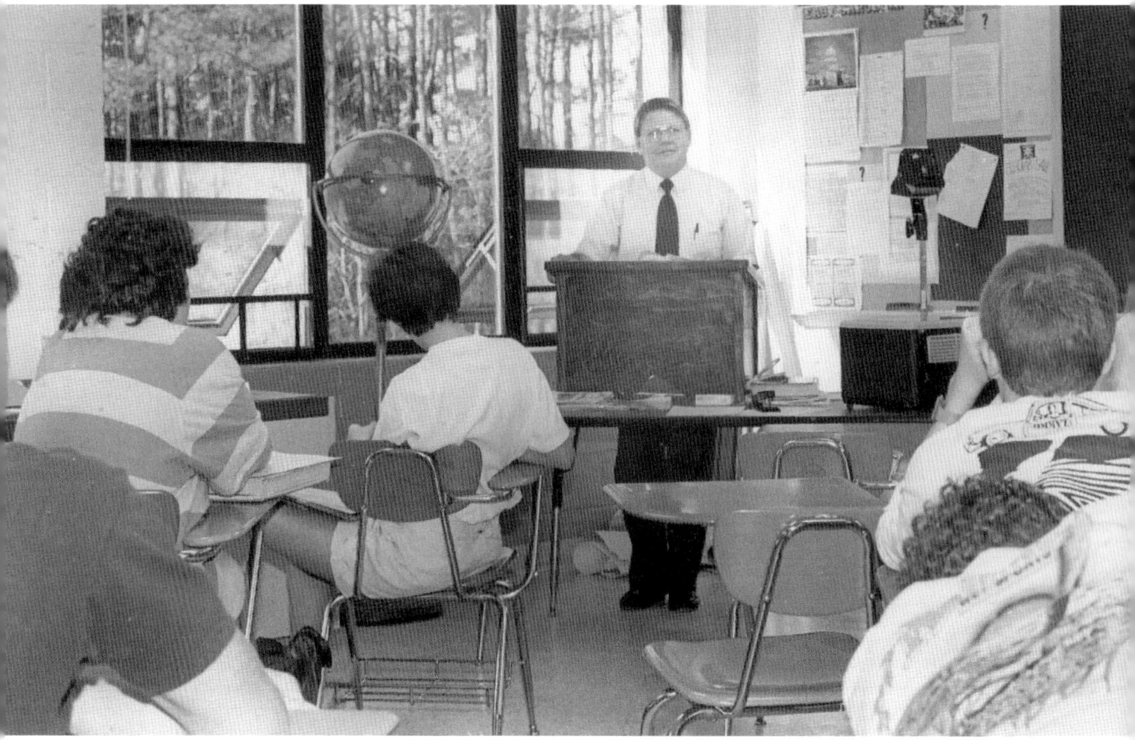

A Lifetime of Education

A message written in adolescent curlicue script on the white board in his Sunday school classroom said, "Mr. Steve, you are the best teacher ever. We love you and wish we could be in your class forever!" Was the high compliment paid to a youthful and awesome instructor? Yes it was, for 80 year-old teacher and former superintendent of Dare County Schools Steve Basnight.

During his career, Basnight also served as teacher, coach, counselor, assistant principal, and assistant superintendent. His tenure took place at a time when the county was experiencing tremendous population growth (1976–1988). During his watch, Dare schools received many awards for meeting and maintaining high standards.

There has been no retiring from teaching Sunday school, a post he has faithfully held since the late 1960s. Basnight has been to Haiti and is planning to go on the next mission trip, where a new group of children wait to sit under his teaching. (Courtesy of Steve Basnight Jr.)

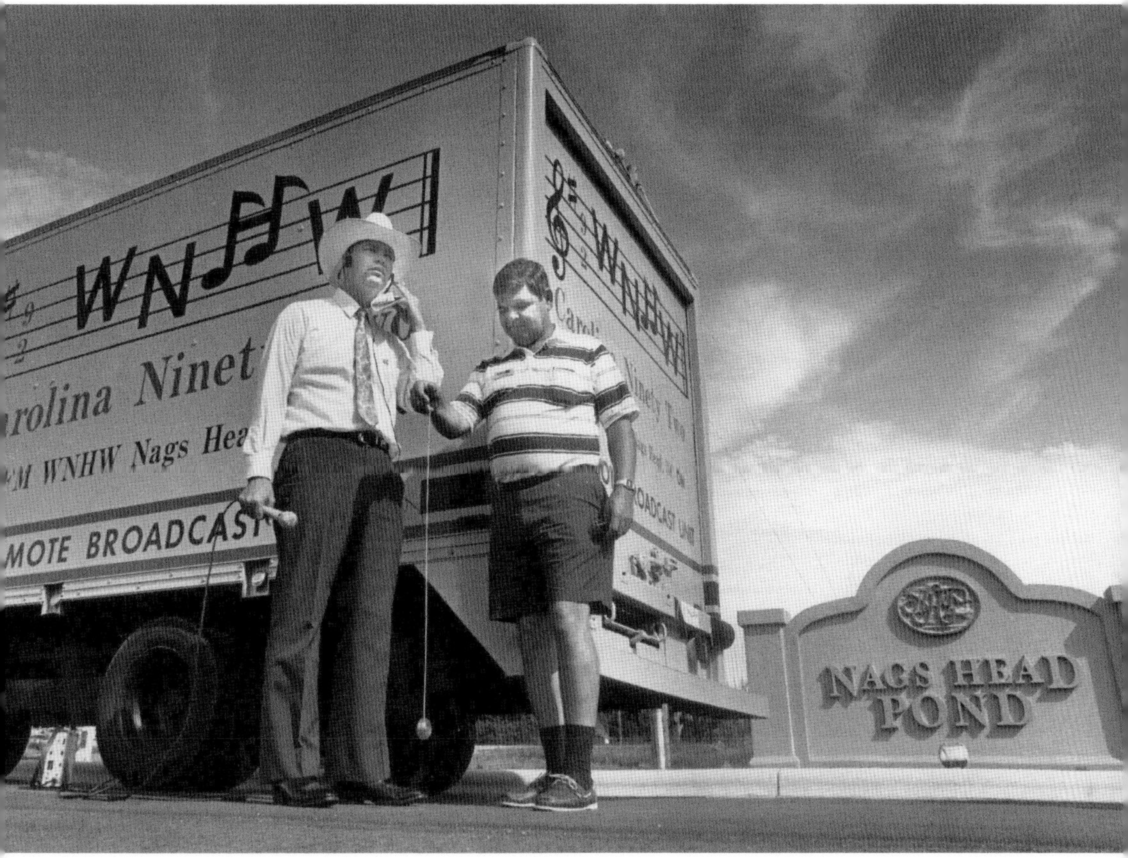

Broadcasting the Good News

Ken Mann (left) got his start in radio in 1970, when, at 15, he did a radio spot selling light bulbs for Manteo High School's Key Club. The Outer Banks' first radio station, WOBR 1530, hired him soon after. Years later, when Ken owned and operated his own station, he always made it a point to employ high school students.

Ken held jobs in other fields—he ran Oregon Inlet fishing center and sold real estate—but he always seemed to come back to radio, where he invested 30 years. He started videoing a weekly news program and then Outer Banks travel shows. Eventually, he started his own company that produced *My Heart Will Always Be in Carolina,* a popular television show that was picked up by UNC TV. With the miracle of the Internet, those shows are still being seen daily.

Ken heard a higher calling and entered into the ministry. He was assigned to pastor Mt. Carmel United Methodist Church in Manns Harbor, North Carolina, where he accepts the challenge of standing in the pulpit and preaching to people he knows and who know him. Ken is now using all of the skills that he developed while in radio and television combined with the gifts God has given him. In his usual humorous way, Ken quips, "Now I'm promoting Jesus instead of the Outer Banks." (Courtesy of Drew Wilson Collection; OBHC.)

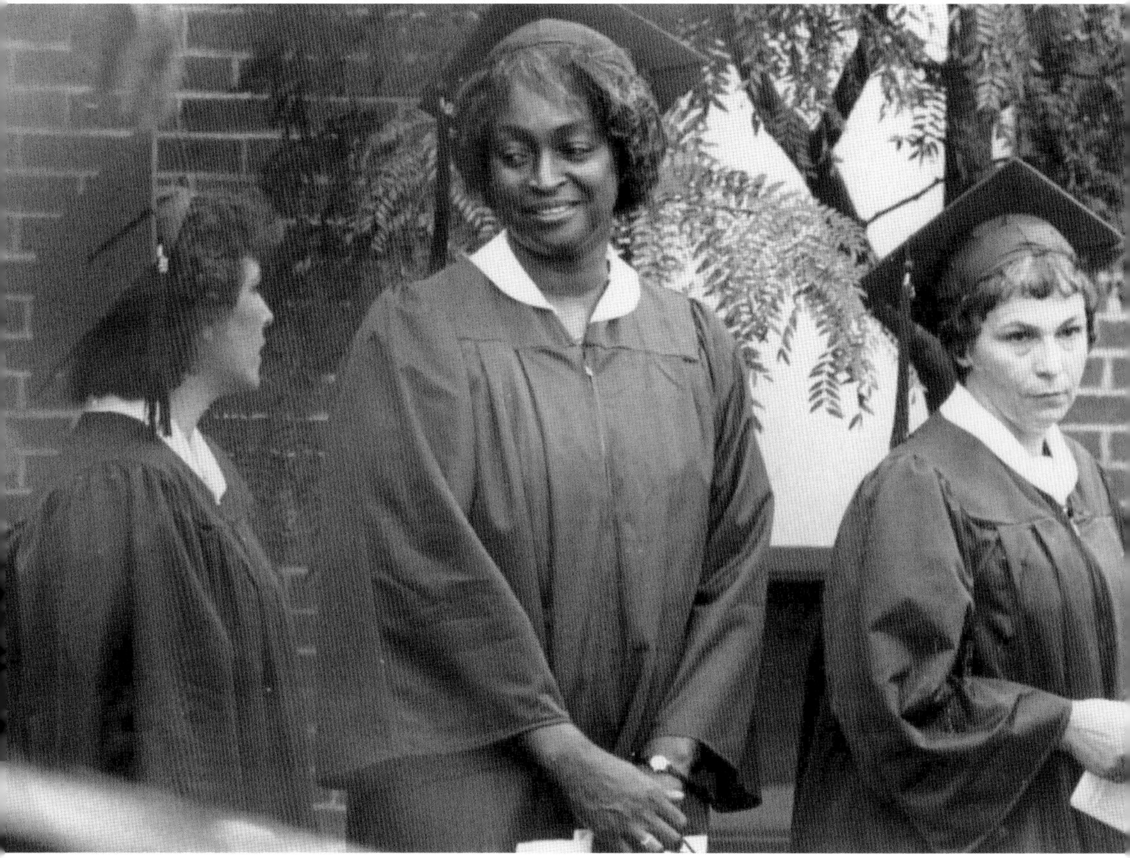

Ready to Listen and Act

Virginia Tillett's interest in education began when she was a teacher's aide at Head Start. She was elected as a school board member back in the 1980s, a major accomplishment for a black woman in a county with less than one percent of a minority population. The board's motto was "Educate Every Child." It must have preyed on her mind that as a teen she had to live with relatives in Elizabeth City so that she could have a senior year and graduate with a high school diploma. The all-black Roanoke School in Manteo only offered classes through the 11th grade.

Currently serving her second four-year term as county commissioner, her desire to pave a way for others to follow has made her an exemplary role model for the community she loves so much. She is pictured here at her graduation ceremony at the College of The Albemarle. (Courtesy of Virginia Tillett.)

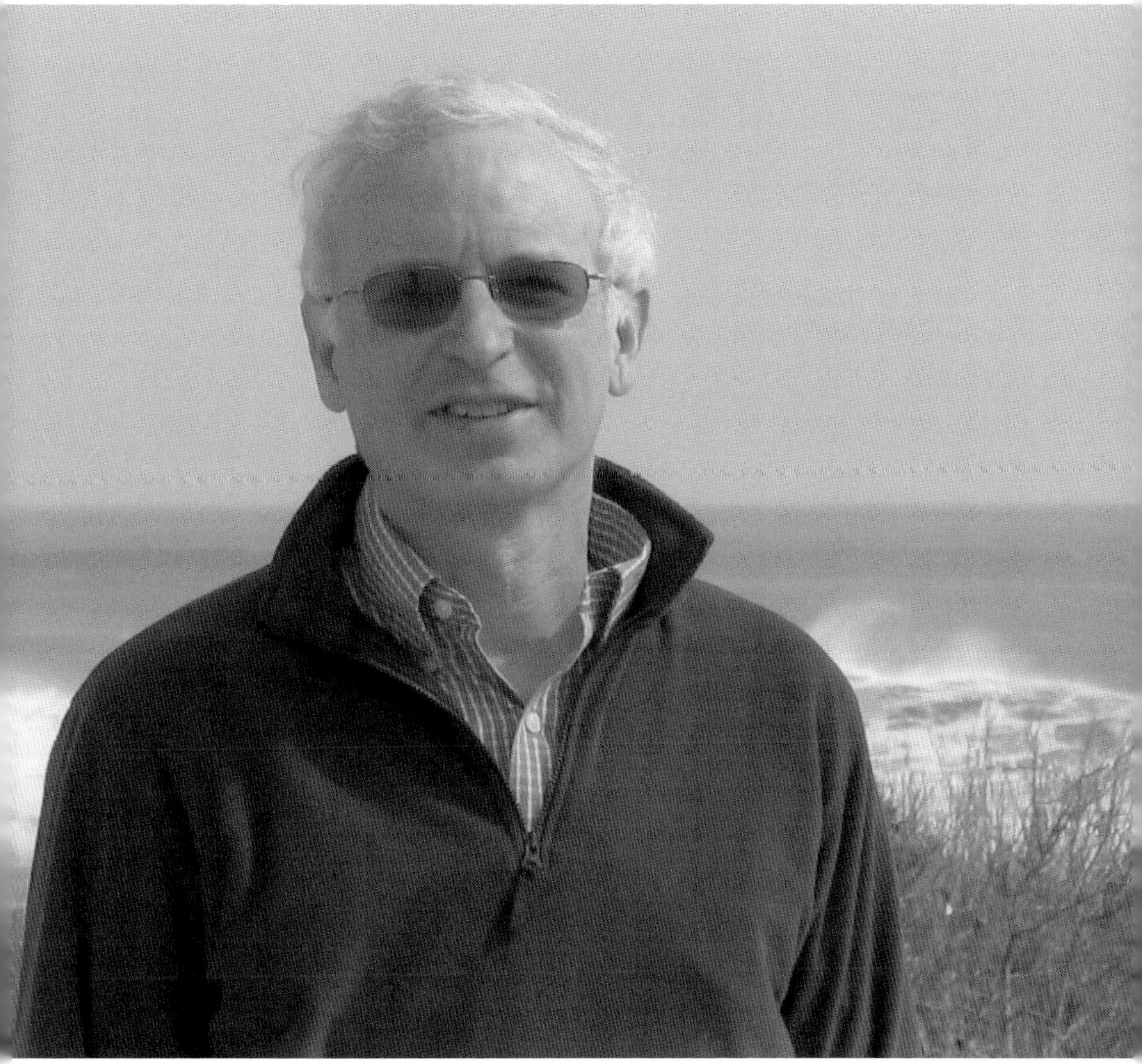

Great and Small
Bill Birkemeier is a study in extremes: he made a career out of understanding the enormity and ferocity of waves and hurricanes while also working as a tinsmith of miniature dollhouse accessories.

He moved to the Outer Banks in 1980 from Washington, DC, to be a coastal engineer at the Field Research Facility (FRF) in Duck. The FRF is a coastal observatory that has a 1,840-foot pier with specialized vehicles to study the impact of storms on the beach. He retired in 2012.

Bill comes from a Massachusetts family that crafted miniatures for dollhouses. He chose tin as his medium and made small candlesticks and lanterns. Their Studio B Miniatures company is no longer in business, but the delightful vignettes can be viewed on a website created by his daughter Sarah. (Courtesy of Bill Birkemeier.)

Preserving Environmental Heritage

Growing up in mainland Manns Harbor, Ladd Bayliss and her brother John spent their days on the Croatan Sound, fishing and crabbing from a rowboat. The sound became her teacher at an early age.

While in college, she studied in Kenya for five months to better understand small communities where natural resources were the basis of the economy. The rural villages had a unique reliance on traditional industries such as animal husbandry and agriculture, in addition to a heavy dependence on tourism. She soon realized that this mirrored her own hometown where fishermen, boat builders, and businessmen rely on their waters and land for provision in an area that is attractive to tourists.

She now works as a coastal advocate with the North Carolina Coastal Federation. This nonprofit organization has as its first priority the preservation of water quality along the state's shores. (Photograph by Ray Matthews; courtesy of Ladd Bayliss.)

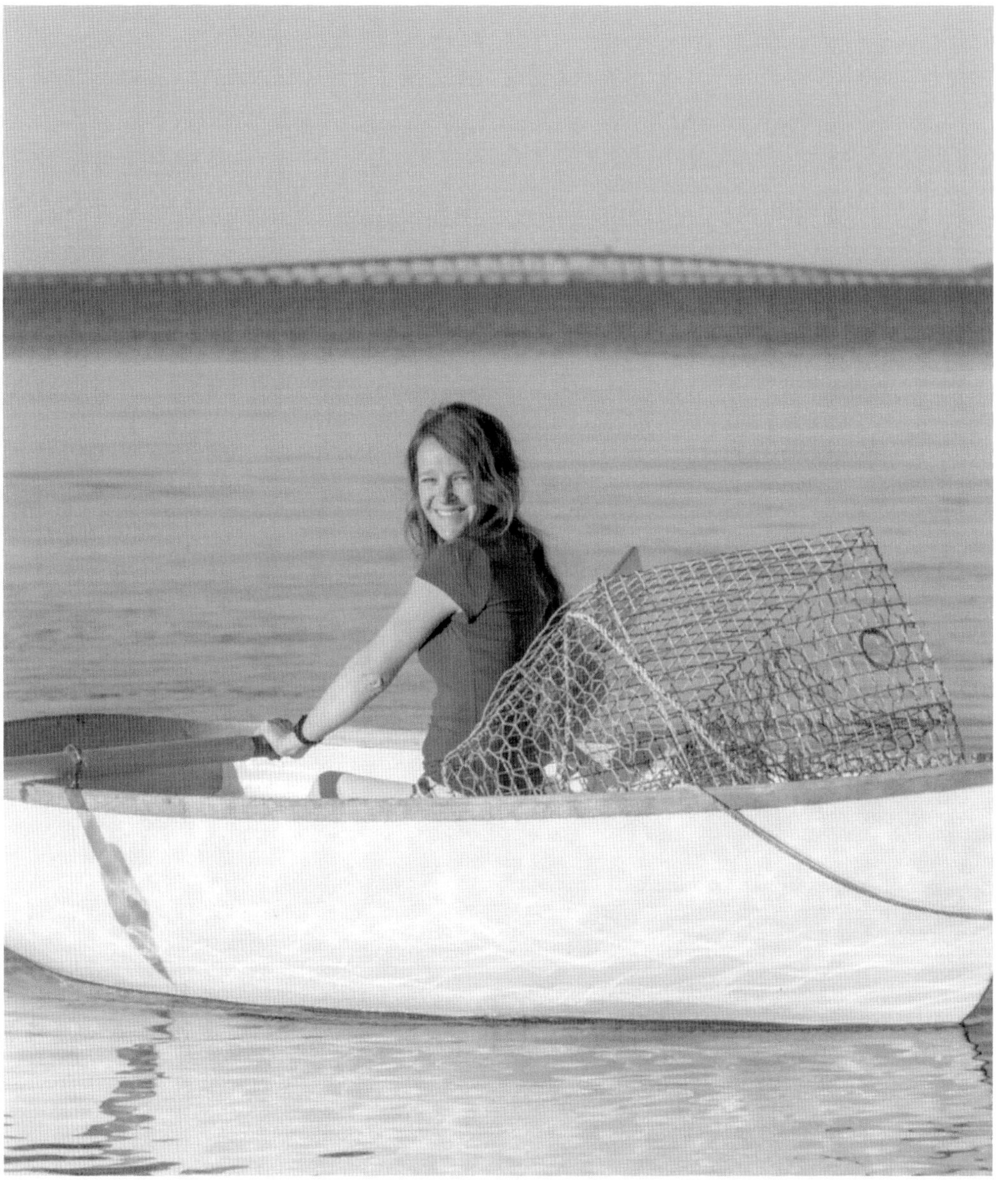

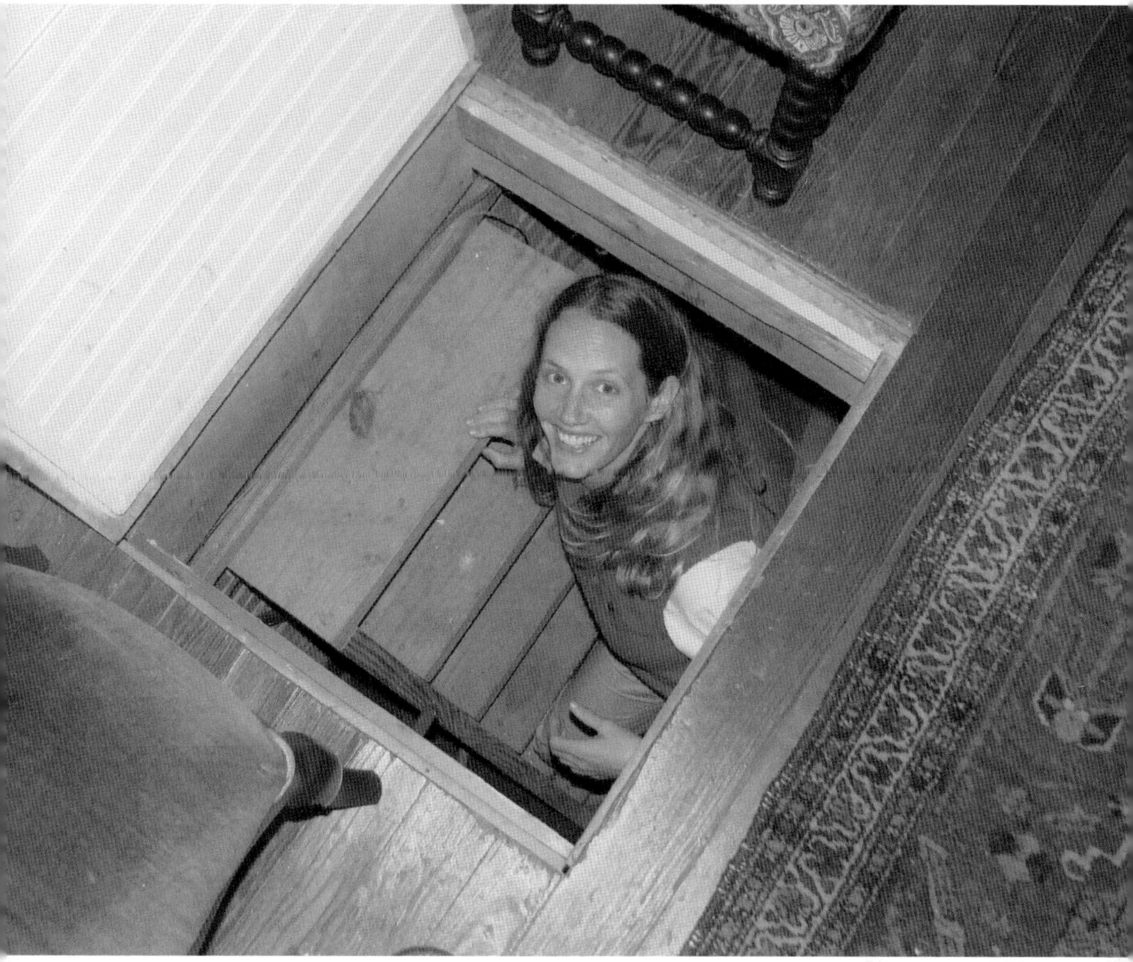

Corolla's Dynamo

Being around Meagan Agreste is like trying to keep up with a small tornado. Bubbling over with ideas, she speaks so fast that it is hard to discern what she is saying. She describes herself as "extremely extroverted, a type-A person, who works well with people and knows how to get things done." That might be an understatement.

She has been the manager of the Currituck Banks Lighthouse in Corolla for almost a decade. Through this nonprofit foundation, she employs about 15 seasonal docents who work hard and have fun interpreting for the 100,000 lighthouse climbers that they meet annually.

Meagan worked hard to get people on the bandwagon for having a Corolla charter school. As a result, a nonprofit educational organization was created, two teachers were hired, and the school was formed. She spends a lot of time there as a volunteer, which is not a sacrifice considering her two boys are enrolled there. (Courtesy of Meagan Agreste.)

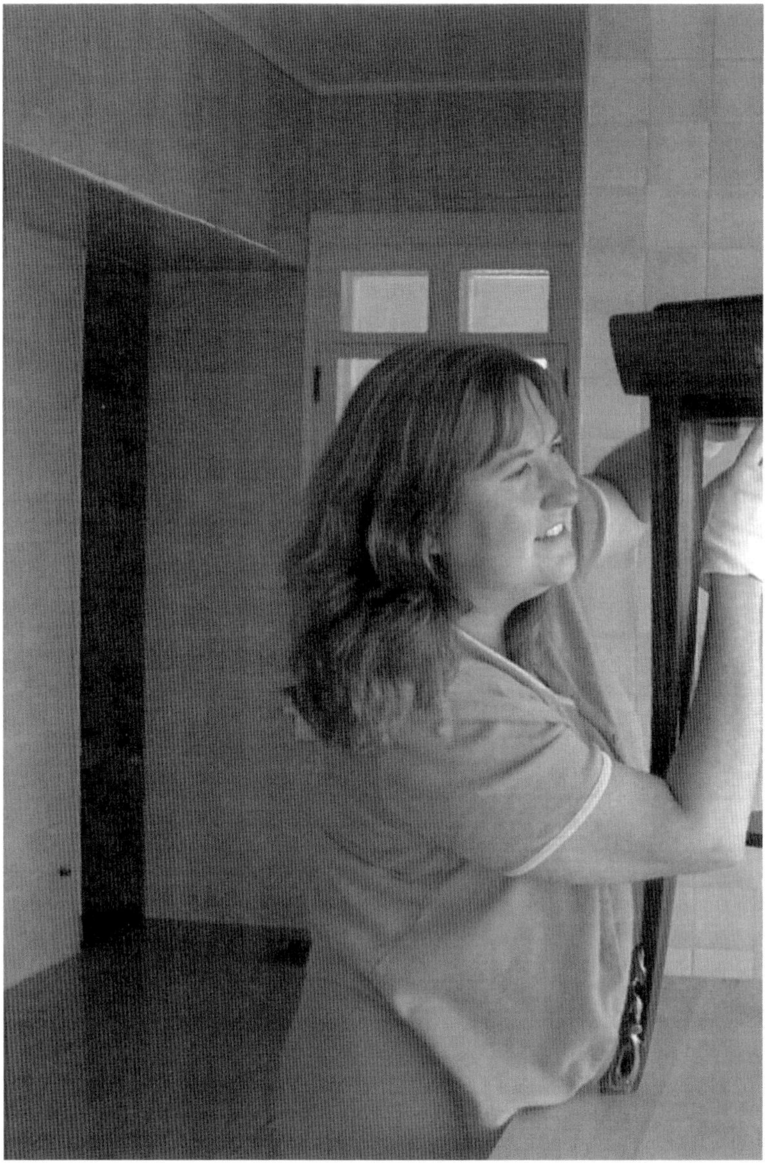

Caring for the Past

When she accepted the job as curator at the Whalehead Club in historical Corolla, Jill Landen walked into a building almost empty of artifacts. While the art nouveau mansion sat uninhabited, curious interlopers and treasure seekers took what they wanted, right down to the Tiffany glass lampshades. Jill and a team undertook careful research to discover exactly what had been in the house. Armed with information, original artifacts or matched pieces were acquired. In the case of the Tiffany shades, an anonymous citizen quietly returned what did not really belong to him.

Jill is also proud of the restoration of the historic boathouse that, along with the mansion, looks much like it did during Whalehead's glory days in the 1920s and 1930s. She has developed a number of interpretive tours, including audio devices that visitors can use. Thousands of tourists have been able to see what an elite hunt club looked like due to her attention to detail during her watch. (Courtesy of Jill Landen.)

CHAPTER SIX

Arts, Music, Entertainment, and Sports

"When the springs of the world run dry, I shall not."

Artists have been attracted to the Outer Banks since John White came over with Sir Walter Raleigh's colonists and made the region famous with his magnificent drawings and paintings. Many of the area's performers, creators, and artists can be linked to White in that they became involved with the drama *The Lost Colony*, which began in 1937. Manteo has become an artists' colony during the summer months when the pageant is playing. Artists, musicians, and actors from New York City's best galleries, theaters, and opera houses can be seen all over the town. Many of these artists, such as Joe Layton and William Ivey Long, had second homes in Manteo. In addition, artists like Glenn Eure, John Silver, and Hubby Bliven are locals and live here year-round, have galleries, and are able to paint outdoors during all the changing seasons.

Tshombe Selby, a native-born singer, is training with a famous opera tenor in New York City while working at the Metropolitan Opera. He still lives at his home in Manteo part of the year. Roy Murray, a rock-and-roll horn player, is now a wedding musician and has a permanent home on the beach.

Andy Griffith was one of the first performers in the Outer Banks to become famous. In a smaller way, Cora Mae Basnight, a good friend of his and a native of Manteo, was well known for just the one phrase she spoke playing the role of Agona in *The Lost Colony,* where Andy got his start in acting. Lisa Griggs, one of the first female photographers to capture the sights of the region, is still hard at work preserving and promoting the Outer Banks.

Maynard Daniels was the only native to become a nationally ranked professional heavyweight boxer. But the Outer Banks is now home to other athletes, surfers such as Jim Vaughn and young skateboarders Durand Beasley, Dan Tugwell, and Beach Gray.

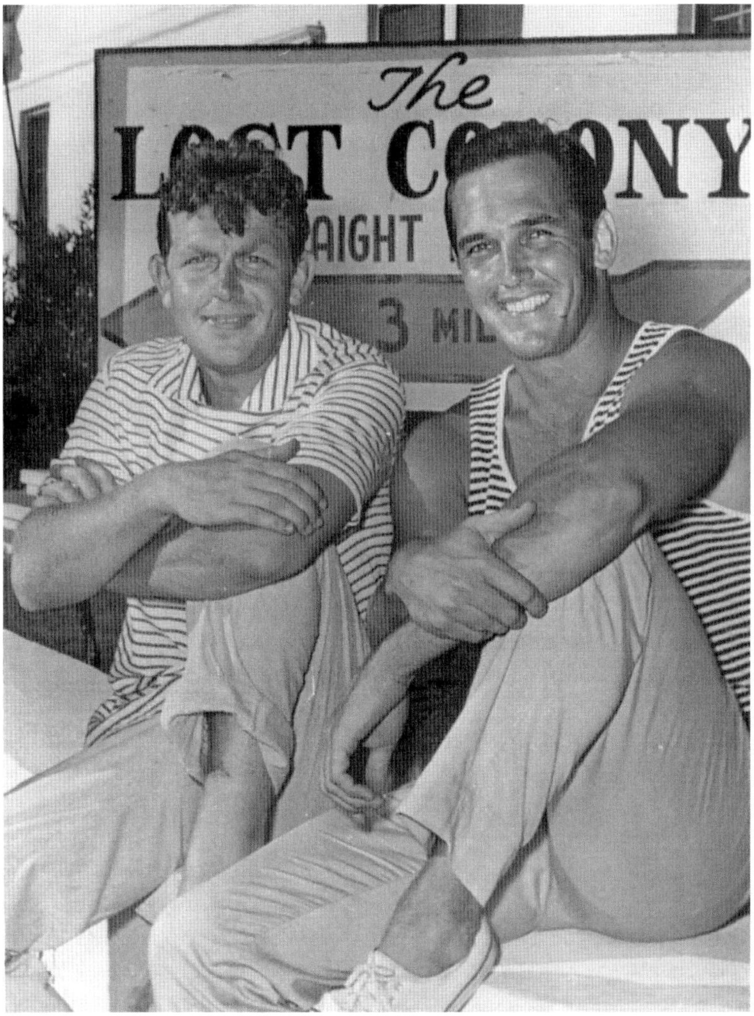

Adopted Native Son

Originally from Mt. Airy, North Carolina, Andy Griffith (left) came to Manteo in the summer of 1947 to play the part of the first soldier in *The Lost Colony.* He fell in love with Roanoke Island and kept a permanent home on the north end all of his life. Upon his death, he was laid to rest in the sandy soil where the colonists once trod.

Andy spent his summers performing at the Waterside Theatre from 1947 to 1953, playing the part of Sir Walter Raleigh for four of those years. He later looked back on those carefree and shoeless summers as some of the best of his life.

He recorded an album of his comedy monologue, *What It Was, Was Football*, a folksy tale of a deacon seeing his first football game. The hit album was his ticket to stardom. Movies such as *No Time for Sergeants* and *A Face in the Crowd* soon followed.

His two most popular television series, *The Andy Griffith Show* and *Matlock*, often drew heavily from the influence Manteo had on him. The fictional town of Mayberry was patterned after Manteo, and many people recognized themselves in the characters portrayed. He promoted Manteo whenever he could and filmed an episode of *Matlock* there.

To the public, Andy Griffith will always be known as Sheriff Taylor or lawyer Ben Matlock. To Outer Bankers, he will always be known as Andy. (Courtesy of Aycock Brown Collection; OBHC.)

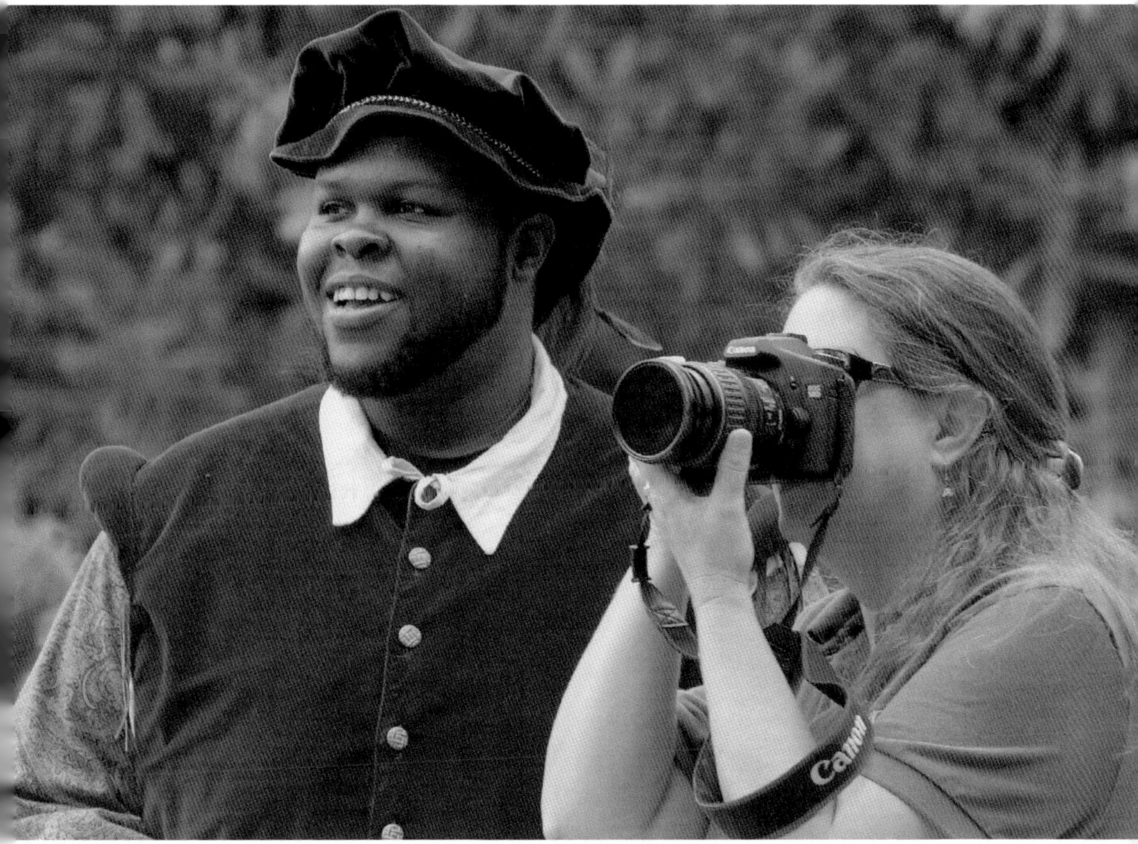

Next Stop–the Metropolitan Opera

A giant of a man, Tshombe Selby moves gingerly and speaks quietly. When he sings, however, his tenor voice bursts forth with controlled power and polish. One gets the sense that he is destined for great things. Other people have that feeling, too, and are working hard to see this young man's dreams fulfilled.

Growing up in Manteo, Tshombe started singing in the junior choir at Haven Creek Baptist Church when his grandmother Annie Drake first took him to church. He participated in musically oriented activities in his school years and went on to graduate from Elizabeth City State University with a degree in music and a concentration in voice. He auditioned for *The Lost Colony* and won a place in the choir.

Two friends gave him tickets to the Metropolitan Opera in New York City. Tshombe told a newspaper writer that "it was the most memorable experience of my life." Again, friends stepped in and arranged for him to study at the New York Opera Studio with the famed tenor Nico Castel. He also studies with Nico's wife, Carol, a renowned opera performer and acting and diction coach. Another piece of the dream puzzle is that Tsombe is working as an usher at the Metropolitan Opera.

A number of organizations have raised money to help pay for opera lessons and living expenses in New York. Hundreds of Outer Bankers have supported him with donations in the hope that the first native-born opera singer will headline at the opera. (Courtesy of Melody Leckie.)

Because It Is Fun

Don Bridge says that to him, theater is "a passion, a hobby, a social life, and sometimes a living." After working in a successful children's theater venture in the Raleigh-Durham area, Don and his wife, Lisa, decided to make Roanoke Island their home. They owned a toy store in downtown Manteo by day and played key roles in *The Lost Colony* by night. Don played Old Tom, Governor White, Father Martin, and the oldest Ananias Dare.

He joined the nonprofit community theater company Theatre of Dare and has been involved in 18 productions since 1995 as an actor and a director. His most recent project was *Oliver!*, which he produced while also expertly playing the role of Fagin.

After 10 years of being a part of *The Lost Colony* cast, he knows firsthand that being an actor in the drama can be all consuming. Whenever he gets nostalgic about those days, he only has to walk out of his house bordering the Waterside Theatre parking lot and take a stroll down memory lane. (Courtesy of Don Bridge.)

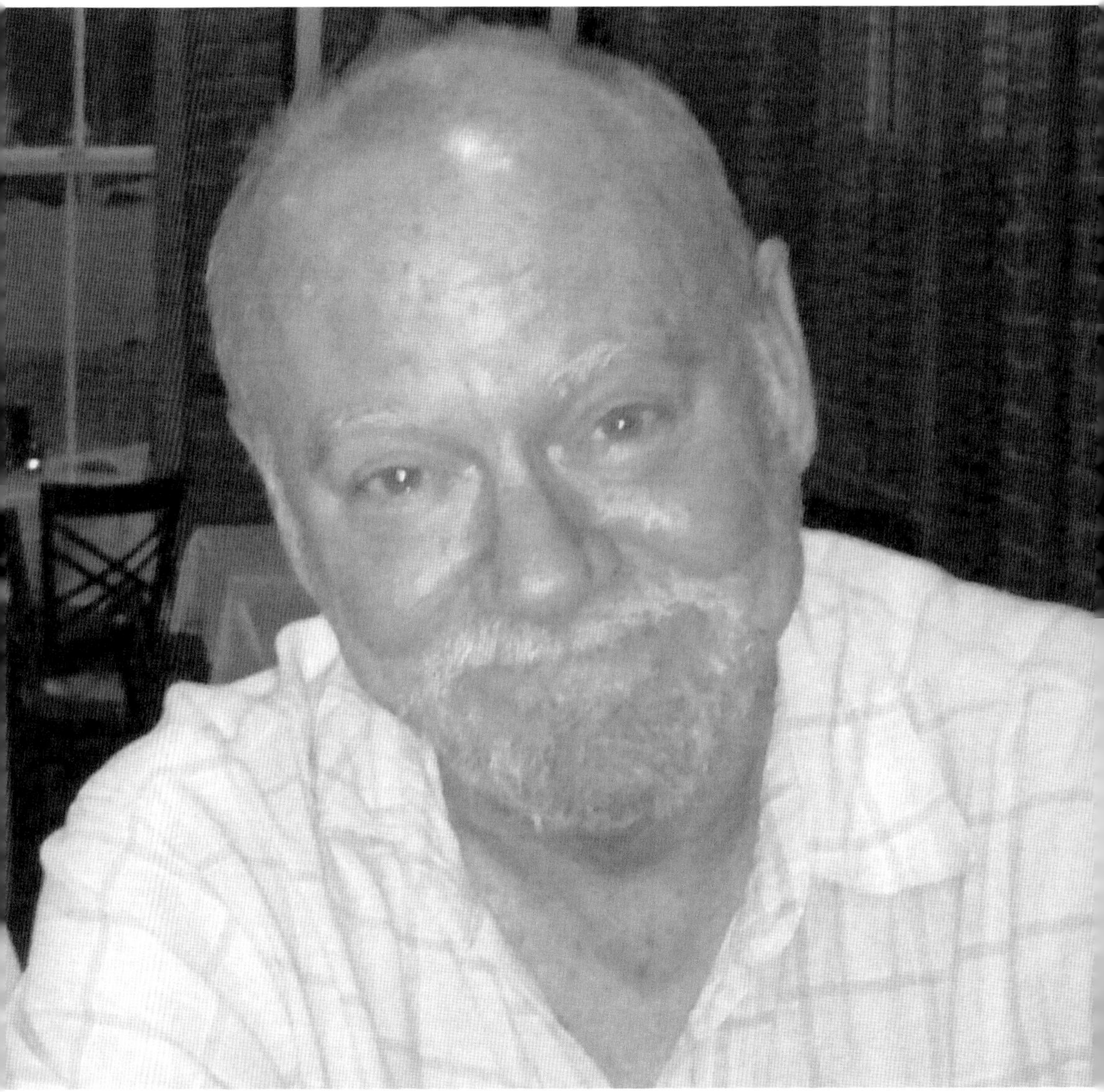

Forever Agona

Even in grade school, Cora Mae Basnight was known as a clown. At 14 she was a self-proclaimed hot-rodder, and since her father, Moncie Daniels, had a gas and oil business, she had plenty of fuel to put in her Model T coupe. Cars pulled off the road when they saw Cora Mae coming.

As a child, she had a part in the 1921 silent movie *Lost Colony*. In the late 1950s, she became part of the live drama's cast, often doubling parts but always a natural fit for the comical Agona. She drew much applause for her acting, even though her speaking part was one phrase: "Tee-hee!" Daniels once described Agona as "an old squaw gal like myself with a prune face." She filled the role of Agona for 25 years, a record for an American actress playing one part. Cora Mae Basnight's hometown of Manteo named a street for Agona and a bridge for her. (Courtesy of the OBHC.)

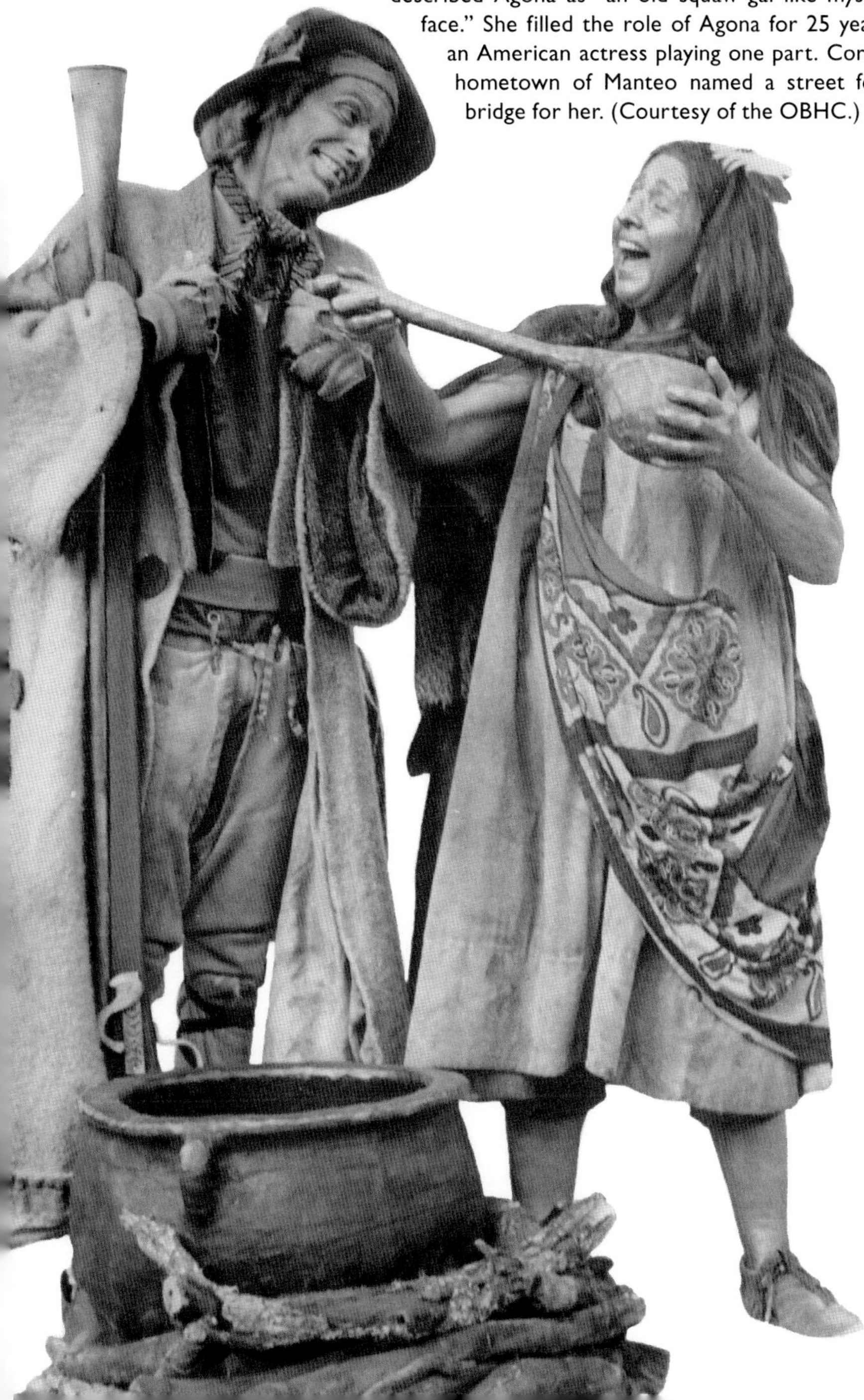

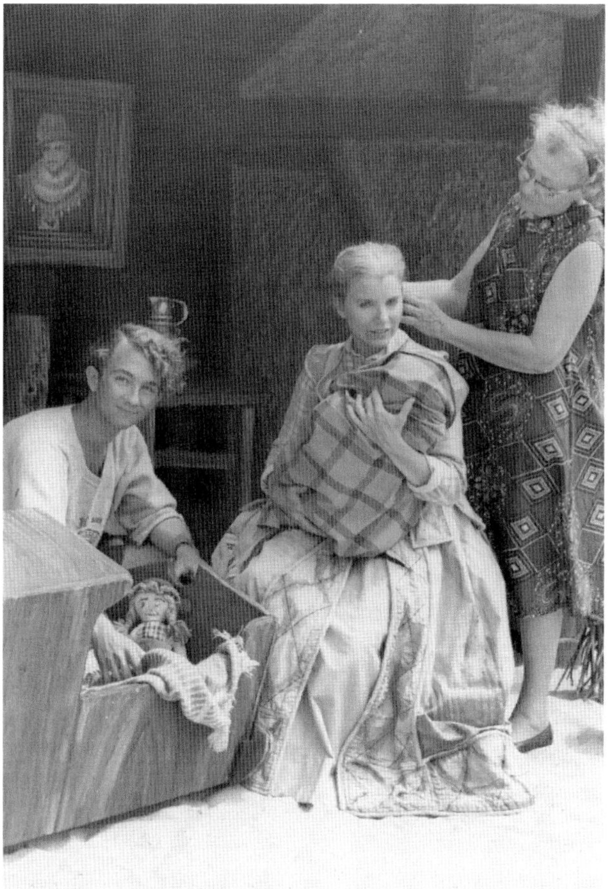

Bringing Broadway to the Colony

When a fire destroyed *The Lost Colony's* costume shop and its contents in 2007, award-winning Broadway costume designer William Ivey "Billy" Long came to the rescue, turning out over 50 elaborate period pieces in a matter of months. How did the outdoor theatre command the attention of such a big name and talented costumer? The answer is easy: Billy Long has the play's lifeblood running through his veins.

Long's family spent their summers on Roanoke Island. His mother played Queen Elizabeth, and his father served backstage and eventually became director in the drama. Long played a colonist boy at age eight, but gravitated to legendary costumer Irene Smart Rains. He played in her scrap boxes, creating little costumes, once making an Elizabethan ruff for his dog's neck.

He always thought he'd be a professor like his father, but teaching and later studying for a PhD in art history were unsatisfying for him. Playwright Betty Smith, who befriended him in Chapel Hill, encouraged him to apply to design school at Yale. After a master of fine arts degree from Yale, he was such a sensation when he made it to Broadway that he has not lacked for work since.

He has been nominated 13 times and has won six Tony Awards. In 2005, he was inducted into the Theatre Hall of Fame and was also elected chairman of the American Theatre Wing. Humbly, he still returns to Manteo every summer to help with scenery and costume design.

A critic once drily described Long's costumes as "hovering between taste and travesty." In characteristic good humor, Long has embraced this description. He has poured himself into *The Lost Colony* where his impeccable eye, meticulous research, and strict attention to detail shine in the footlights. (Courtesy of Aycock Brown Collection; OBHC.)

Another Broadway Joe

The Lost Colony has been a starting point in the careers of many actors and technicians. In Joe Layton's case, however, he already had a reputation as the most skilled young director and choreographer in American theater when he came to the production. Emma Morrison sought Joe out in New York City during a time when *The Lost Colony* was in a slump. When he was hired in 1964, he was told to bring the professional standards up any way he saw fit. He revolutionized the play with new costumes and scenery and implemented new ideas, such as having the previously dry historian become a vibrant part of the scene on stage.

He produced and directed *The Lost Colony* for 20 years. He established an innovative theatrical education program in summer workshops where young performers could learn what it was like to work in professional theater. A large and athletic man who often reminded people of quarterback Joe Namath, he was considered a genius in his field, although he had no formal training.

On Broadway, he designed musical sequences in hits like *Annie*, which were also featured in a film directed by John Huston. He was a three-time Emmy Award winner for *My Name is Barbra*. One of his greatest accomplishments was choreographing the 1984 opening ceremony of the Los Angeles Olympics.

Pictured here sitting in the second row in a Batman sweatshirt, he is often remembered as a charismatic person and as possibly the most talented director ever to guide *The Lost Colony*. (Courtesy of Aycock Brown Collection; OBHC.)

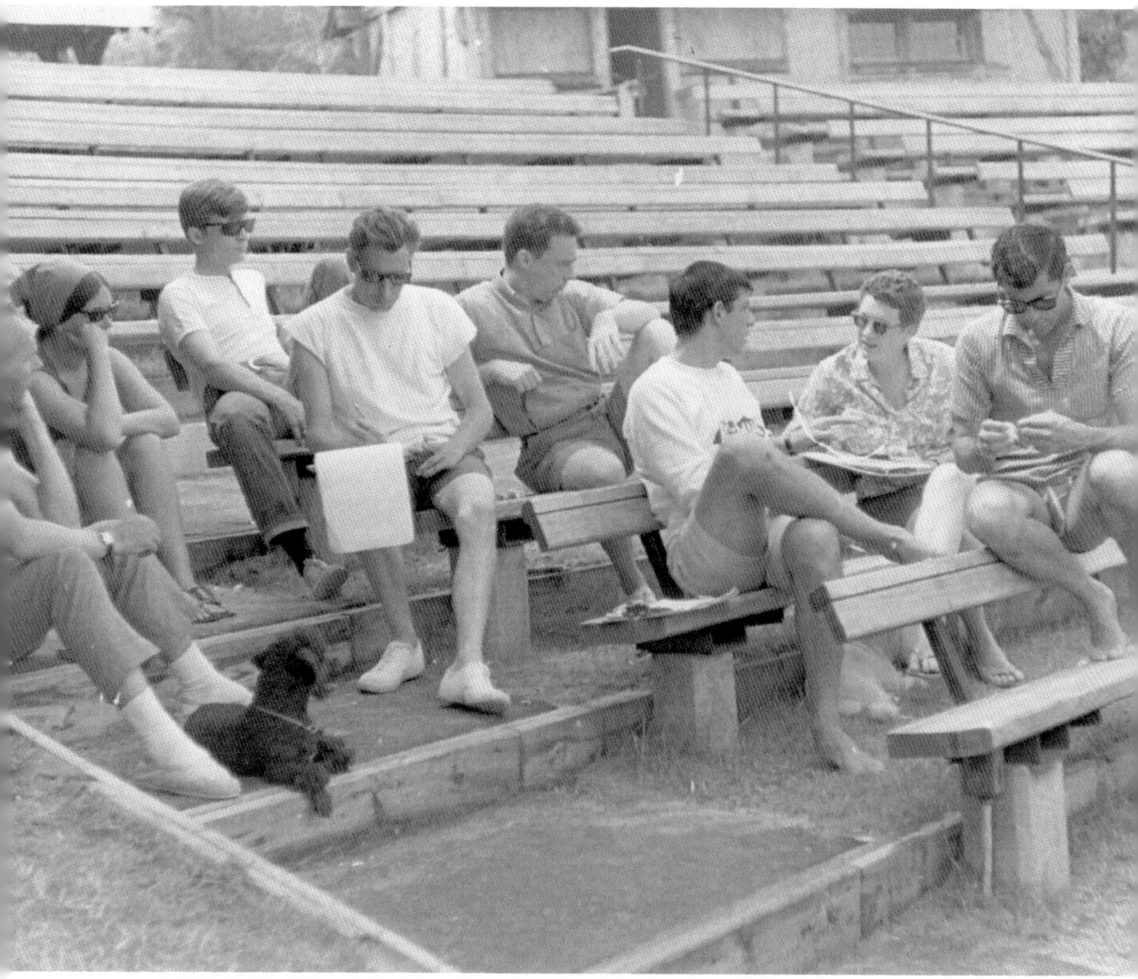

Eleanor Dare One Day

As a flower girl, Marjalene Thomas remembers standing up on costumer Irene Smart Rains's cutting table. "Stand still," Rains said, "One of these days I'll be making you an Eleanor Dare costume." Her words were prophetic, and Marjalene is perhaps the most recognizable face of Eleanor Dare. A public school teacher for 30 years, she and her family would come home to Manteo every summer to take part in the drama. She said, "I was able to have my cake and eat it too." (Courtesy of OBHC.)

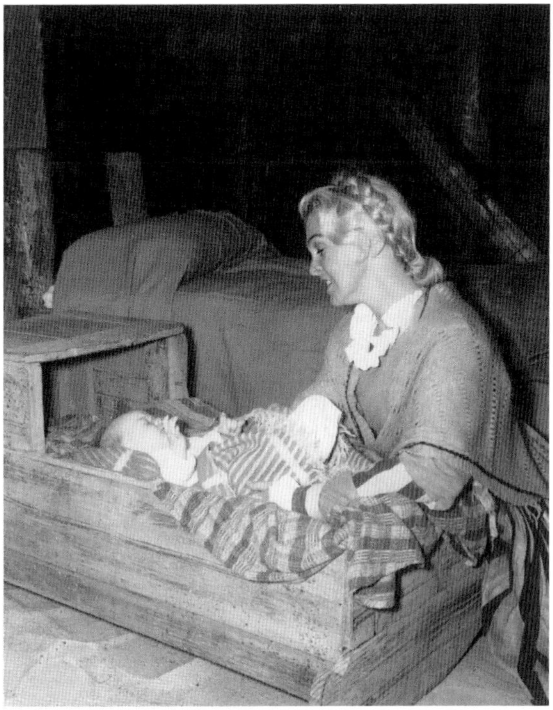

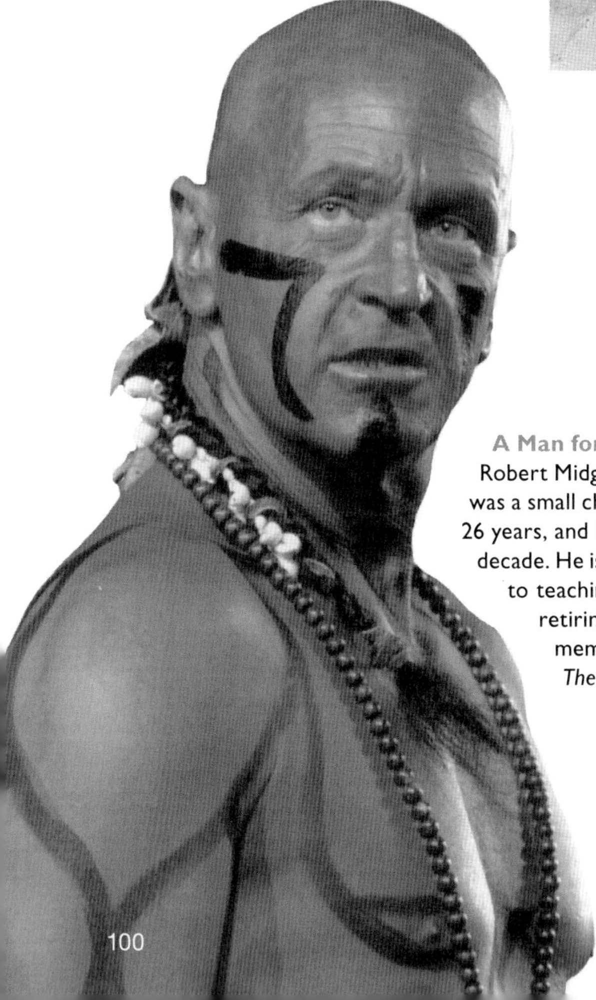

A Man for All Seasons

Robert Midgette has been in *The Lost Colony* every year since he was a small child. He played the coveted role of Chief Manteo for 26 years, and has been the fight scene choreographer for the last decade. He is as disciplined and dedicated to the drama as he was to teaching and coaching in the public school system before retiring. Midgette can entertain friends by reciting from memory all the players' lines in the script. (Courtesy of *The Lost Colony*.)

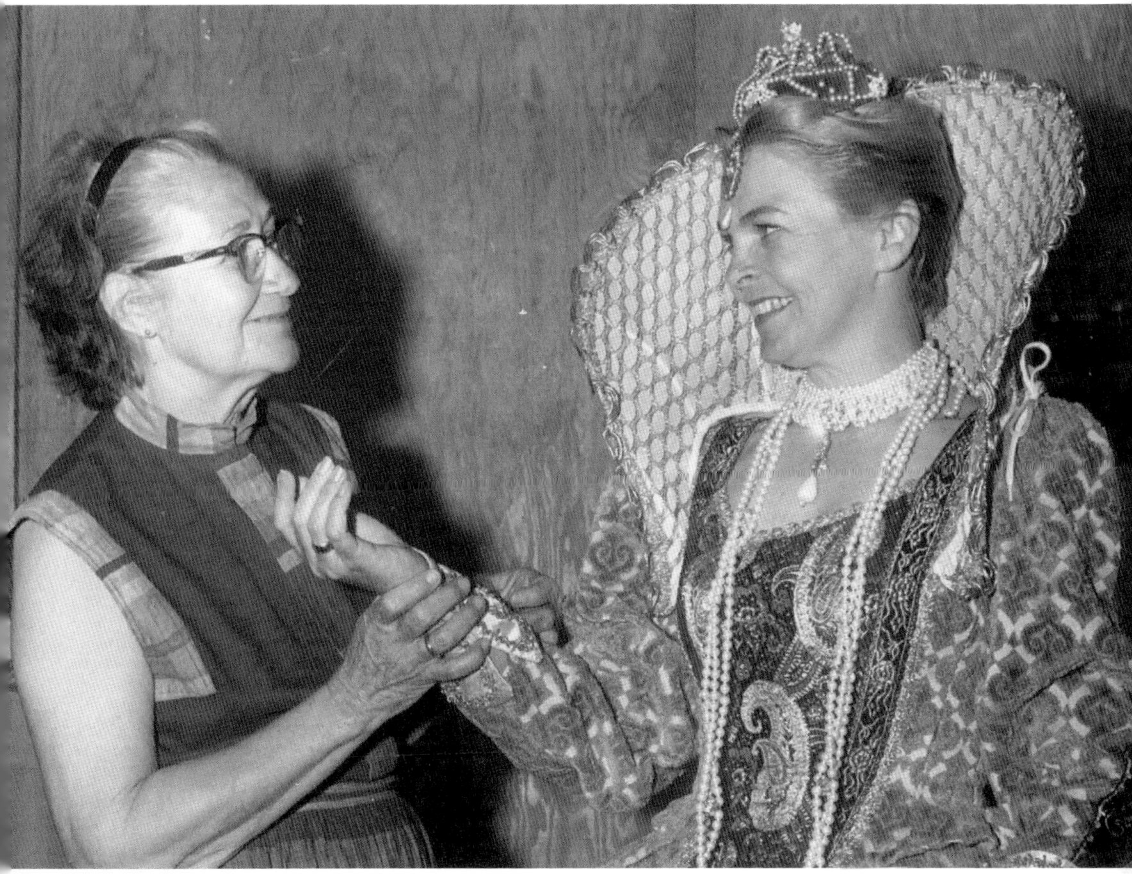

A Stitch in Time

Spunky, stern, and with a no-nonsense demeanor, Irene Smart Rains spent long hours making and maintaining all of the costumes for *The Lost Colony* outdoor drama. She began in 1937, working for Oramae Davis as a wardrobe assistant. She became Davis's personal assistant four years later. In 1946, she became the play's head costumer.

A native of Wanchese, Rene (pronounced "Ree Nee") studied costuming in New York City. She was an associate professor of theatre arts at the University of North Carolina at Chapel Hill, where she taught full-time for 25 years. She was associated with professor Fred Koch's Carolina Playmakers, which fed many actors and technicians to Manteo's summer drama.

Many young people went to her costume shop on the edge of the sound behind the stage for advice, consolation, or encouragement. *Colony* alumnus Pat Fearing remembers that Rene was very strict about how the costumes were to be washed and handled so that the "fibers didn't break down." She even insisted that the boy Indian costumes laden with "Texas dirt" make-up be washed separately from the girl Indian costumes in an effort to maintain propriety.

Rene always referred to the actors she worked with as "her people" who wore "her costumes." Two of her students became very famous and successful: actor Andy Griffith and costume designer William Ivey Long both credited Irene Smart Rains for her influence. She was well loved by all who worked with her. (Courtesy of Aycock Brown Collection; OBHC.)

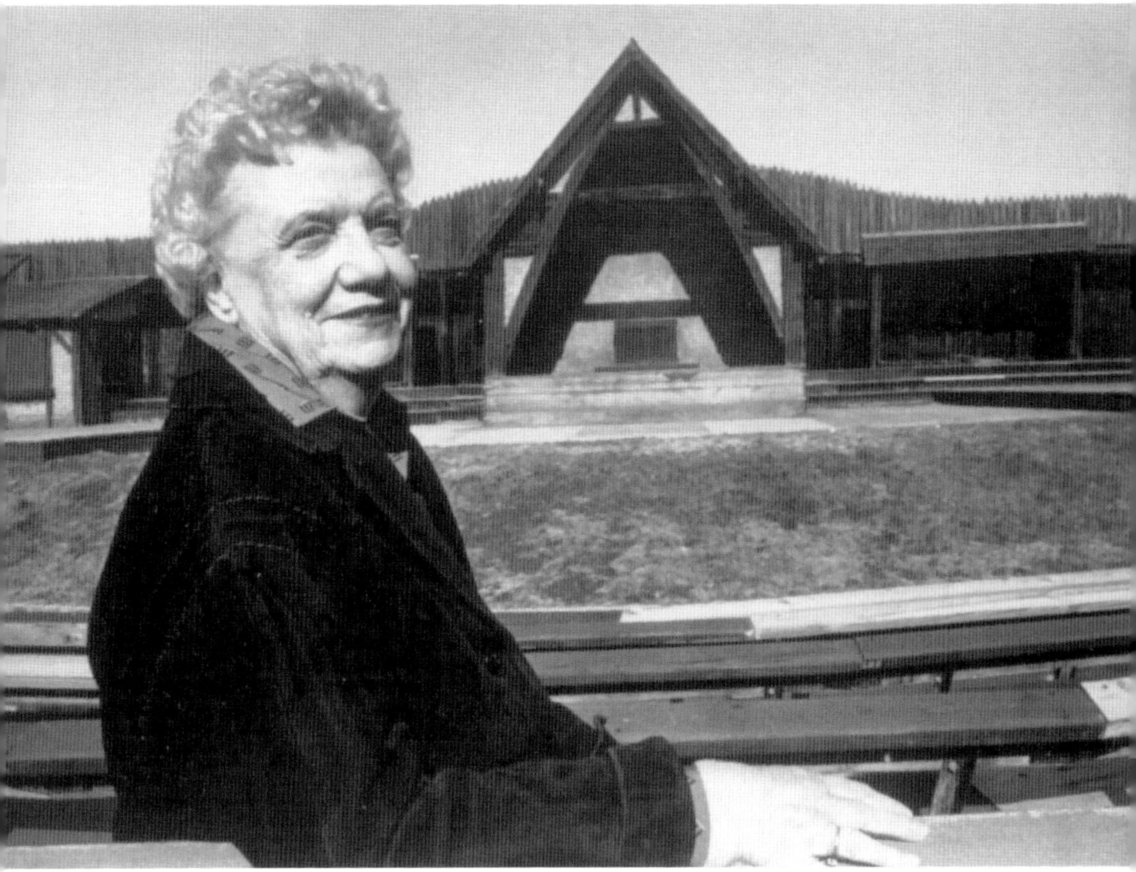

Guardian of a Dream

Mabel Basnight's lifelong cause was heritage tourism on the Outer Banks—particularly the creation and perpetuation of *The Lost Colony*. Shortly after graduating from college, she became enraptured with Sen. Bradford Fearing's dream for Dare County and cast her lot with his, becoming executive secretary for all his civic, political, and nonprofit positions.

Through the successes and problematic years of the show's long run, she steadfastly guarded the dream, working closely with managers, particularly with producer and board chair Emma Neal Morrison. Her professional career was centered in downtown Manteo, working primarily with the Fearing enterprises and Dominion Power, but she always made it clear: when spring comes, it is *Lost Colony* time. And so it was for her, for 57 years. (Courtesy of Lebame Houston.)

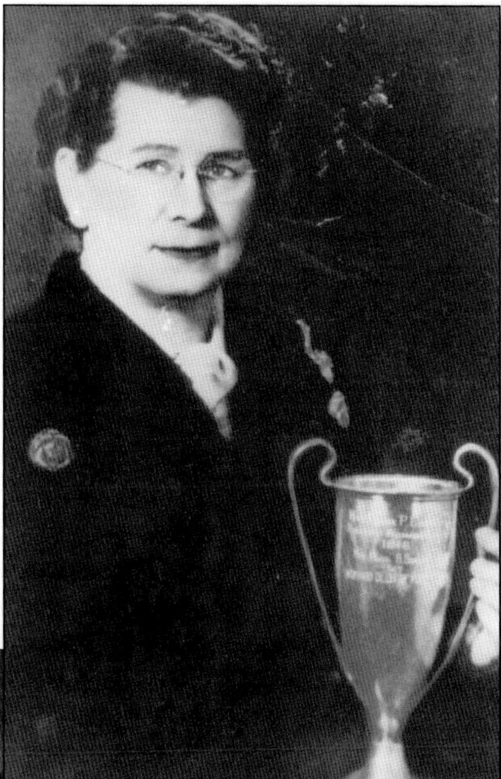

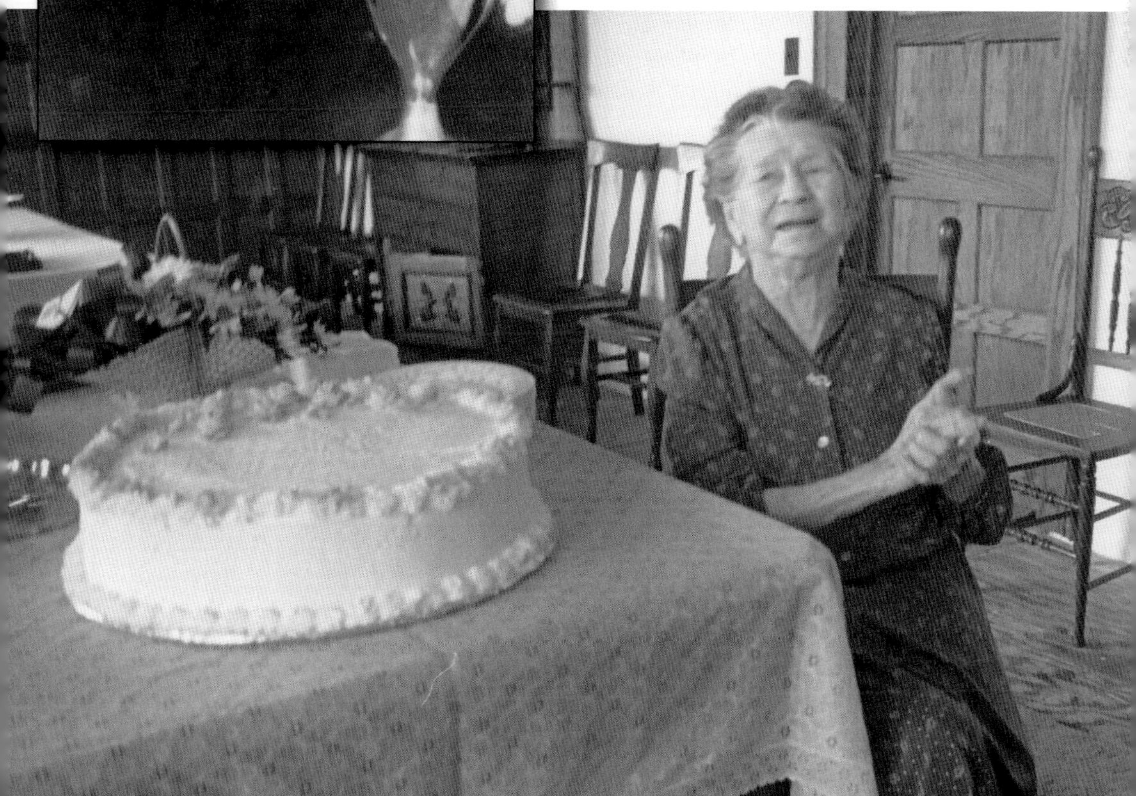

A Musical Pearl

Pearl Scharff composed the *Virginia Dare March* in honor of the first English child born in the New World. She was the winner of the North Carolina Florence Cooper Cup for writing music and lyrics. Her composition was played by the US Marine Band and was also used as a full-score symphony number. After her husband died, she lived with her sister Rena Tillet, who was also a widow. Pearl played the piano, and Rena played the organ at the Methodist Church in Wanchese until they were in their 90s. (Courtesy of Minta Meekins.)

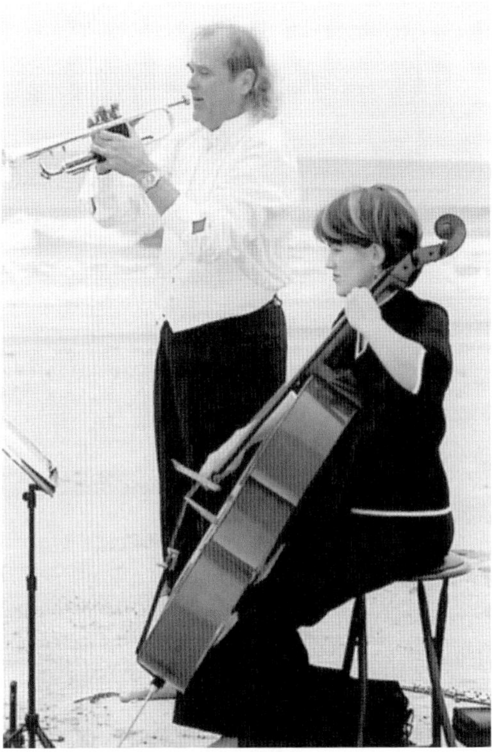

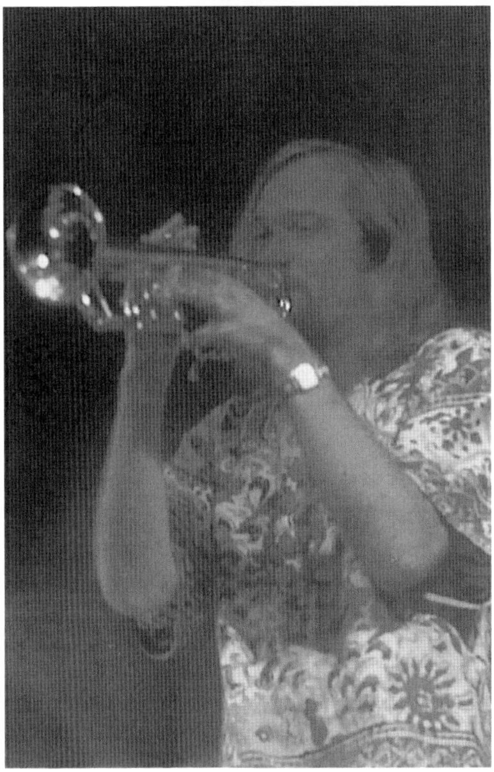

2,500 Weddings and Counting

Now a wedding musician and private music instructor, Roy Murray still radiates the energy of the rock-and-roll horn player who spent 15 years touring with bands, most notably Jorge Santana and his Latino band Malo. His students have gone on to perform, attend music universities, and serve as worship leaders in their churches. However, he says, "The biggest thing by far that happened to me on the Outer Banks was meeting people who called themselves 'Christians.' That is really when new life began." (Both images courtesy of Roy Murray.)

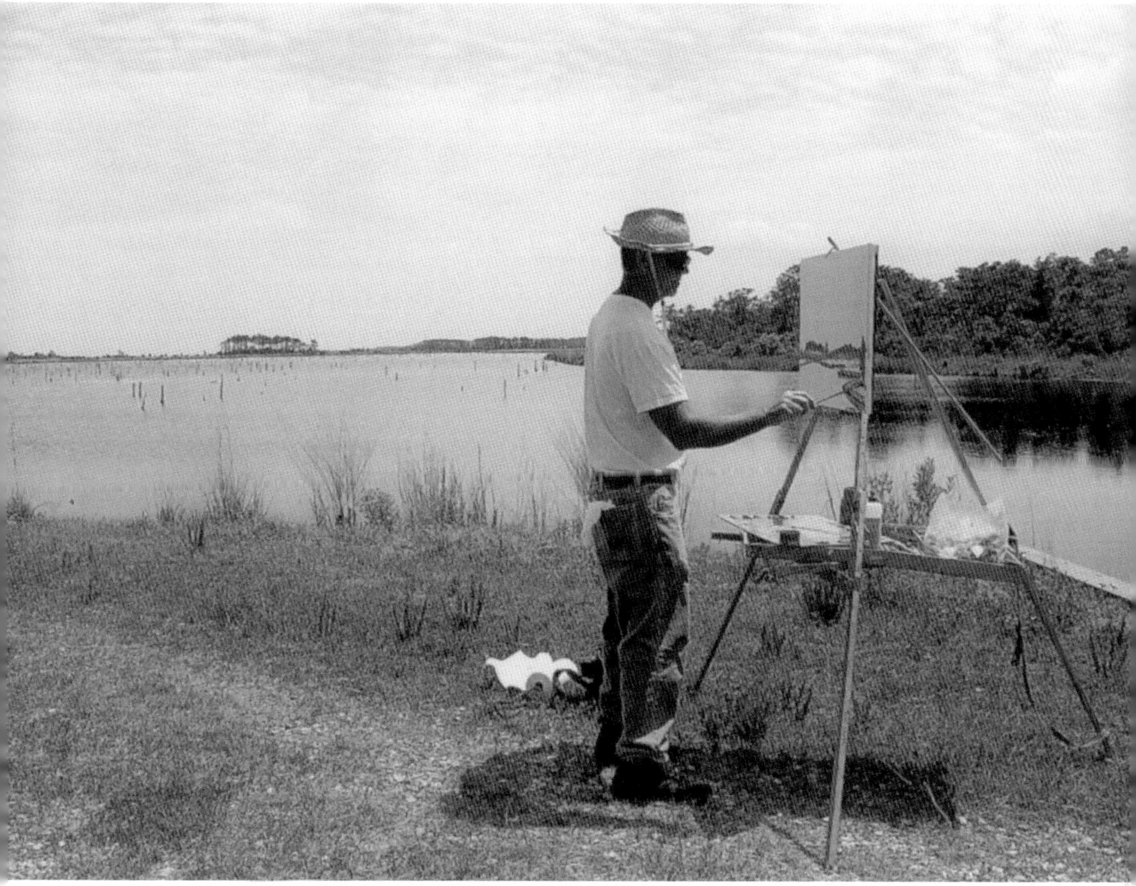

Possum's Pseudonym

John "Possum" Silver does not fit the stereotypical image of an artist. He has been a commercial fisherman, carpenter, house builder, and boat restorer. Possum jokes so much that it seems he would never get anything done, but, in fact, he is a very prolific and very successful artist.

In 1980, his wife, Sheila, gave him a gift of his first painting class, with Ralph Smith, who painted big, bold abstract figures full of color. "It was like a magic wand was waved before me," he says.

There was a fork in the road, and he took it in 1994, when he put 60 paintings in an art show and 50 were sold. His watercolors represent life the way he sees it on the Outer Banks: beach fishermen setting nets, the ocean, the marsh, and anything "furred, finned, or feathered." (Courtesy of John Silver.)

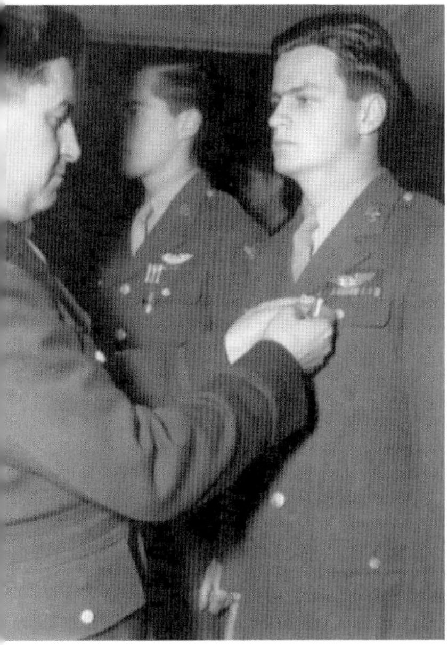

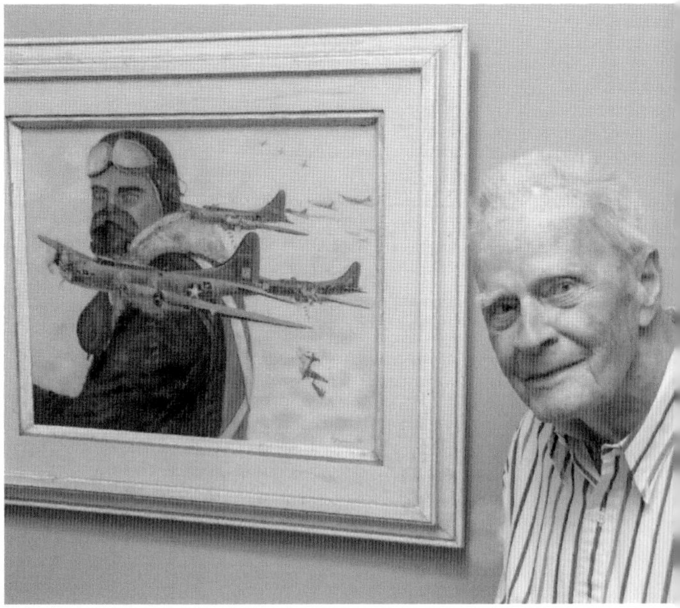

A Life of Service

Don Bryan came to Nags Head after spending 30 years in the US Air Force and fighting in three wars. He survived 25 missions over Germany as a tech sergeant and gunner in a B-17 "Flying Fortress" bomber. Later, as a pilot, he saw action in Korea and Vietnam. He served with NATO and in the Pentagon before retiring as an Air Force colonel.

He was elected to the Nags Head Board of Commissioners in 1975, and served as the town's mayor from 1978 to 1991. Friend and colleague Bob Muller said, "During that time, the face of Nags Head was truly set. When Don came into office, the town was about 30 percent developed. When he left office, it was probably 75 percent developed."

However, there was a third integral part of this warrior and political figure. He was an award-winning artist and promoter of the arts. He had studied painting while stationed in Germany and found his muse in the Outer Banks. In his final years, he established the Don and Catharine Bryan Cultural Series. The series will bring a broad spectrum of cultural events from all artistic disciplines to the community. Muller, who also served as mayor of Nags Head and acknowledged Don's great foresight in community planning, described the cultural series as "Don's ultimate legacy."

Sgt. Don Bryan was awarded the Distinguished Flying Cross by Gen. Curtis LeMay in England in 1943. An older Bryan stands in front of a self-portrait. (Both images courtesy of Bob Muller.)

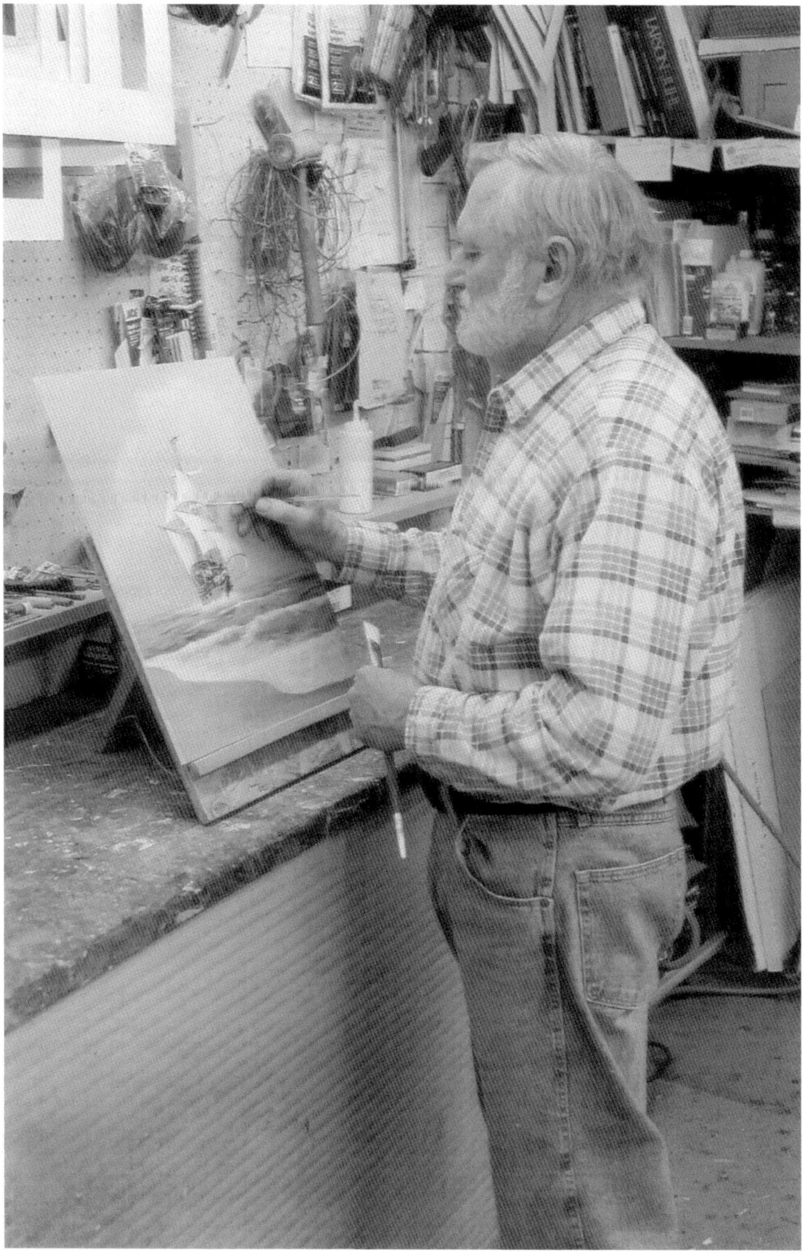

Artist and Historian Extraordinaire

Many of the Civil War artifacts in Hubby Bliven's Roanoke Heritage Art Gallery and Military Museum were actually found by the owner. Bliven has found much of his collection along the shore of the Croatan Sound. Extensive scuba diving, metal detecting, and combing the narrow shoreline with his wife and sons has yielded cannon balls, bullets, clay pipes, and Civil War–era bottles.

He is also a renowned artist who sells his original paintings and prints that he frames himself in the gallery and museum that sits beside his ancestral home. When his son Jeremy wrote a children's book, he did not have to look far for an illustrator. After some arm-twisting, he convinced his father to collaborate with him on three popular books about Stumpy, the pirate cat. (Courtesy of Hubby Bliven.)

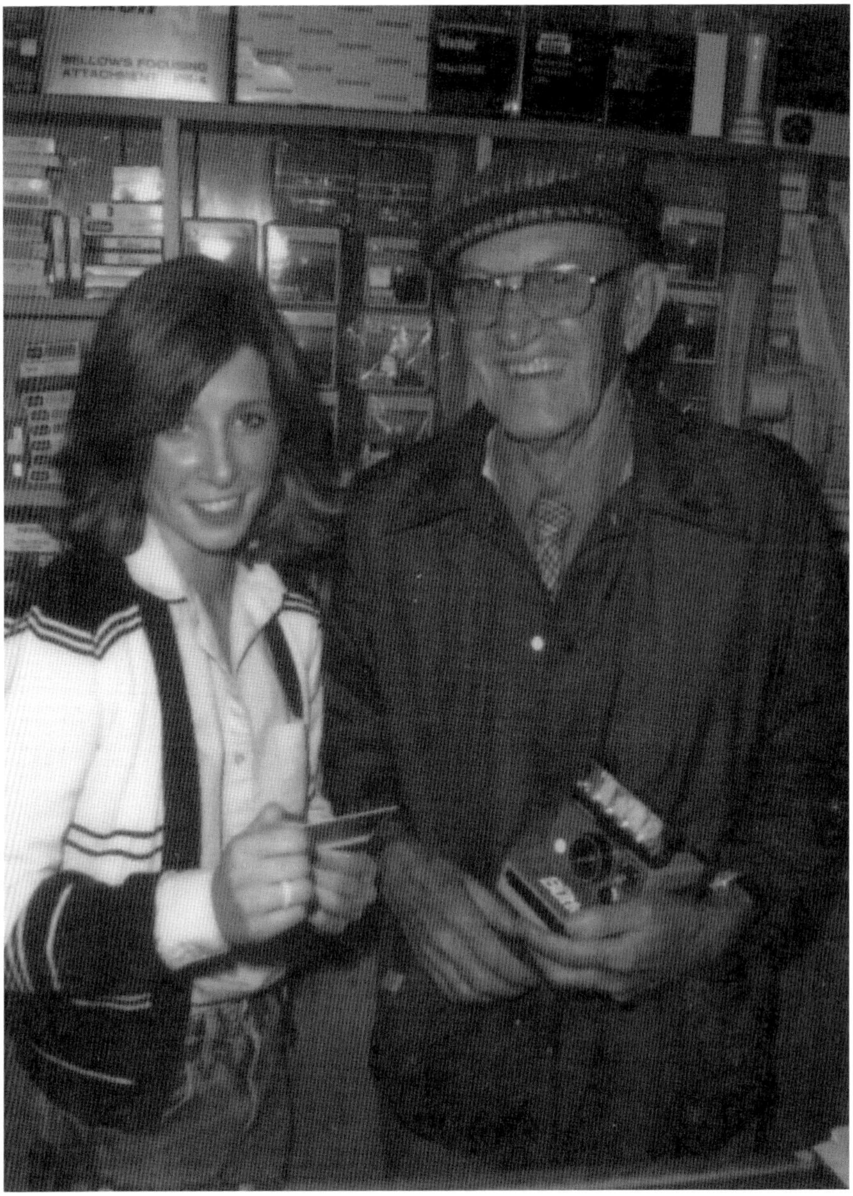

Outer Banks as a Backdrop

It was at the fishing docks where Lisa Griggs first saw photographer Aycock Brown with two Yashica twin lens cameras around his neck, taking pictures of everything. She was officially bitten by the shutterbug.

In high school, Griggs was encouraged by her Distributive Education Club leader to find a job in her dream vocation. She called on her friend Brown, and he arranged for her to start at Jim's Camera House in Kill Devil Hills. Jim Lee became her instructor, teaching her all aspects of the trade, including aerial photography. She was 15 when she shot her first wedding and 16 when she began doing family portraits on the beach.

Lisa Griggs was the first woman to open her own studio, Griggs Best Shot, on the Outer Banks. In almost 40 years of professional photography, she has a renewed appreciation for having been an apprentice to the very best in the field. (Courtesy of Lisa Griggs.)

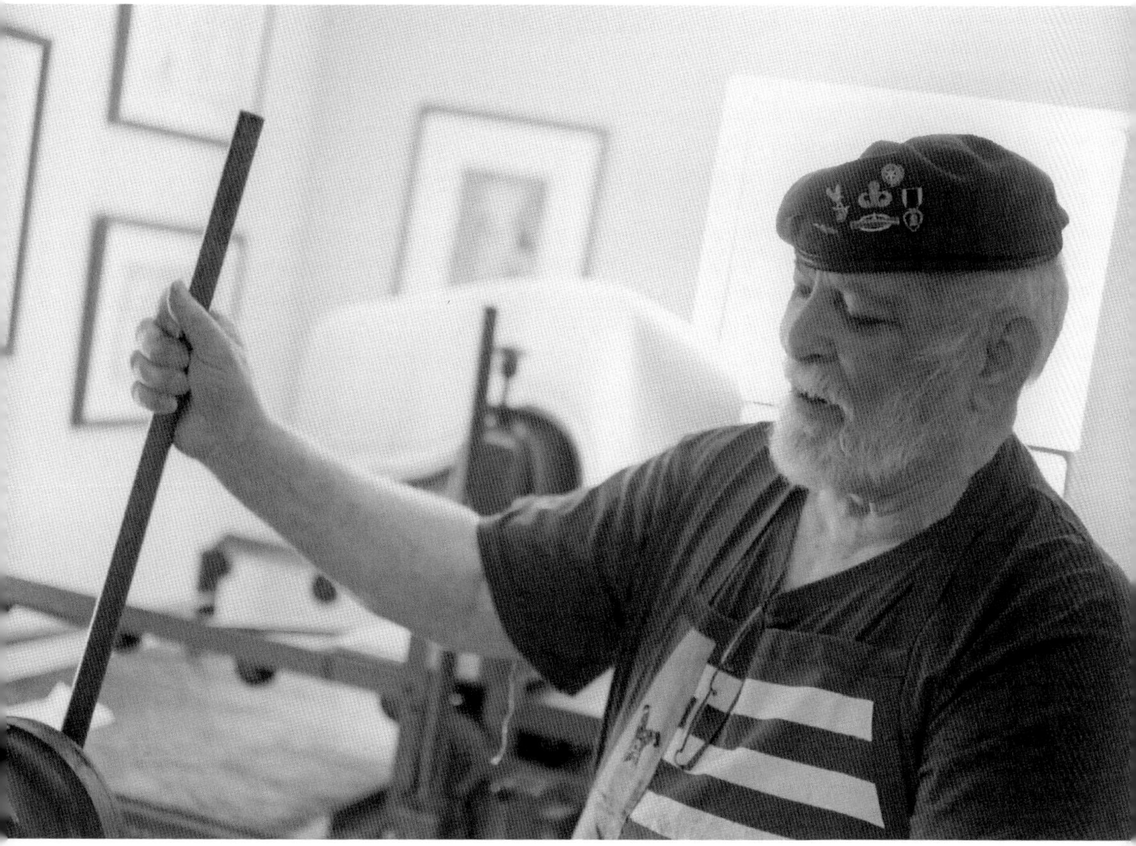

Creating from Chaos

As the owner of the Ghost Fleet Gallery in Nags Head, artist Glenn Eure has been an encouragement to artists in every stage of their careers. He has been described as having a whale-sized imagination and a heart to match his talent. His self-designed gallery exhibits his wide variety of work and is the epicenter of art shows and demonstrations on the Outer Banks.

He conceptualized the Kitty Hawk Monument to a Century of Flight and was one of the design artists for the massive sculpture dedicated in 2003. Another giant-sized project came to life when, at age 78, he completed carving the 14 Stations of the Cross for the Holy Redeemer Catholic Parish, his church in Kitty Hawk. The labor is teasingly referred to as "Glenn Eure's Redemption."

In 2010, he was awarded the Outer Banks Living Legend Award. Still a prolific artist in his 80s, Glenn uses whatever is at hand as tools and medium for expression. (Courtesy of Linda Lauby.)

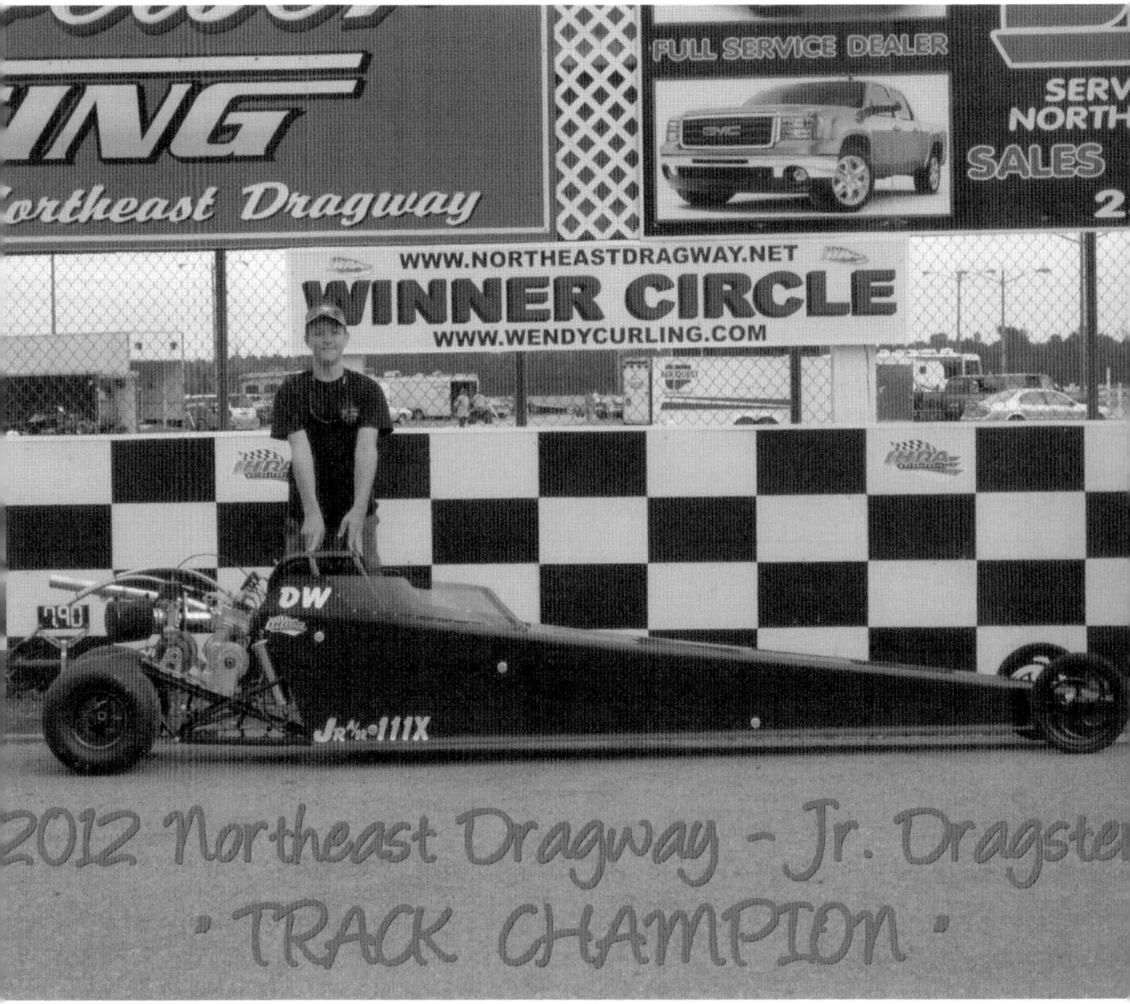

All in the Family

At an age when most boys are driving go-carts, David Wayne Light is already a junior dragster track champion. With the help of his parents, who own and operate Lighthouse Automotive Repair in Wanchese, this teenager has been racing since the age of eight. He won his title at the 2012 Northeast Dragway competition in Hertford, North Carolina. The Light family travels to races almost every weekend during the season that spans April to September. One can only imagine his instructor's surprise when Light recently completed his high school driver's training course. (Courtesy of David Light.)

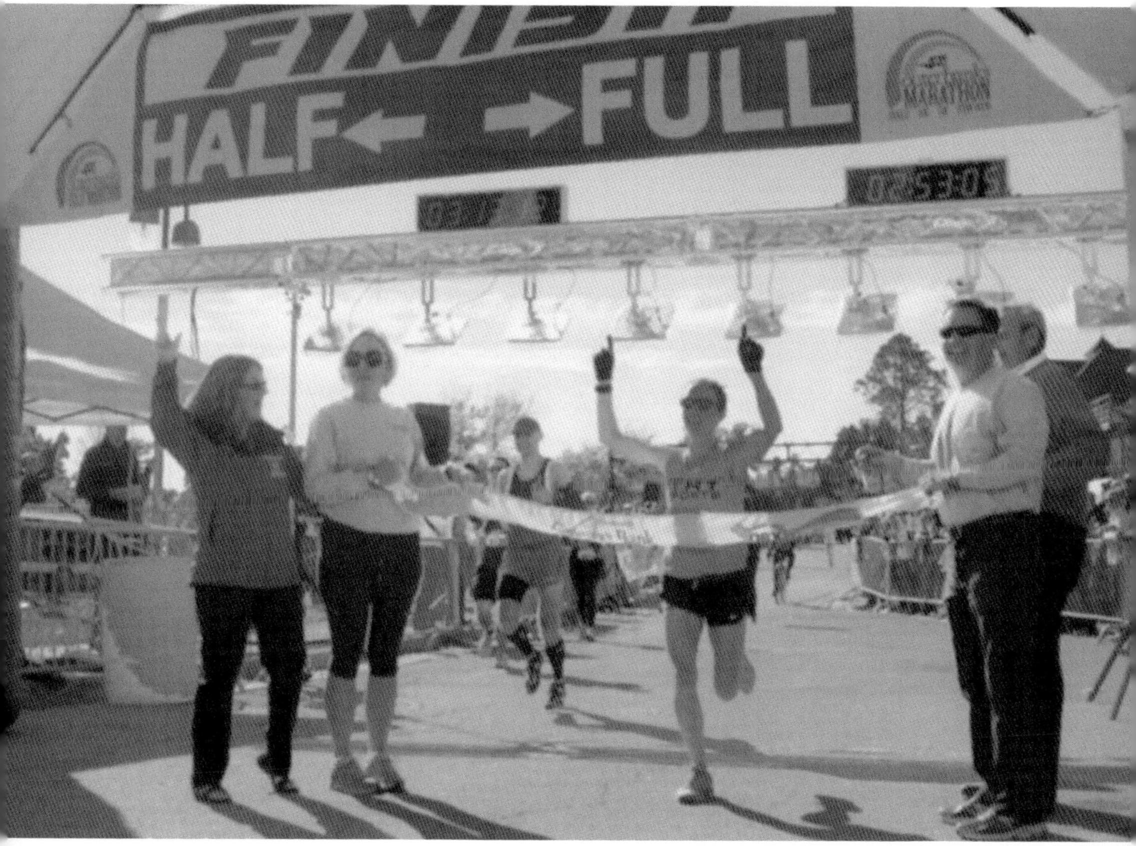

Sentinel at the Finish Line

Lynda Wood (left) is the executive director of the nonprofit Outer Banks Sporting Events (OBSE). OBSE currently sponsors four major events: the Flying Pirate Half Marathon, an obstacle course called Storm the Beach, the Outer Banks Triathlon, and the Veterans Day Weekend Marathon. Besides raising money for the Dare Education Foundation and the Outer Banks Relief Foundation with entrance fees, the events have provided an estimated $6.2-million economic impact through restaurant, hotel, and rental home earnings. (Courtesy of Lynda Wood.)

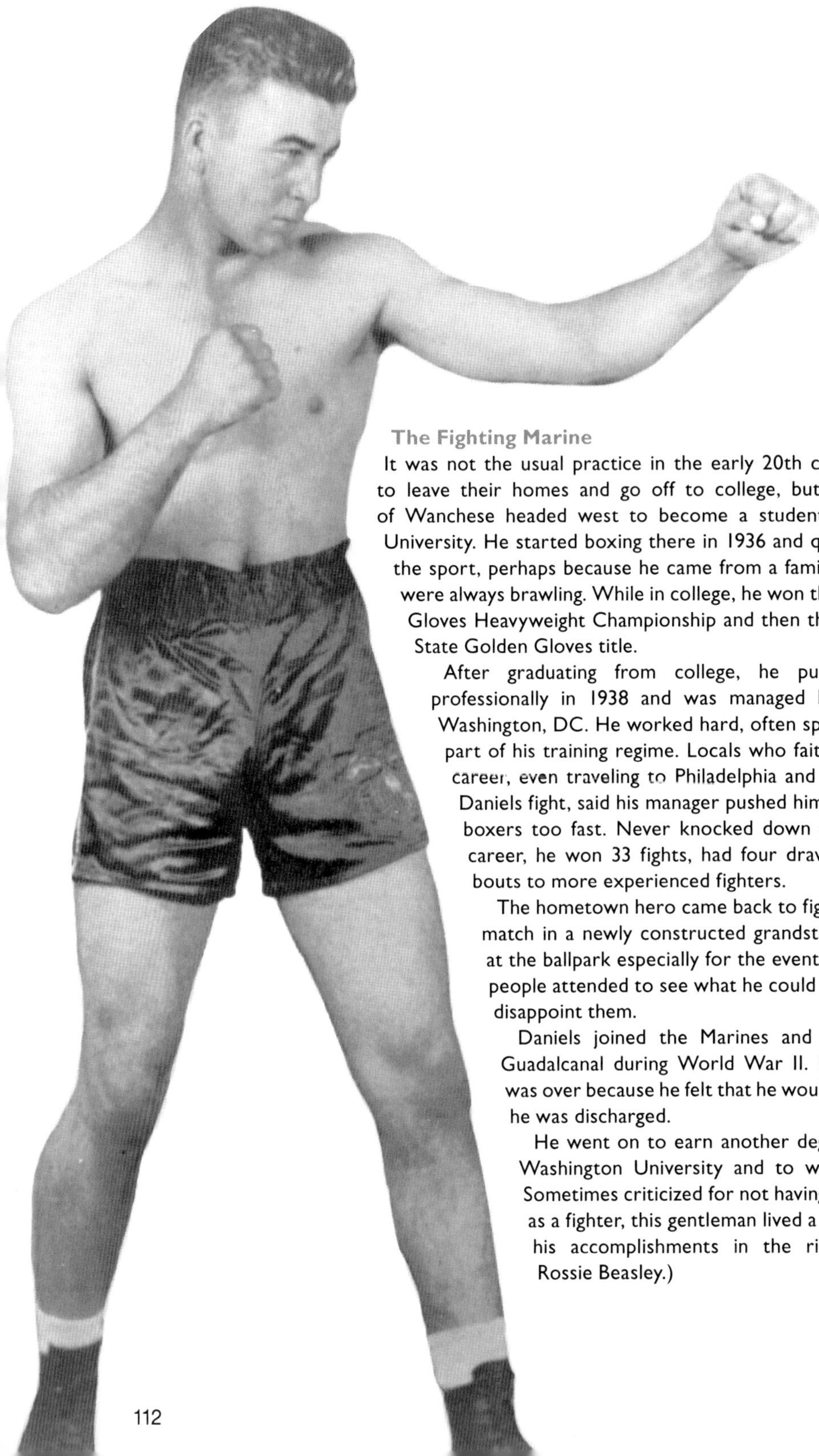

The Fighting Marine

It was not the usual practice in the early 20th century for natives to leave their homes and go off to college, but Maynard Daniels of Wanchese headed west to become a student at Wake Forest University. He started boxing there in 1936 and quickly advanced in the sport, perhaps because he came from a family where the boys were always brawling. While in college, he won the District Golden Gloves Heavyweight Championship and then the North Carolina State Golden Gloves title.

After graduating from college, he pursued the sport professionally in 1938 and was managed by Sid Fischell of Washington, DC. He worked hard, often splitting firewood as part of his training regime. Locals who faithfully followed his career, even traveling to Philadelphia and New York to see Daniels fight, said his manager pushed him to fight seasoned boxers too fast. Never knocked down during his fighting career, he won 33 fights, had four draws, and lost three bouts to more experienced fighters.

The hometown hero came back to fight in an exhibition match in a newly constructed grandstand that was built at the ballpark especially for the event. Several thousand people attended to see what he could do, and he did not disappoint them.

Daniels joined the Marines and was a soldier in Guadalcanal during World War II. His boxing career was over because he felt that he would be too old when he was discharged.

He went on to earn another degree from George Washington University and to work with NOAA. Sometimes criticized for not having the killer instinct as a fighter, this gentleman lived a life that outshined his accomplishments in the ring. (Courtesy of Rossie Beasley.)

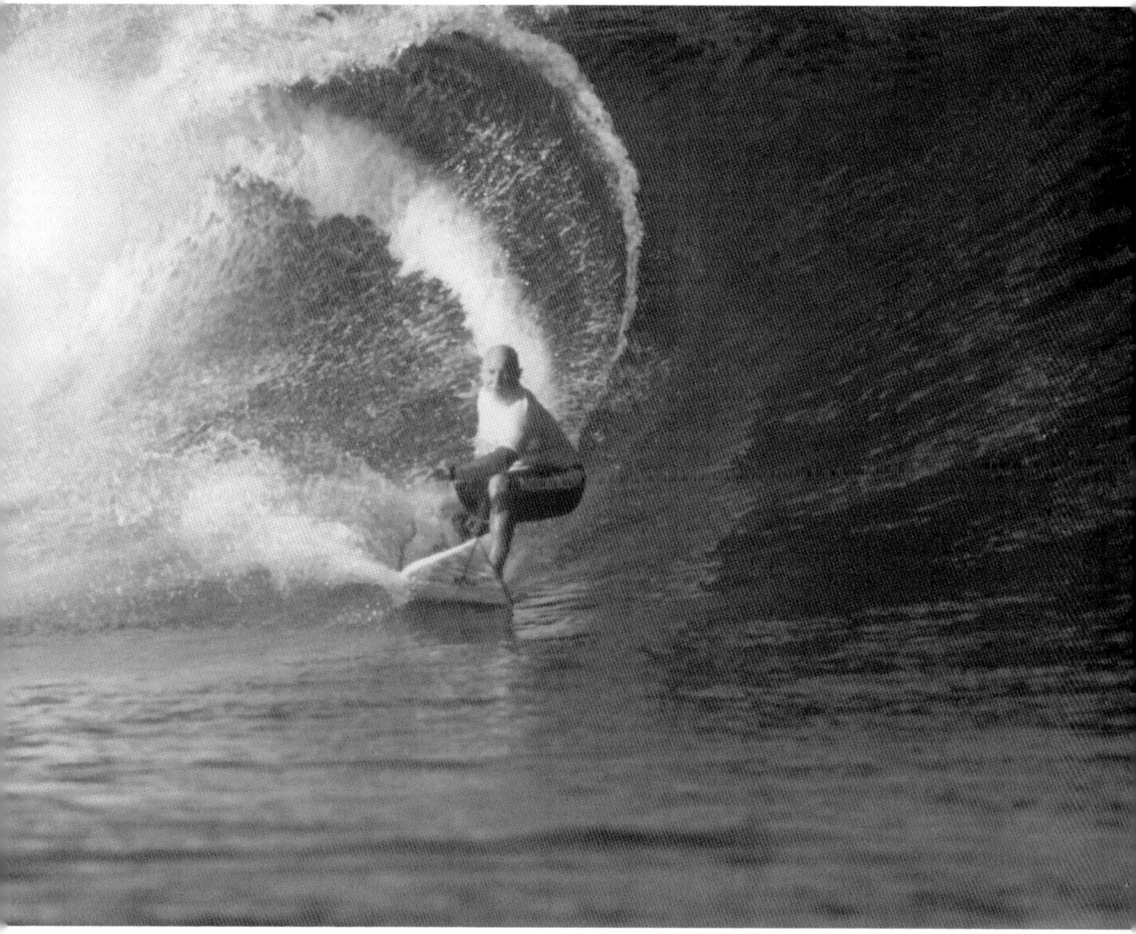

Riding the Swell

Somehow, Jim "Biggie" Vaughn has maintained a cool persona even though he is a successful businessman, a devoted husband and father, and over 50 years old. It may be a state that only surfers can achieve.

Floridian Vaughn came to the Outer Banks to surf during summer breaks from the Citadel. He had a lucrative job in construction after graduation but desired to open a surf shop and give it a go. With no background in retail, he and his roommate opened a surf shop out of a little house next to the Catholic mission at Whalebone Junction in 1975. He soon discovered the pitfalls of being in a business that relied on just 10 weeks of hustle and bustle and an almost nonexistent shoulder season. He and his wife, April, have since worked hard to build Whalebone Surf Shop storefronts that bring customers in year-round to purchase boards, clothing, and lessons. Three structures—one in Nags Head, one in Virginia Beach, and an urban shop in Raleigh—now fly the skull and cross surfboards flag. Whalebone has its own surf team and helps to sponsor surf competitions.

And, of course, Biggie still surfs. One of his dreams was realized when he surfed in the tropical paradise of Fiji. Here he executes a bottom turn on Cloudbreak Reef in Tavarua. (Courtesy of Jim Vaughn.)

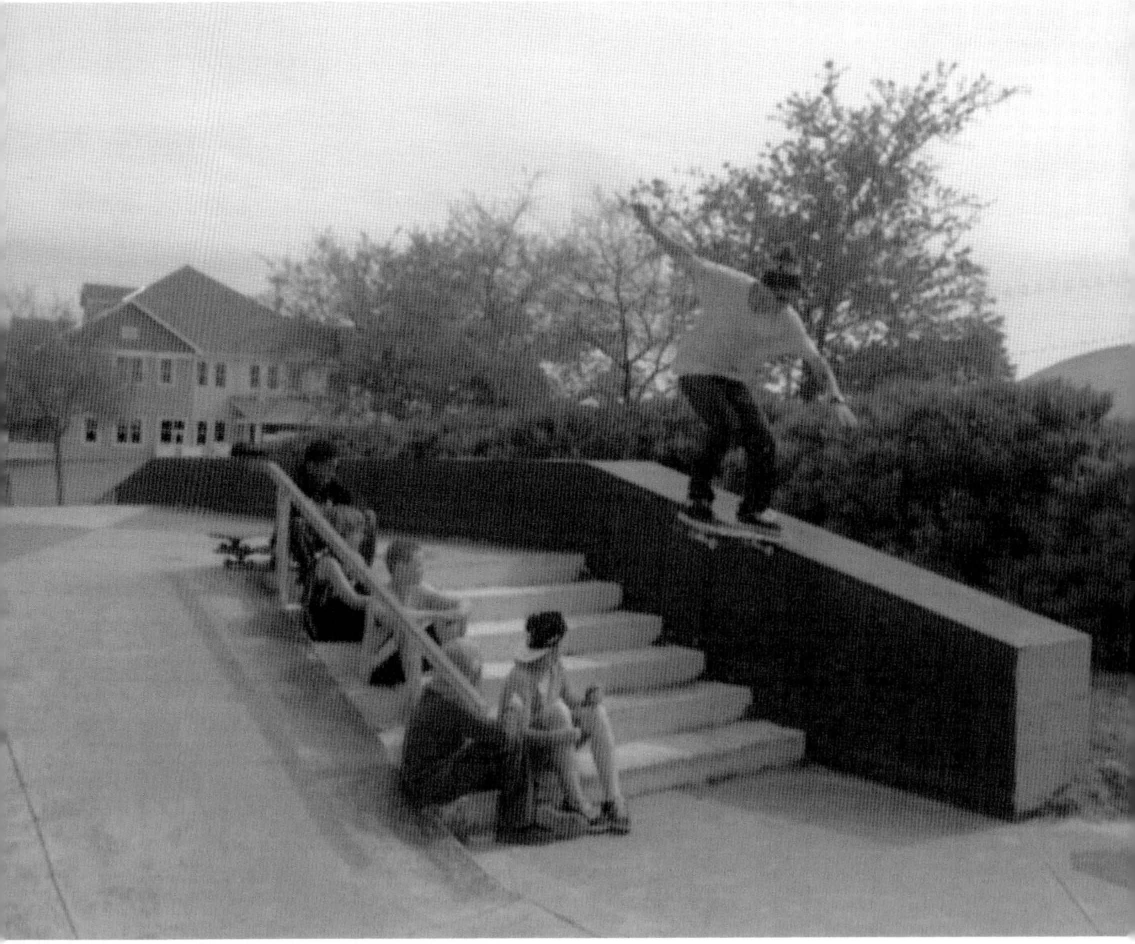

Carving out a Spot

Since the mid-1980s, Outer Bankers have been skateboarding on ramps in each other's yards, in the parking lots of churches, or wherever they could find a smooth patch of concrete. There was no sanctioned public area for people to skateboard.

In 2007, this finally changed with the establishment of the first free public skateboard park in Manteo. A group of skateboarders attended town meetings from the time they were age 13 to 22 and finally convinced the town that the park was something that was needed. Daniel Tugwell recalled, "Not only did the Manteo City Skatepark alleviate the problems among business owners, the public, and skaters, it also set the standard for other towns in Dare County to fund and build their own parks."

This particular group of skateboarders is turning 30, but they continue to skate the park when they come home to visit. Wanchese native Beach Gray takes a respite from doctorate studies at the University of Pittsburgh through skateboarding. His distant cousin Durand Beasley has gone on to make a living designing and constructing skateboard parks in national and foreign cities. (Courtesy of Daniel Tugwell.)

CHAPTER SEVEN

Visionaries

"I hardly know thee in thy greatness."

One of the first Outer Banks visionaries was Sir Walter Raleigh, who never stepped foot ashore in America. However, he envisioned what settlement in the new world would be like, and, against great odds, he carried through with his plans to establish a colony on Roanoke Island.

Visionaries appear when there is a need (or that is the way it seems). George Washington Creef saw the need in the late 1880s for a workboat that had a shallow draft, would carry heavy loads, and take rough seas. He built what came to be called a shad boat during a time when commercial fishing for shad fish became big business in a place that eventually became known as the shad capital of the world.

Later, men like Orville and Wilbur Wright made Kitty Hawk and themselves famous with their heavier-than-air flying machine that changed transportation for the world. About the same time the Wright brothers were carrying out their flying experiments on the sand dunes, Reginald Fessenden, a few miles across the sound on Roanoke Island, was conducting his own tests with wireless transmissions that would bring him fame.

Modern-day visionaries like Frank Stick and Huntington Cairns used their influence to introduce the first National Seashore to the area. Others, like Percy and Elizabeth Meekins and Diane Baum St. Clair, would make possible many present-day grants and scholarships with their generous philanthropy. The Outer Banks seems an inherently fertile breeding ground for visionaries.

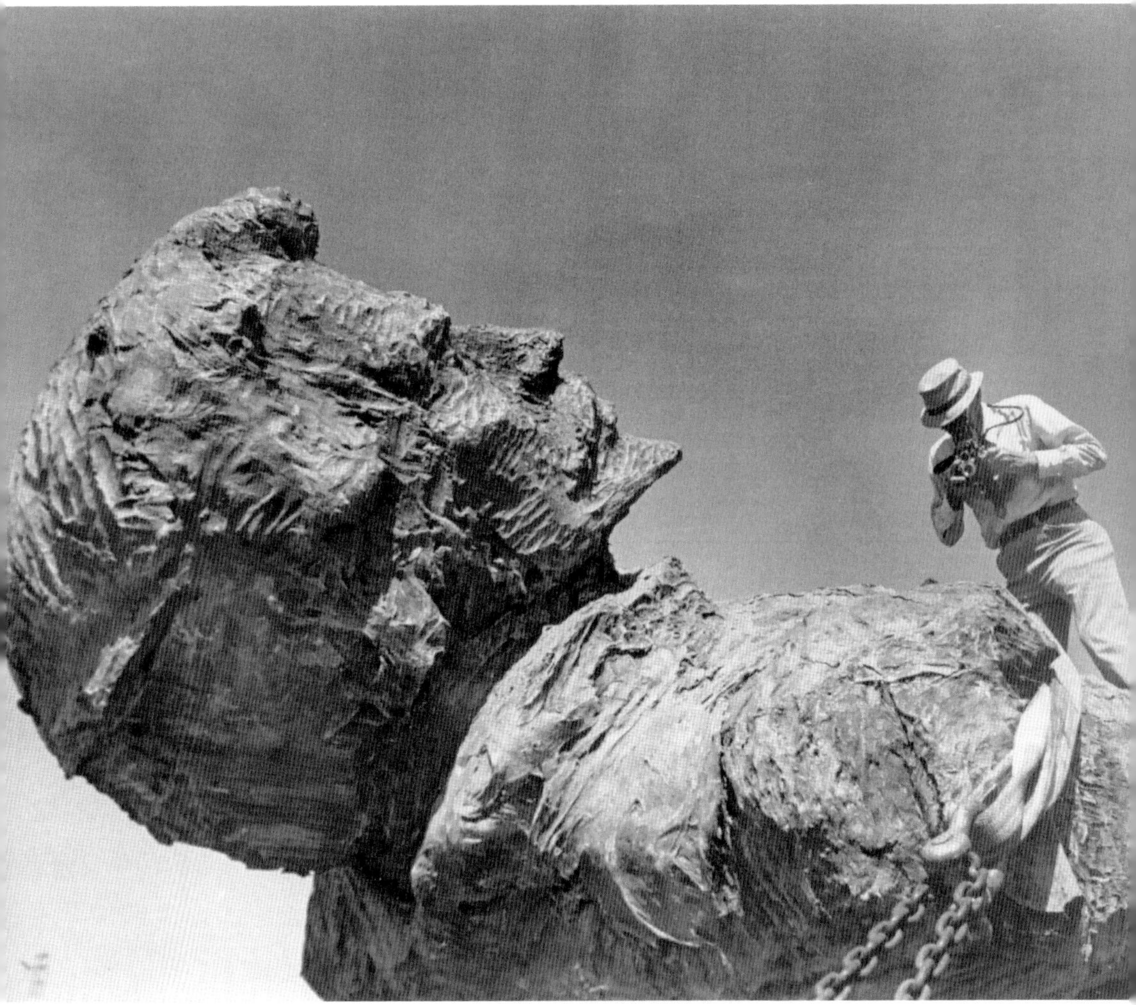

Beheaded Twice

Queen Elizabeth helped Sir Walter Raleigh fulfill his dream of settling a colony by giving him a royal patent to develop land along the American coast from North Carolina to Florida. He backed the colony on Roanoke Island with his money, power, and prestige. Although the first colony ended in failure, the way was paved for other settlements to succeed.

He was in and out of favor with the Virgin Queen. Later, he was executed, some think unnecessarily and unjustly, for being involved in a plot against Elizabeth's successor, King James.

From 1976 to 1990, a 24-foot wooden statue of the poet, courtier, and soldier overlooked the town of Manteo. The sculptor, Robert K. Harniman, fashioned the figure from a 500-year-old cypress tree. But, alas, Roanoke Island termites got the better of it. When the decision was made to take it down, one woman was given Raleigh's head as a souvenir. As it was being taken to her home, the head fell out of the back of a truck and broke into pieces. Raleigh lost his head more than once.

Aycock Brown photographed Raleigh on the day he arrived in Manteo. (Courtesy of Manteo Centennial Exhibit Collection, OBHC.)

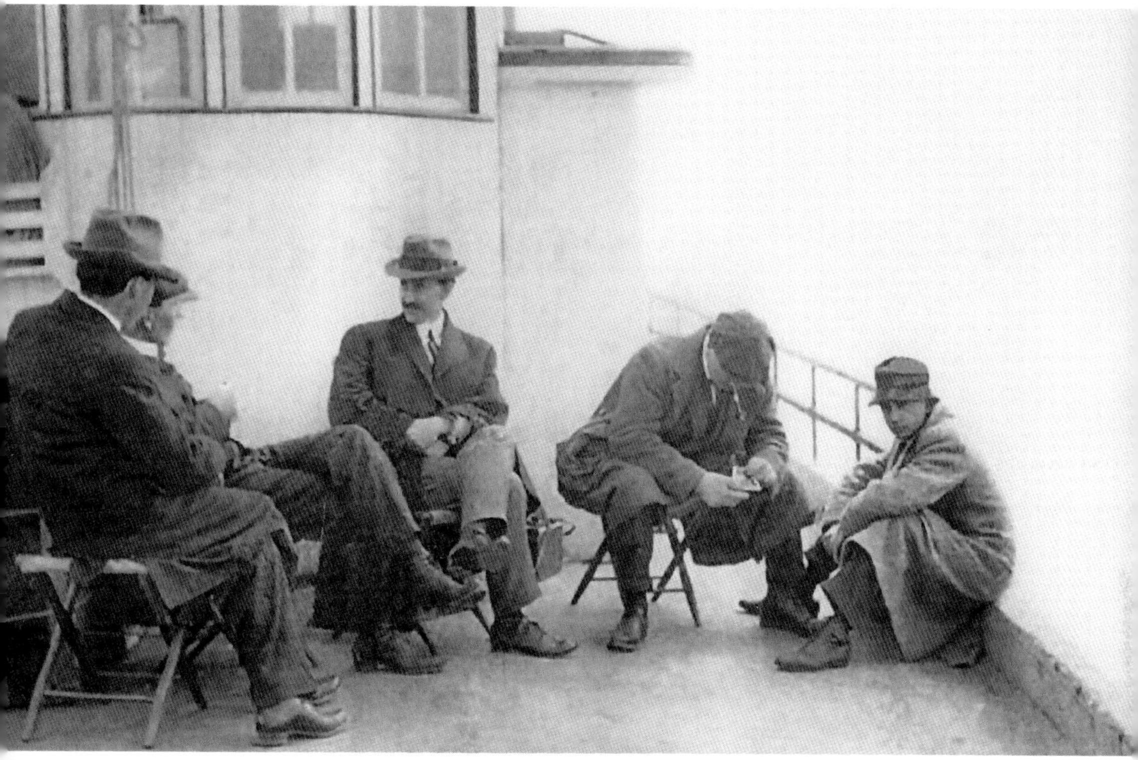

Lift Off

On December 17, 1903, in Kitty Hawk, North Carolina, Wilbur and Orville Wright accomplished what they set out to do—successfully fly an engine-powered heavier-than-air machine. Their lifetime dreams came true in doing what men had attempted to do for centuries: fly. During their many attempted flights, a number of locals befriended and helped them. John T. Daniels snapped the photograph as the plane lifted into the air. The Tate family and the members of the Kill Devil Hills lifesaving station were always ready to help them carry the plane and assist as ground crew. They became friends of the Wrights and helped them make aviation history.

Five of these locals were the only witnesses to man's first flight. Because the Wrights were so secretive and the eyewitnesses so loyal, it would be five years before the world came to know what happened that day in 1903. The Wright brothers kept the only image of the flight hidden during that time. The world did not discover their secret until the Wrights wanted to make it public knowledge.

In this photograph, the Wright brothers are sitting on the deck of the well-known *Hattie Creef*, the vessel that transported them and their equipment to Kitty Hawk. (Courtesy of Museum of the Albemarle.)

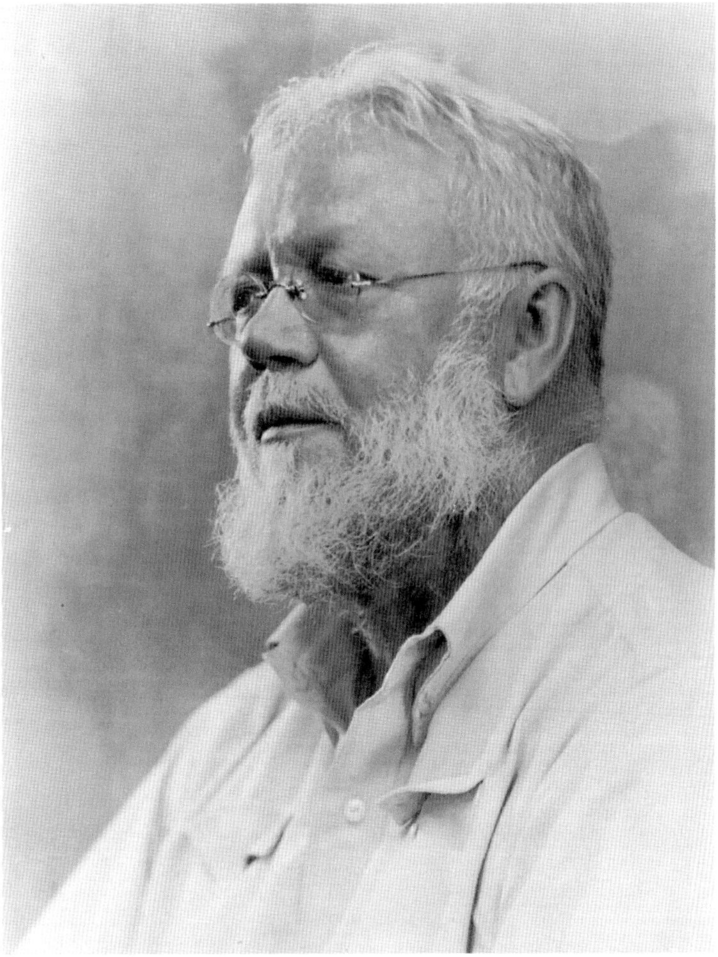

Father of Radio Broadcasting

About the same time that the Wright brothers were working on their flight experiments, another inquisitive mind was testing out his theories a few miles away.

Dr. Reginald Fessenden was hired by the weather bureau to set up telegraph stations on the Outer Banks. With varied funding, he returned to the area and stayed in Manteo at the Tranquil House and Hotel Roanoke around 1900.

Fessenden has gone down in history as "the originator of the continuous wave principle of wireless transmission." To achieve this accolade, he had 50-foot towers built at the north end of Roanoke Island near the foot of where the Croatan Bridge is now and sent the first audio transmission by radio. He went on later to transmit in Buxton and receive on Roanoke Island. He is also credited for sending the first two-way transatlantic transmission and the first radio broadcast of entertainment and music. The Fessenden Center in Buxton is built in his honor at the visible base of one of his long-gone towers.

He could have been a name-dropper since he worked with both Thomas Edison and George Westinghouse at different times. However, he was known for often being quarrelsome and temperamental and not taking advantage of available publicity. He patented over 500 inventions, but he was also embroiled in many bitter fights with people in his field. He was a professor at Purdue University and was chair of what is now the University of Pittsburgh.

He died in Bermuda. On the stone across the top of two columns over his grave is inscribed, "*By his genius, distant lands converse and men sail unafraid upon the deep.*" (Courtesy of OBHC.)

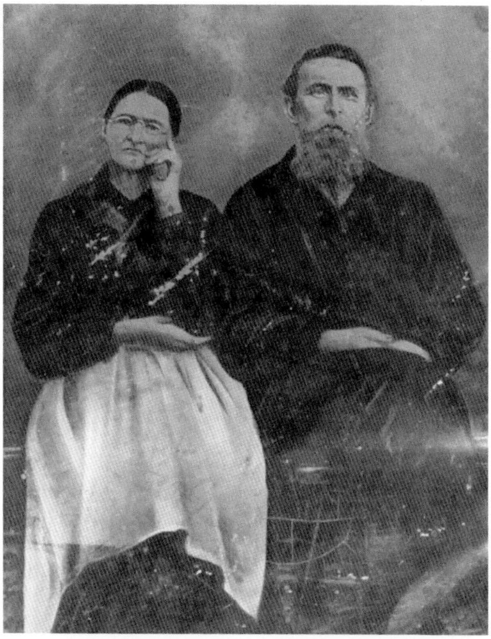

An Unusual Creditor

E.R. (Ezekiel Roscoe) Daniels founded the very successful Globe Fish Company in 1911. He also owned a tremendous mercantile store that stocked equipment needed by fishermen that he allowed to be bought on credit. Daniels possessed a fleet of vessels known as the Wanchese Line that delivered passengers, freight, and seafood to numerous locations along the Outer Banks. The editor of the local newspaper stated, "His greatest achievement was in lifting his people out of the class of tenants." His death truly marked the end of an era. (Courtesy of Vickie Simpson.)

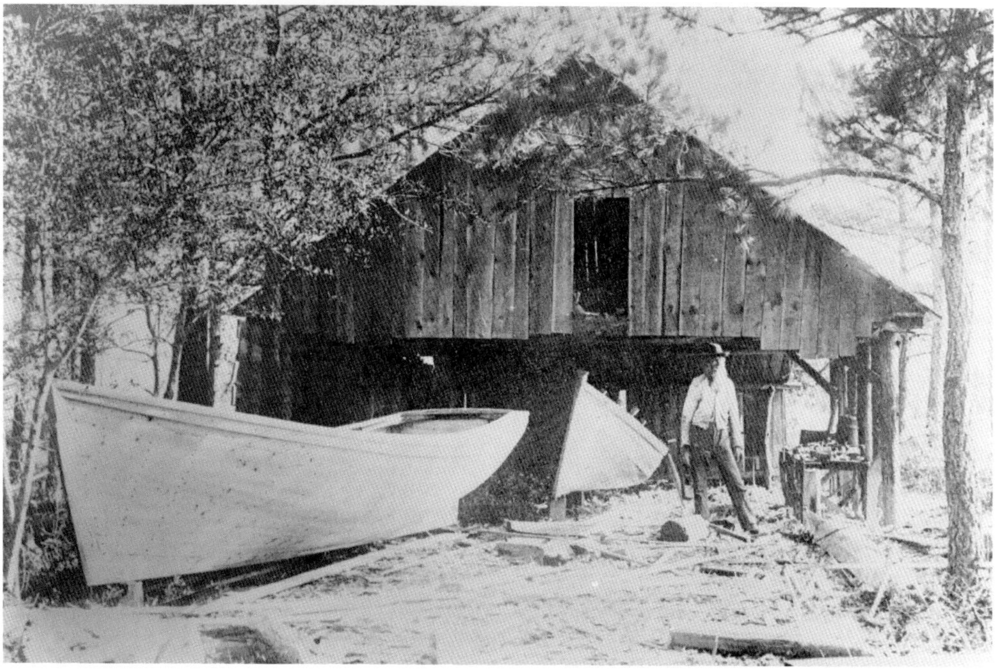

Wash's Creation

George Washington "Wash" Creef designed and built a shallow draft juniper boat with a round bottom and a wide beam for hauling heavy loads of shad fish. A century later, North Carolina would call it the official boat of the state. His most famous boat was built in 1899, and it was named for his 10-year-old daughter. The *Hattie Creef* was a two-mast schooner with Wash's round bottom signature. She was first used for oystering and later for transporting mail, freight, and two humble passengers, Orville and Wilbur Wright, from Elizabeth City to Manteo. (Courtesy of OBHC.)

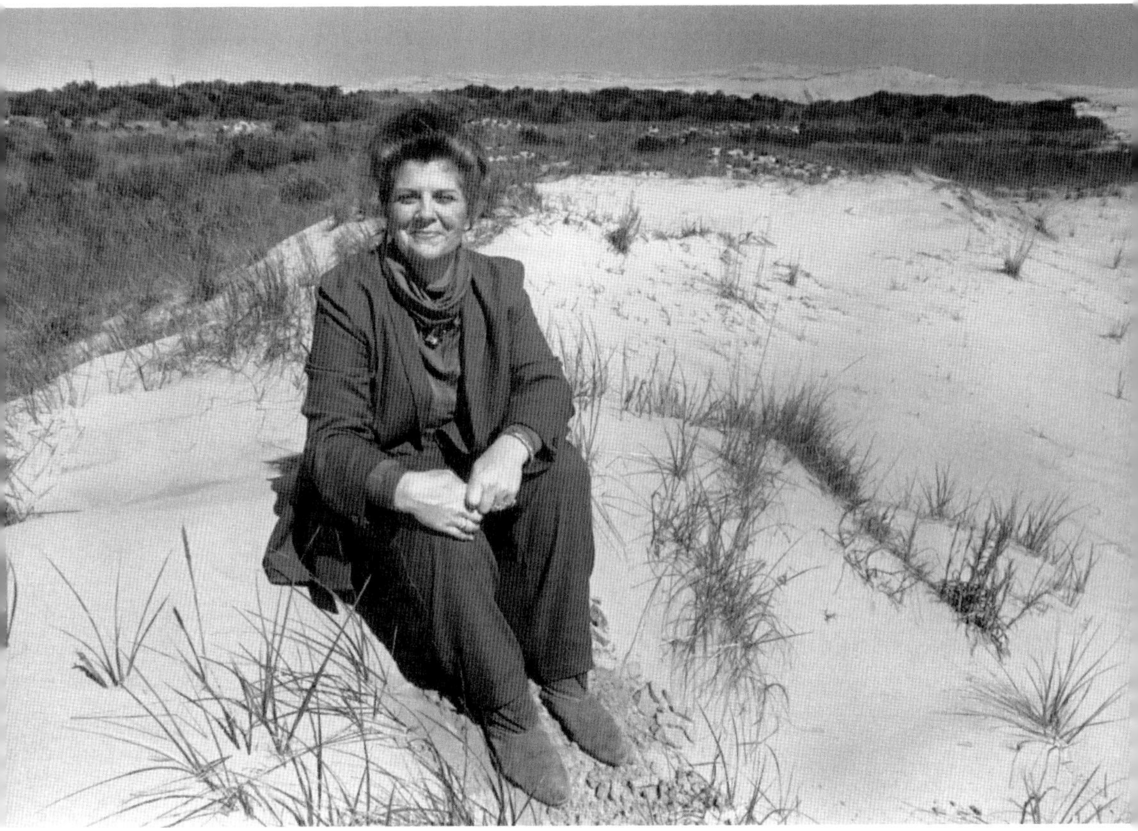

Securing a Precious Gem

As the granddaughter of North Carolina historical novelist Inglis Fletcher, Carolista Golden was attuned to the rich heritage of the eastern part of the state. She spent her summers at Nags Head as a child and called it her home as an adult.

To describe her as a free spirit would just begin to capture her bold personality. She was an artist, a sculptor, and made her living as a jewelry designer and maker in a studio just a shell's throw from Jockey's Ridge, the tallest natural sand dunes on the Atlantic Coast. When developers had plans to build homes around the base of the dunes, Golden raced to the site and stood in front of a bulldozer until the driver conceded by getting off of his seat and leaving. The development stopped long enough for citizens to gather 25,000 signatures on a petition in just a few days.

Golden set up and organized a hue and a cry throughout the county and state. She helped to persuade the general assembly to appropriate $500,000 to acquire land and set it aside as a state park. She made a video about saving Jockey's Ridge with former governor Luther Hodges as narrator. Matching federal funds were donated and used to purchase additional land around the dunes. A group called S.O.S. (Save our Sand Dunes) was formed that ingeniously sold a square foot of sand for $5, which was donated back to the cause. Many other individuals and groups joined the effort.

Today, the 414-acre state park is a national landmark where a million people visit yearly. When a visitor stands at the top of the ridge where he or she can see both the sound and the ocean, it is not hard to visualize a strong, beautiful woman with long hair streaming in the wind, standing down an encroaching bulldozer. (Courtesy of Drew Wilson Collection; OBHC.)

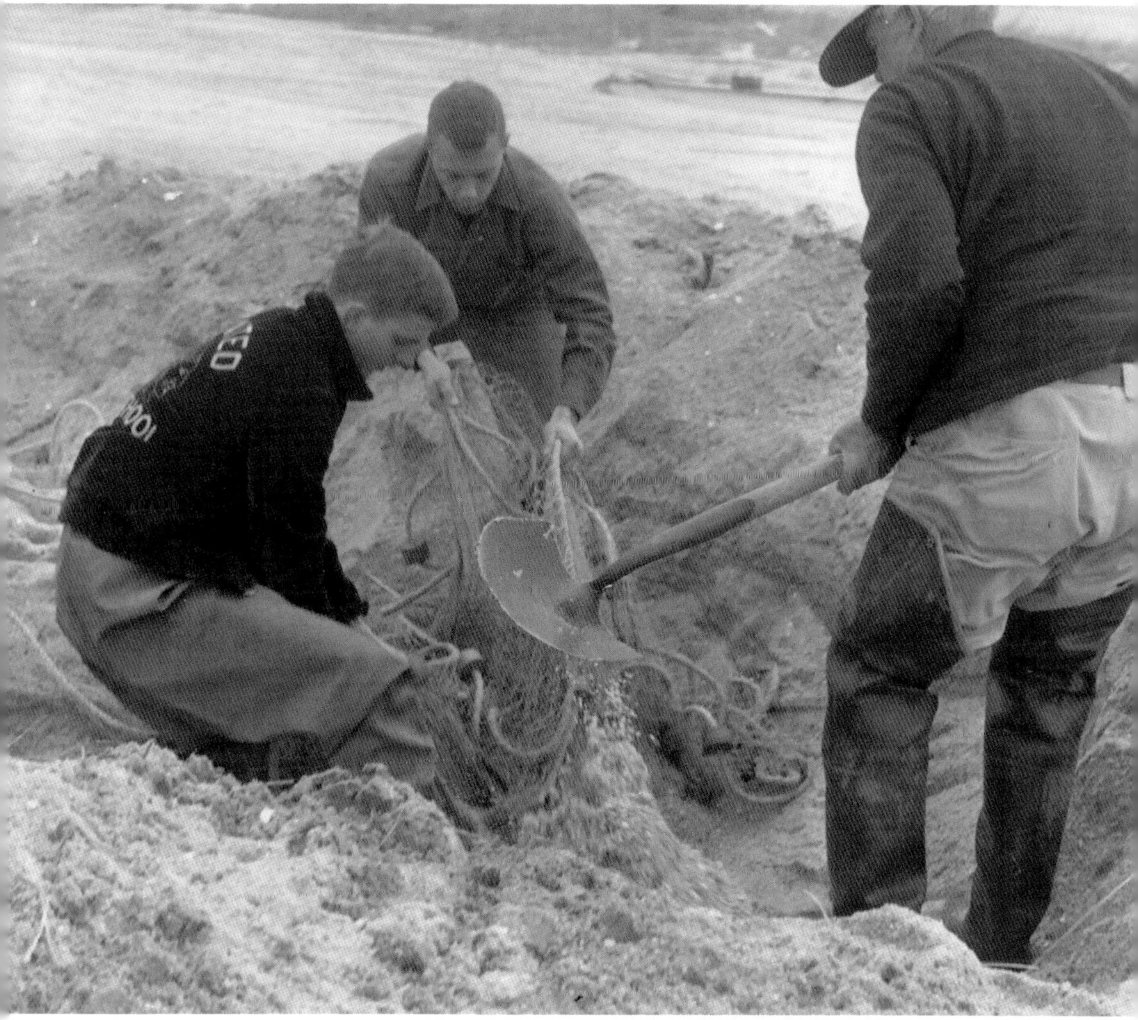

Prophesying the Future

Commercial seine fisherman Jethro Midgett Sr. had seen what hurricanes—specifically the storm of 1933—could do to the beach. In the 1950s, when talk began of building a bypass highway parallel to the beach road and seven feet higher, Midgett became alarmed, thinking it would act as a dike when the next storm hit. He argued that it was best for the waters to sweep over, and then recede across the Outer Banks. He took up the crusade, protesting loudly, even traveling to Raleigh by bus to discuss his fears in an unproductive appointment with the governor.

During the disastrous Ash Wednesday Storm of 1962, the high water came up to the bypass, which acted as a dam just as he had predicted. When the water broke through the dam, it was a fast-moving river that took out everything in its path as it rushed to the sound. Midgett (right) and his crew are pictured digging out nets after the storm.

When the bypass was rebuilt, he advocated that it be built lower. He was again ignored. Today, the highway dam awaits another storm. (Courtesy of Aycock Brown Collection; OBHC.)

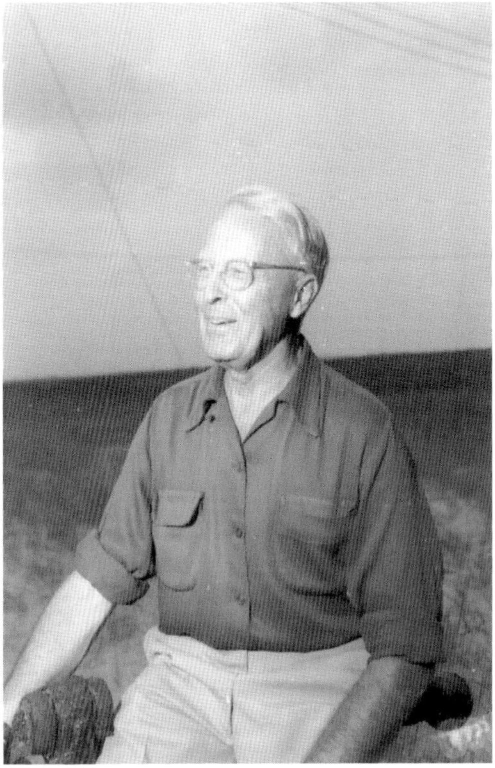

Painter of Wildlife and Dreams

An ardent sportsman, commercial artist Frank Stick became famous for painting covers for prominent hunting and fishing magazines. In 1929, he moved his family from New Jersey to Skyco, and became a real estate developer, buying a large piece of land from the ocean to the sound that is now known as Southern Shores.

Stick transitioned from developer to conservationist. His visionary acts include proposing the Cape Hatteras National Seashore, promoting beach stabilization, restoring the "Cittie of Raleigh" on Roanoke Island, and establishing the Pea Island Wildlife Refuge. (Courtesy of OBHC.)

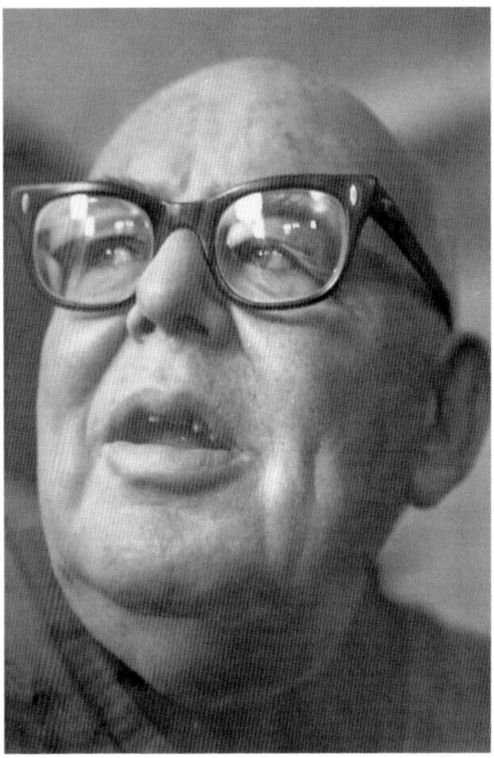

An Intellectual with Generous Friends

Prominent lawyer, writer, philosopher, and Shakespearian scholar Huntington Cairns retired from his job at the National Art Gallery and moved to Southern Shores in 1965. He and his wife, Florence, moved next-door to longtime friends Maud and Frank Stick.

He remained intellectually active and convinced his friend and philanthropist Paul Mellon to put up $617,000 from Mellon Foundations to acquire needed land for the Cape Hatteras National Seashore. He promoted writers and wrote two books, earning the nickname "the Socrates of the Outer Banks." (Courtesy of Aycock Brown Collection; OBHC.)

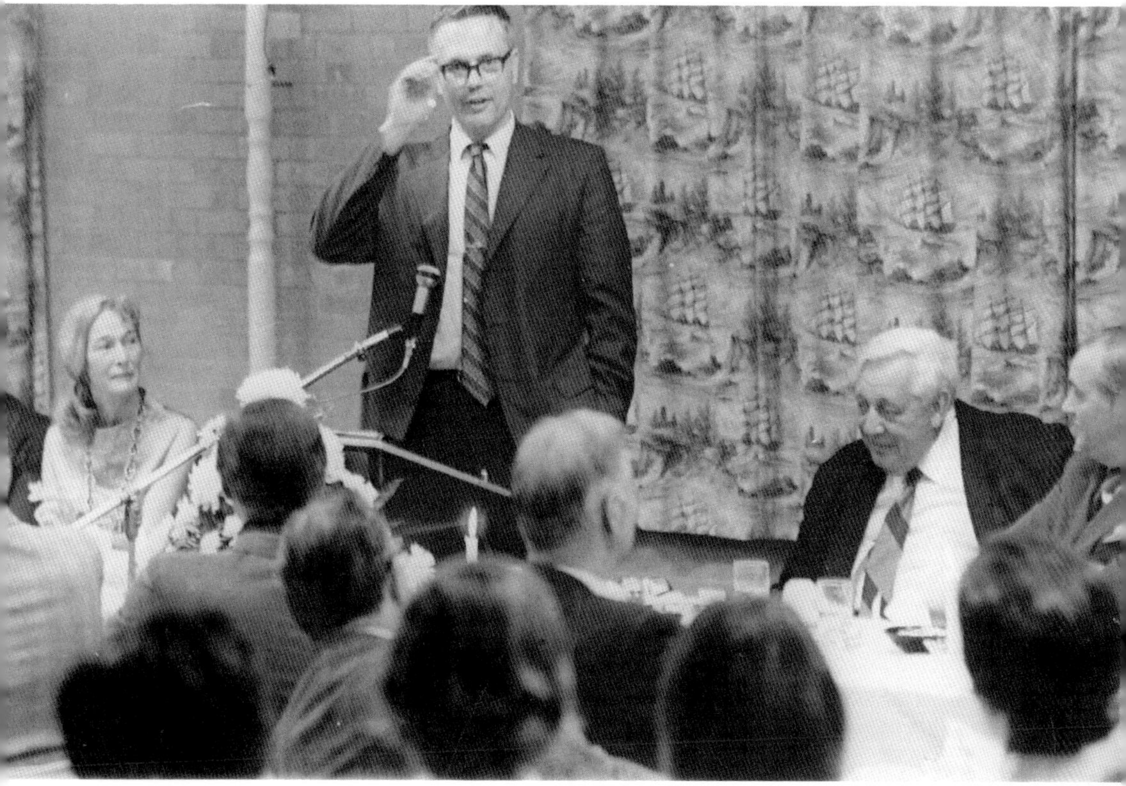

Grand Dame of the Outer Banks

The Baum family name is seen on signs all over the northern Outer Banks and in Kill Devil Hills, in particular. This is due in part to the generous benefaction of Diane Baum St. Clair, a feisty and perceptive businesswoman pictured here second from left.

Diane ran off to New York City from her Tidewater Virginia home as an 18-year-old and became a high-income model for Saks, Bergdorf-Goodman, and Stein and Blaine. She graduated from Johns Hopkins University with a degree in abnormal psychology and followed that with postgraduate studies at Yale. Besides starting a school for abnormal psychology in California, she was a dancer, appeared in television commercials, and raced horses.

Diane would come to Kill Devil Hills in the summers to help run the family business, the Wilbur Wright Hotel, on the oceanfront. Her father, Tom Baum, was occupied with operating his ferry business that provided transportation from Currituck to the northern Outer Banks. In the late 1940s, she began to become involved in community activities that eventually led to her serving terms as town commissioner and as mayor of Kill Devil Hills. With an eye on the future, she started buying parcels of land and became a real estate developer.

After becoming a wealthy woman, she found a new source of pleasure and fulfillment. Always a supporter of education, she gave thousands of dollars to the College of The Albemarle, Dare County Campus, and a specific $300,000 allotment for which they named the Technology Education Center for her. She sold and partially gifted a 320-acre tract to Kill Devil Hills where a library, a senior citizens' center, a town hall, the Outer Banks Chamber of Commerce, and two schools were built.

She made the old Kill Devil Hills Coast Guard Station her home with little renovation. At 75, she was described as having a touch of "Hepburn and Bacall wearing well in the lines of the face and blue eyes that snap." Although married four times, she left no children, but 12 heirs were the recipients of her continued generosity. (Courtesy of OBHC.)

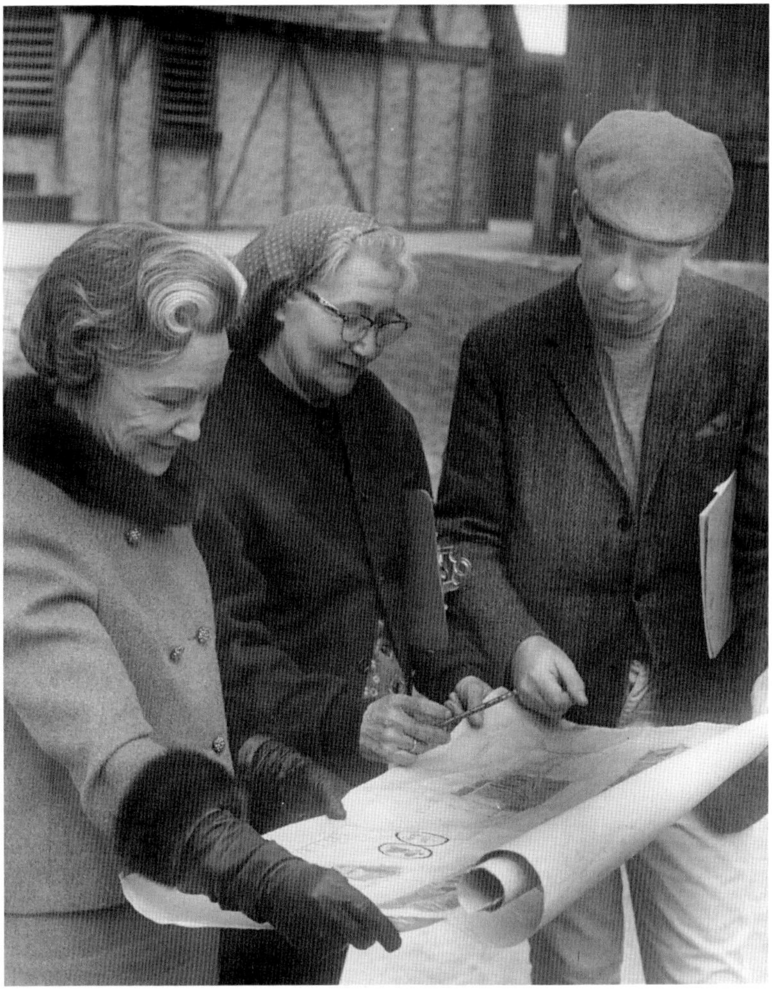

A Heart for the Colony

In the over 75 years that *The Lost Colony* has been presented, there have been many times that the continuation of the outdoor drama was uncertain. In those instances, it seems that just the right person came along at a critical moment to provide the right creativity, connections, or resources to breathe life into the symphonic play. One such person was Emma Neal Morrison.

Headquartered in her Kill Devil Hills cottage every summer, Morrison always fought to keep alive the difficult process of *The Lost Colony.* She was involved with the people and the production for over 50 years, serving 20 of those years as producer. She chaired the Roanoke Island Historical Association and created the Roanoke Voyages Stamp. A consummate giver, she was responsible for having Morrison Groves built, an apartment complex that houses 90 *Lost Colony* cast members.

She was constantly steeped in all areas of need for the drama, but perhaps her most creative contribution was convincing Broadway director Joe Layton to come help *The Lost Colony* when it was in a flat state, and its future looked bleak. Layton brought a fresh outlook and a genius that revived the play.

During a celebration of "Emma Neal Morrison Day," the humble lady was presented with many awards. She paraphrased the *Lost Colony* character Old Tom by saying, "I hardly know me."

Morrison, in gloves, looks over plans with the stage set in the background. (Courtesy of Aycock Brown Collection; OBHC.)

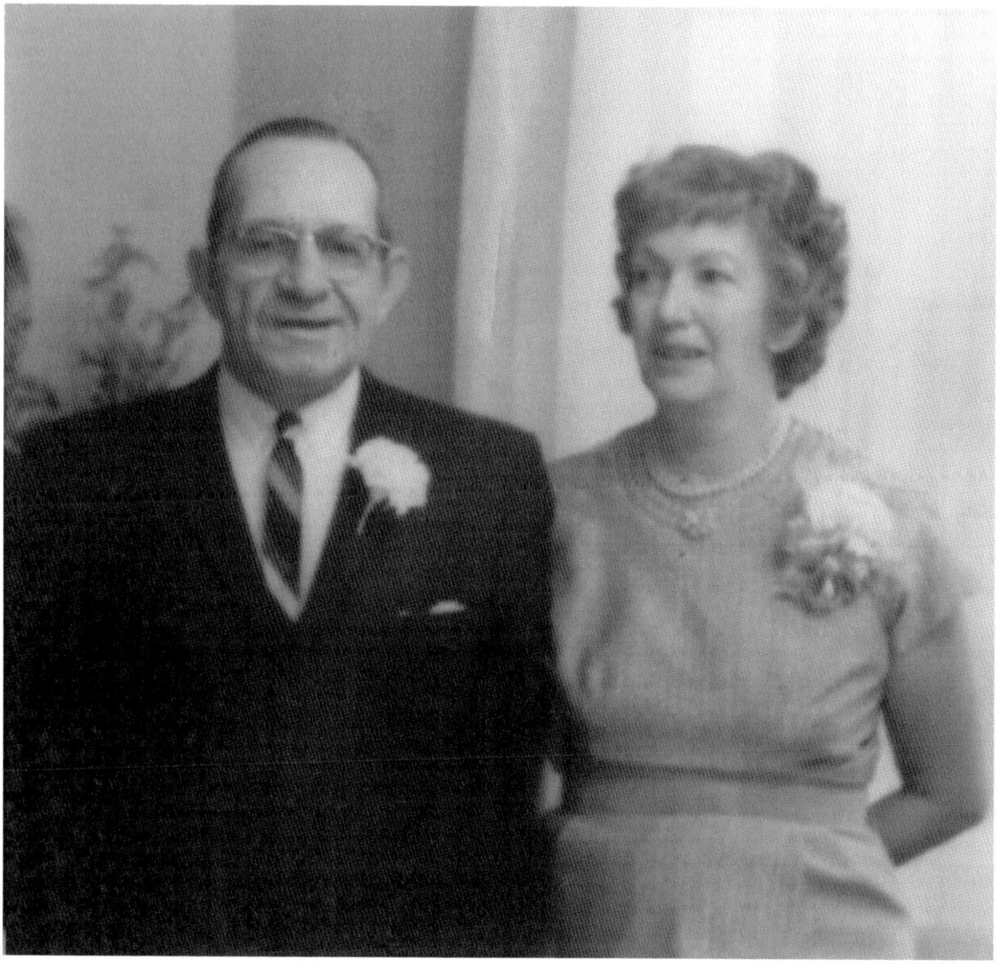

Philanthropists beyond the Grave

Hailing from Manteo, Percy Meekins won a seat in the North Carolina Assembly when he lived in Lenoir. There, he became lifelong friends with fellow legislator Hugh Alexander. After his term, Meekins moved to Washington, DC, and was an administrative aide to a prominent congressman and later to his friend Alexander, who succeeded a popular congressman.

Meekins's father bought large amounts of land on the beach when most people thought it was a worthless wasteland. This inheritance, combined with his wife, Lib's, wise investments, made for a healthy nest egg. Alexander and Meekins made a pact that whoever outlived the other would look out for the interests of the deceased one's wife. When Meekins died first, Alexander, his wife, and Lib came up with the idea of creating a trust. Alexander, being an attorney, drew up the proper legal papers to create the Percy W. and Elizabeth G. Meekins Charitable Trust.

As of 2014, the trust has disbursed over $2.5 million to worthy causes in Dare County that promote the health and well-being of the people of the community. Museums, churches, historical associations, parks, and health centers have all benefitted from grants, and this generosity will benefit the citizens of Dare County for generations to come. (Courtesy of Bill Alexander.)

BIBLIOGRAPHY

Bailey, Anthony. *The Outer Banks*. New York: Farrar, Straus and Giroux, 1989.

Conoley, Neal, John, and Jim. *Carolina Flair Outer Banks Boatbuilding & Sportfish Heritage*. Wendell: Carolina Flair, LLC, 2007.

Conoley, Neal. *Waterfowl Heritage North Caroline Decoys and Hunting Lore*. Wendell: Webfoot, Inc., 1982.

"Dave Driscoll Does a Good Job Testing Aircraft for War," *Dare County Times*. May 12, 1942.

Davis, Susan Joy. *The Whalehead Club*. Virginia Beach: Donning, 2004.

Keller, Neel. "Nags Head Mourns Loss of Renaissance Man," *Outer Banks Sentinel*. September 27, 2013.

Khoury, Angel Ellis. *Manteo: A Roanoke Island Town*. Virginia Beach. Donning, 1999.

Lewis, Jim. "The Winds of Change," *News and Observer*. January 2, 1970.

MacNeill, Ben Dixon. "Putting Wings To Groceries," *News and Observer*. March 26, 1936.

McAdoo, Donald and Carol. *Reflections*. Manteo: Island Publishing House, 1978.

McCoy, Anne Griffin. Unpublished memories, 1955.

Morris, Travis. *Duck Hunting on Currituck Sound*. Charleston: The History Press, 2006.

Morris, Travis. *Stories of Old Currituck Outer Banks*. Charleston: The History Press, 2013.

Powell, William S. *Paradise Preserved*. Chapel Hill: The University of North Carolina Press, 1965.

Stick, David. "Outer Bankers To Be Remembered." Unpublished paper.

Tate, Suzanne. *Memories of Manteo and Roanoke Island*. Nags Head: Nags Head Art, 1988.

Wright, David & Zoby, David. *Fire on the Beach*. New York: Oxford University Press, 2006.

INDEX

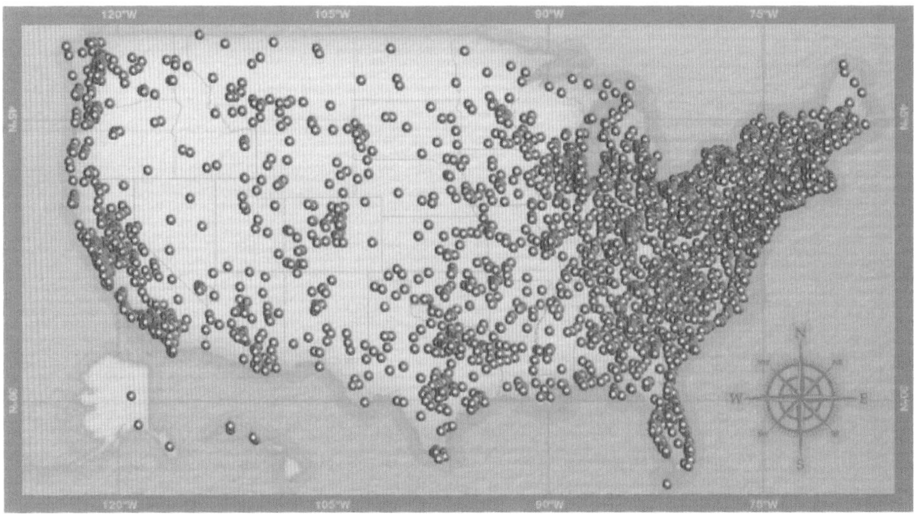